AF903696

FINANCIAL ACCOUNTING

Dr. Risha Khandelwal

TAP

Toronto Academic Press

Financial Accounting

Dr. Risha Khandelwal

Toronto Academic Press
224 Shoreacres Road
Burlington, ON L7L 2H2
Canada
www.tap-books.com
Email: orders@arclereducation.com

© 2024 Toronto Academic Press

ISBN: 978-1-77469-704-7

This book contains information obtained from highly regarded resources. Reprinted material sources are indicated and copyright remains with the original owners. Copyright for images and other graphics remains with the original owners as indicated. A Wide variety of references are listed. Reasonable efforts have been made to publish reliable data. Authors or Editors or Publishers are not responsible for the accuracy of the information in the published chapters or consequences of their use. The publisher assumes no responsibility for any damage or grievance to the persons or property arising out of the use of any materials, instructions, methods or thoughts in the book. The authors or editors and the publisher have attempted to trace the copyright holders of all material reproduced in this publication and apologize to copyright holders if permission has not been obtained. If any copyright holder has not been acknowledged, please write to us so we may rectify.

Notice: Registered trademark of products or corporate names are used only for explanation and identification without intent of infringement.

Toronto Academic Press publishes wide variety of books and eBooks. For more information about Toronto Academic Press and its products, visit our website at www.tap-books.com.

ABOUT THE AUTHOR

Dr. Risha Khandelwal has expertise in finance and global business as an academician and researcher. She has been teaching and conducting research for more than six years. She has held positions at JECRC University in Jaipur and GL A University in Mathura. She received the UGC fellowship after passing the NET-JRF. She has written case studies, book chapters, and research papers that have been indexed by Google Scholar and SCOPUS. She is proficient in utilizing econometrics to analyze secondary data. She is currently a freelancer, helping academics with their research projects.

Contents

6 Stakeholder's Equity 147

7 Financial Ratio Analysis and Performance Evaluation 175

8 Challenges and Prospects of Financial Accounting 217

Index 245

List of Figures

List of Tables

List of Abbreviations

AI	Artificial Intelligence
AP	Accounts Payable
AR	Accounts Receivable
ARR	Accounting Rate of Return
CCE	Cash and Cash Equivalents
CFF	Cash Flow From Financing
CFI	Cash Flow From Investing
CFO	Chief Financial Officer
CFS	Cash Flow Statement
CSR	Corporate Social Responsibility
DDB	Double-Declining Balance
DPS	Dividend Per Share
DSCR	Debt Service Coverage Ratio
EPS	Earnings Per Share
ESG	Environmental, Social, and Governance
ETFs	Exchange-Traded Funds

FCF	Free Cash Flow
GAAP	Generally Accepted Accounting Principles
GDPR	General Data Protection Regulation
IFRS	International Financial Reporting Standards
IoT	Internet of Things
IRS	Internal Revenue Service
ML	Machine Learning
NPM	New Public Management
P/E	Price-Earnings Ratio
PP&E	Plant, Property, and Equipment
PPE	Property, Plant, and Equipment
REITs	Real Estate Investment Trusts
ROCE	Return on Capital Employed
RPA	Robotic Process Automation
RRR	Required Rate of Return
SMBs	Small and Medium-Sized Businesses
SYD	Sum-of-the-Year Digits
TVM	Time Value of Money
UFCF	Unlevered Free Cash Flow
UTC	Unamortized Investment Tax Credits

PREFACE

Financial accounting is a critical component of modern business management. It provides a framework for recording, reporting, and analyzing financial transactions essential for decision-making. A sound understanding of financial accounting is vital for business leaders, investors, and stakeholders, enabling them to evaluate a company's financial health and make informed decisions.

This book is designed to provide a comprehensive introduction to financial accounting, covering the essential concepts and practices that underpin this field. It suits students, professionals, and academics seeking a deeper understanding of financial accounting's fundamental principles and practices.

The book is organized into eight chapters. The first chapter provides an overview of financial accounting, highlighting its importance and relevance in business management. The second chapter focuses on accrual accounting concepts, explaining how companies use the accrual method to record and report financial transactions. It covers the accounting equation, debits and credits, and the double-entry accounting system. It also explains how companies adjust their financial records for accruals, deferrals, and estimates.

The third chapter delves into the fundamentals of financial statements, exploring how companies prepare and present these documents to stakeholders. It covers the balance sheet, income statement, and statement of cash flows, explaining the purpose and content of each. The fourth chapter focuses on cash flow within a company, explaining the importance of cash flow management in financial accounting. It covers the different types of cash inflows and outflows a company may experience and explains how companies use cash flow statements (CFS) to track and analyze their cash flow.

The fifth chapter covers assets, liability, and depreciation, providing a thorough understanding of these key concepts and their role in financial accounting. It explains the different types of assets and liabilities, how they are classified, and how they are reported in financial statements. It also covers the concept of depreciation, including the different methods of calculating it, and explains how companies account for impairments and disposals of assets. The sixth chapter focuses on stakeholders' equity, examining the various types of equity and how they are reported in financial statements.

The seventh chapter provides an overview of financial ratios and performance evaluation, exploring how companies use financial ratios to assess their performance and make informed decisions. The final chapter of the book focuses on the challenges and prospects of financial accounting, highlighting the emerging trends and opportunities in this field.

The book provides a comprehensive overview of financial accounting's key concepts, theories, and practices, making it a valuable resource for students, scholars, and professionals. By reading this book, readers will gain a deeper understanding of financial accounting, enabling them to make informed decisions confidently.

—***Author***

CHAPTER 1

INTRODUCTION TO FINANCIAL ACCOUNTING

UNIT INTRODUCTION

Financial accounting assesses a firm's performance for a specific time period in the denominated currency in which the firm deals such as, Canadian dollars, U.S. dollars, euros, or any other currency deemed appropriate to the firm (Yu et al., 2018). This evaluation of a company's financial performance and status is carried out for a diverse range of organizations, including small and large businesses, governments at all levels (from the local to the national), universities, charitable organizations, religious institutions, clubs, and international associations.

In addition to the numerical information, these financial statements include comments, spanning dozens of pages and comprising many words that provide explanation and analysis. The annual report compiles different words and statistics required by all publicly traded firms (Muda et al., 2013). It also contains the company's financial statements and any accompanying remarks. (Listed firms must provide reports more frequently than once a year, such as quarterly or further "interim" reports). The statements provide a report on the financial and economic aspects of the situation and are primarily intended for individuals not affiliated with the firm. Examples of these individuals include investors, club members, regulatory agencies, and taxes authorities (Hopwood, 2000).

In short:

- Financial performance is a measure of success or failure over time, giving rise to fresh supplies from everyday operations;
- A company's financial position is its current combination of financial resources and obligations.
- Financial statements are reports that describe a company's status and financial performance.
- *Notes* are included in the sentences to explain the numbers.
- Quarterly and annual reports contain statements, notes, and other information (Alexander & Nobes, 2007).

High performance usually results in a strong financial situation: hypothetically, you are more likely to have money in the bank if you earn good money at work. A strong financial position also supports performance: having cash in the bank allows you to carry out the tasks that result in good performance while avoiding the risks and concerns that come with being broke (Annand, 2008) (Figure 1.1).

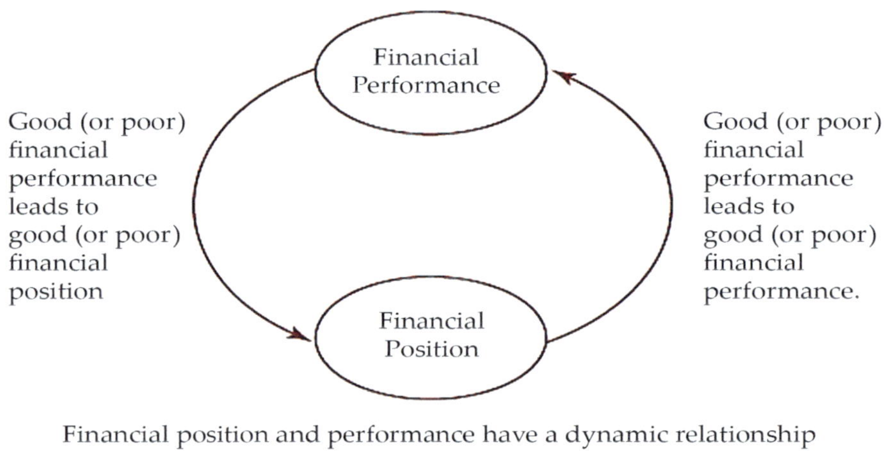

Figure 1.1. Illustration of the relationship between financial position and financial performance of the company.

Source: Anni Britton & Chris Waterston, Creative Commons License.

Learning Objectives

At the end of the chapter, the reader will be able to understand

1. The social significance of financial accounting
2. The key principles of financial accounting
3. The importance of financial accounting

4. The main types of financial accounting
5. The key difference between financial and managerial accounting

Key Terms

1. Accrual Accounting
2. Auditors
3. Cash Accounting
4. Credibility Enhancers
5. Decision Maker
6. Economic Equity
7. Financial Accounting
8. Recording Transaction

1.1. THE SOCIAL SETTING OF FINANCIAL ACCOUNTING

The growth of commerce and society has influenced financial accounting in various ways. The following are just a few of the many tasks that financial accounting performs:

Remember

The financial statements, which are the reports generated by financial accounting, provide a concise summary of the measurements of financial performance and position in ways considered beneficial for determining whether or not the enterprise has been successful.

- It assists investors in the stock market in determining whether to purchase, sell, or buy shares of corporations.
- It aids in managing businesses on behalf of shareholders, members, or citizens.
- It offers fundamental financial records for daily administration, control, insurance, and fraud protection needs.
- Governments employ it to keep tabs on how businesses act and calculate taxes like income and sales tax (Hussein, 1981).

The enterprise's financial accounting functions in and supports a complex social environment. It aims to track and report financial events that the organization either starts or experiences. Accounting is not inactive since it informs us of what is happening and impacts our choices and behavior, affecting what is happening because these events originate from and affect the social context (Dopuch & Sunder, 1980).

Numerous people make up the social environment. At least following four parties are immediately affected by what the company's financial accounting indicates about it.

- The company's owners, such as its stockholders
- The management, who are in charge of running it on their behalf
- The external auditors, who the owners hire to assess the managerial and financial reports
- All governmental levels for revenue and regulation-related purposes (Fogarty et al., 1994)
- The bankers and financial institutions who lent to the business entity.

Shareholders can buy and sell shares that make up the business; nonetheless, the organization is a separate legal institute from its shareholder owners. On behalf of the company's owners and other parties, auditors provide a report on the accuracy of its financial accounts. The following parties and financial accounting are connected to one another (Wang et al., 2018).

- Managers, for instance, might work for a firm for the entirety of their careers and, as a result, might feel just as much ownership as do shareholders, who might only be a company's partial owners for a short period through the trade of shares on the stock market before relocating on to another investment.
- Owners and managers may overlap in smaller businesses (Hines, 1991).
- Although the owners officially choose external auditors, they work closely with the managers daily. They may also guide on tax, accounting, and other matters pertinent to managers' day-to-day activities aside from their work as auditors.
- However, an organization's external auditor is not allowed also to be a manager or owner of the same organization. This is done to guarantee that the auditor is morally and financially impartial and can, thus, be unbiased regarding the company's economic issues.

Aside from these three key partners, many teams, firms, institutions, and parties are intrigued by or impact the company's financial accounting. They may even be in rivalry or disagreement with one another. Most will be located in the same nation as the business and its management, but more companies and other enterprises are operating in an international market. As a result, the other parties interested in and influencing the company's financial accounting may be located worldwide. (Muniandy & Ali, 2012) (Figure 1.2).

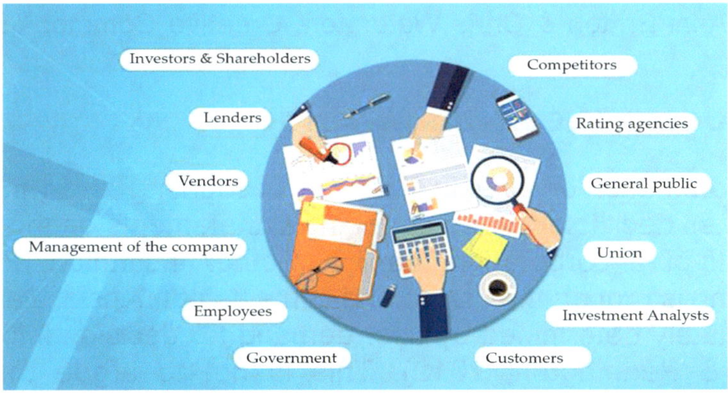

Figure 1.2. Schematic of users of financial accounting.

Source: Madhuri Thakur, Creative Commons License.

1.2. PEOPLE INVOLVED IN FINANCIAL ACCOUNTING

The art of financial accounting has numerous practitioners.

- The information users – decision makers;
- The information makers who assemble the information to help the users make decisions;
- The auditors help the users by improving the credibility of the information and issuing a professional opinion that the information is appropriate and reliable (Noor et al., 2020).

These people collaborate and affect one another, and their dynamics shape financial accounting. Financial accounting, on the other hand, influences their engrossment and behavior. These relationships are significant in accounting (Tugas, 2012) (Figure 1.3).

Figure 1.3. Flow diagram of the relationship of people with financial accounting.

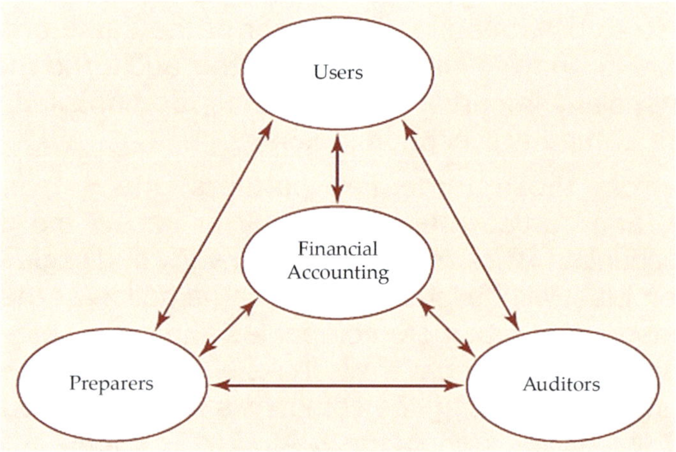

Source: Anni Britton & Chris Waterston, Creative Commons License.

1.2.1. Users (Decision Makers)

A decision-maker or user in financial accounting is an individual who makes decisions based on financial statements on their behalf or behalf of a corporation, bank, or other institution. Financial accounting is proper: the nature and contents of financial statements are ultimately determined by user demand for decision information (Kelton & Pennington, 2012). This is not to argue that such individuals are the only ones who are significant in the process. They are constantly vigilant regarding the required information or are always content with what they receive. However, user demand is the underlying reason for financial statements; thus, knowing demand is critical (Young, 2006).

The primary requirement of a user is trustworthiness and periodic reporting of a firm's economic situation and performance, which is explained below.

- The term "credible" refers to how well-prepared and trustworthy the information in the statements (the financial accounts) seems to be for use in making judgments. There is a trade-off between cost and benefit in this situation. It could cost a lot of money to render the reports flawless, but as those funds would have to come from the company's resources, doing so would worsen the performance and position of the company. Credibility is relative, not absolute, because users, like owners and managers, might not want that to happen. Accounting data must be cost-effective (Socea, 2012).
- "Periodic" refers to the fact that customers can anticipate reports regularly (for instance, annually or quarterly). The information is more reliable the longer you have to wait. The users are typically ready to accept some informational imprecision in exchange for periodic reports containing timely, decision-relevant information; nevertheless, waiting a long time for information is unacceptable. Therefore, accounting information takes a regular picture of occurrences (McNally et al., 1982) (Figure 1.4).

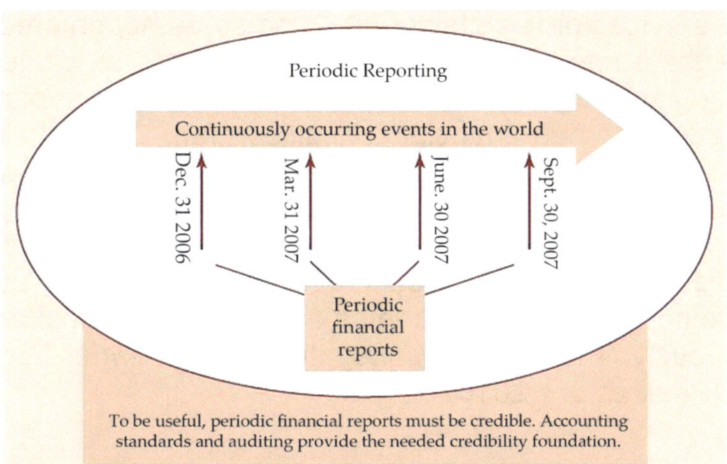

Figure 1.4. Illustration of periodic financial reports.

Source: McGraw Hill, Creative Commons License.

The main groups of users are illustrated below:

1.2.1.1. Owners

Individual business owners, such as proprietors, partners, and other businesspeople; individual stock market shareholders or investors with voting rights; businesses that put money in other industries; pension plans and other companies that invest in businesses; individuals with quasi-ownership interests, such as club members or municipal voters; and so forth, are considered the 'owners" (Weidner, 1999).

KEYWORD

Stake is partial ownership or a position in which you stand to gain when the company performs well.

1.2.1.2. Potential Owners

Like the owners mentioned above, these individuals may be considering investing in the business but do not currently have a financial stake in it (Sian & Roberts, 2009). There is frequently a massive difference in outlook between present owners, who want to sell their shares for as much as possible, and potential owners, who want to pay as little as possible, because potential owners frequently buy shares from current owners, for example, by trading shares on the stock market rather than investing precisely. Not all customers will have identical demands, despite the fact that claims accounting reacts to user requests (Holmes & Zimmer, 1994).

1.2.1.3. Creditors And Potential Creditors

Distributors, banks, employees, and anybody else who has provided financial support to the business, is owed money in exchange for goods or services or is considering doing so. Although creditors do not have the same legal control over a business as owners, they frequently play a significant role in business decisions, particularly when a business has financial difficulties (Tan, 2013). In extreme circumstances of trouble, creditors may be able to seize ownership of the company from the proprietors. Because it can depend on complex legal issues regarding who has what rights, it cannot be easy to distinguish between creditors and owners in some situations. For instance, an owner who puts money into a business may simultaneously lend it more money, turning the owner becomes a creditor (Peek et al., 2010).

1.2.1.4. Managers

Those who manage the company on the owner's behalf are the company's managers. They are very interested in how accounting documents their operations and outcomes (Sloan, 2001). The financial statements contents directly impact managers' pay, bonuses, and chances of keeping their employment. The owner may also be the primary manager, particularly in small enterprises (Bhattacharyya, 2012).

KEYWORD

Employment is a relationship between two parties regulating the provision of paid labour services.

1.2.1.5. Employees

The employees are concerned about the company's capacity to make payroll, sustain employment, and uphold commitments like pension payments (Roslender, 1997).

1.2.1.6. Taxation Authorities

Those who may use the financial accounts to determine the amount of taxes owed or whether the company abides by certain agreements and guidelines (Cloyd, 1995).

1.2.1.7. Financial and Market Analysts

Financial and market analysts research the performance of firms and use that information to create reports for others. Analysts frequently advise on whether to lend, invest, or do neither (Barniv et al., 2005).

1.2.1.8. Competitors

A few people who receive the accounting statements might be attempting to comprehend how the business operates to make life more challenging for the company. For example, when competitors learn about the information, managers may be reluctant to share it with shareholders since it will hurt their chances of success (Balakrishnan & Cohen, 2014).

1.2.1.9. Accounting Researchers

People who study accounting to understand and improve it (primarily university academics, but some based in public accounting companies and other organizations) (Beattie, 2005).

1.2.1.10. Miscellaneous Third Parties

Numerous additional parties could get and use an organization's financial information differently. Many persons may use remarks once they have been released. Politicians might assess the economy's effectiveness or the level of taxation, for instance. About employment practices, news writers may write. During trials, juries, and judges may assess a company's capacity to pay damages (Kirwan, 1964).

1.2.2. Preparers (Decision Facilitators)

The data contained in the financial accounts is primarily the responsibility of three groups:

1.2.2.1. Managers

People manage an organization's operations, including disseminating accounting and other information and handling its finances. The evolution of the auditing function will be explored in the following section. The reality that managers are also users and have a substantial stake in the results has led to a fundamental interest conflict for them. A common term for managers is "management" (Dye et al., 2015).

KEYWORD

Financial Accounting is the process of documenting, analyzing and reporting every transaction of a business or an organization, in order to assess the financial health and stability of the same.

1.2.2.2. Bookkeepers and Clerks

Bookkeepers are the individuals who, under management's supervision, maintain the company's records and produce the data that serves as the foundation for financial accounting. Nowadays, computers handle a lot of bookkeeping and administrative tasks, with all the advantages and drawbacks that technology brings (Strom, 1987).

1.2.2.3. Accountants

People who work under management's guidance to form financial statements by implementing accounting principles to the company's records are the accountants. Numerous accountants hold certifications as CMAs (certified management accountants), CAs (chartered accountants), CGAs (certified general accountants), and CPAs and are members of professional societies (Glover, 2014). Financial reporting and checking those reports once made are fundamentally distinct. However, accountants, and their communities frequently have auditing skills, interests, and occasionally auditing duties (Medley, 1997).

1.2.3. Auditors (Credibility Enhancers)

Auditors assist the users by suggesting that the financial statements have been drafted effectively, skillfully, and following generally approved standards. The auditing job has a long history and developed due to users' need for assurance that managers' reports on their effectiveness were not biased, self-serving, or outright false (Krishnan & Visvanathan, 2009). There are other auditors (such as tax auditors, who confirm taxpayers' tax calculations) and internal auditors who work within the firm to support the credibility of information being used by management (Satava et al., 2006). Although external auditors may be consulted in compiling the statements, particularly for small businesses, they must abstain from taking ownership of the statements since their mission is to examine the establishment process. They are unable to audit the statements they have created legitimately! (Professional accountants frequently generate financial statements, but they should make it explicit in covering letters and footnotes attached to the statements that they are not serving as external auditors while doing so) (Ali & Nesrine, 2015).

TIPS

A good external auditor must be respected by both the preparer and the user.

To increase the likelihood of acceptance, hiring an objective third party who will get paid regardless of whether the financial results are positive or negative or whether the customers or managers are pleased or dissatisfied is preferable. In most cases, only certified public accountants or other members of a professional accounting organization with competence in auditing are granted permission to carry out the external auditing function (Höglund & Sundvik, 2016).

Most external auditors work for public firms of accounting where they cooperate with colleagues, even if others choose to work individually. Some of these companies are enormous, employing tens of thousands of people across dozens of locations in dozens of countries (Salterio, 1996). In addition to conducting external audits, public accounting firms provide "consulting" services, advising their clients on a wide range of topics related to taxes, finances, and technology. Public accountants are prohibited from being involved in the businesses they audit considering that they are auditing their own work or generating any conflict-of-interest issues through providing such other advice (Hackenbrack & Nelson, 1996). Whether or not this is being handled correctly is a matter of significant debate and calls for a high level of professional expertise and adherence to ethics and principles of professional conduct. Disclosure of auditor fees for both traditional auditing and specialized advisory services became mandatory for large U.S.

firms in the 2000s. The information revealed that many businesses paid their auditors a far higher rate for consulting than auditing. When more money is earned as consultants, how do auditors maintain their independence? According to a survey of senior financial managers published in March 2002 by Business Week, many executives believe auditors should not simultaneously serve as advisors to the companies they audit. Chartered accountants favored stricter independence standards in December 2003 (Manzon & Guo, 2006). The new standard prevents auditors from providing some non-audit services to audit customers to maintain their independence. Accounting, valuation, actuarial, outsourced internal auditing, information technology planning and implementation, human resources duties, and corporate finance tasks all fall outside the purview of an audit (Saeed et al., 2020).

The accounting process flow among the participants is depicted in Figure 1.5. Recurrent financial statements are fashioned from the basic information by the preparers, then audited to lend credibility, and finally sent to the many users (Kinney, 1994).

Figure 1.5. Illustration of people involved in financial accounting.

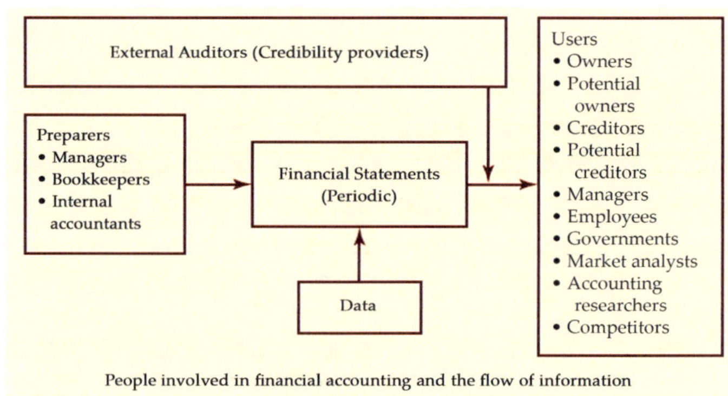

Source: McGraw Hill, Creative Commons License.

1.2.4. People and Ethics

Almost every aspect of accounting has ethical concerns. Here are a few real-world examples:

- A recently sacked employee has filed a lawsuit against the company, alleging that the dismissal was unlawful because it was motivated by the person's age. The company's president disputes improper behavior (Melé et al., 2017). The chief accountant for the company has recommended to the boss that the lawsuit be listed in a letter to the financial statements so that readers of these statements will be aware that there is a possibility for loss if the former employee wins. The chief accountant personally believes the former employee's claim is convincing. To prevent embarrassment and the impression of admitting guilt, the president thinks the chief accountant should disregard the lawsuit when drafting the financial accounts (Gordon, 2011). The president is concerned that such a seemingly admitting could be used against the company in court, resulting in the company losing the lawsuit. The chief accountant should do what?

- While conducting the audit, an outside auditor discovers that a different company might have defrauded one of its clients. Another auditor client is the customer, who is blissfully oblivious to this and content with the situation. The auditor is aware that revealing anything to anyone could lead to lawsuits from all sides and is thus constrained by standards of ethics and manners created to secure the privacy of the data obtained during the audit. Should the auditor not disclose what was discovered (Duska et al., 2018)?
- The president of a third company receives an annual bonus that is determined by taking a portion of the company's revenue. The president is debating whether to alter an accounting procedure to increase revenue and the president's bonus. Therefore, the measure would increase the president's wealth. Should the President accept the greater reward, disregard the accounting change, and appeal that the bonus calculation ignores the change or both (Meymandi et al., 2015)?

No solutions are provided at this time because these illustrated issues do not have simple solutions. They present problems for the president, the auditor, and the chief accountant (Zadek, 1998). But nevertheless, these are serious ethical issues which poses problems and challenges to the management.

KEYWORD

Accountant is a professional who performs accounting functions such as account analysis, auditing, or financial statement analysis.

1.3. FUNDAMENTAL PRINCIPLES OF FINANCIAL ACCOUNTING

A company should handle its business accounting following rules known as the fundamental principles of financial accounting. All accountants must follow these guidelines when doing their tasks to guarantee consistency and responsibility (Schroeder et al., 2022). While many nations adhere to specific norms, a few of these laws are more widely accepted globally. The most fundamental accounting principles—which are complied with by online accounting software—will be covered in this piece (Brunnermeier et al., 2009).

You must fundamentally understand these fundamental accounting principles to practice accounting. It's not as easy to learn financial information for a test and remember it two days afterward. These values are prevalent in accounting research all across the world. These are followed by accounting software for financial services to execute the smooth accounting process for any business, whether big or small (Chiappetta et al., 2009).

Before proceeding with financial accounting fundamentals, let's discuss the trends, statistics, and data for invoicing and online accounting software. Only 1% less than large firms and mid-sized businesses have implemented accounting software, according to AccountingToday.com's "Year Ahead" study from 2018. On the other hand, at 45%, the idea of online billing software is spreading throughout small businesses (Chandra, 2017). Here are some of the most well-known accounting principles and how they relate to accounting software for financial services, the role of an accountant, and their duties (Brigham & Houston, 2021) (Figure 1.6).

Figure 1.6. Image of principles of financial accounting.

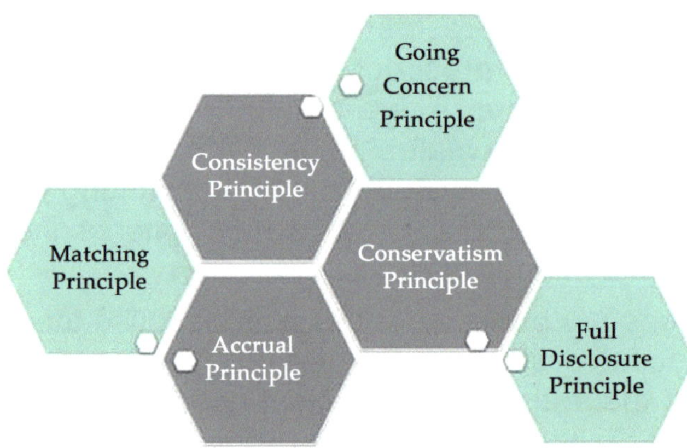

Source: Sayantan Mukhopadhyay, Creative Commons License.

1.3.1. Principles of Conservatism

According to the conservative principle, all liabilities and expenses should be declared immediately. Contrarily, assets, and profits should only be recorded after an accountant is confident they will materialize (Sugiarto & Fachrurrozie, 2018).

Due to delays in identifying assets and revenue, this strategy will cause financial statements to be skewed cautiously, lowering predicted earnings (Hellman, 2008).

1.3.2. Principle of Accrual

According to the accrual accounting theory, all costs should be recorded as incurred rather than when cash flow is connected with them. This idea is particularly pertinent to accrual accounting because it enables the creation of more thorough financial records that show what took place over time. The subsequent cash flow can artificially accelerate or delay the transaction if a business does not follow the accrual approach (Brorströım, 1998).

1.3.3. Principle of Cost

According to the expenditure theory of accounting, a business can track all equity contributions, earnings, and accountabilities at their accurate purchase prices. According to this hypothesis, the reported amounts cannot be modified for inflation or an increase in market value (Boadway, 2006).

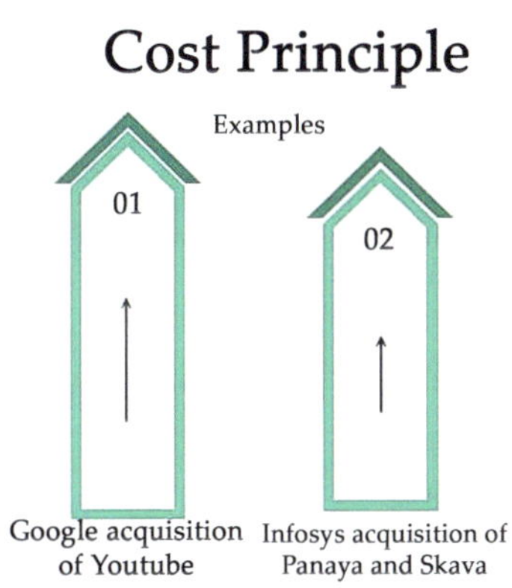

Figure 1.7. Diagram of an example of cost principle.

Source: Sumit Sharma, Creative Commons License.

This regulation is exempt if there has been a shift in the market valuation following a short-term transaction of a corporation's capital stock. This exception, however, only applies if the securities are listed for public trading on a single global stock exchange. A company's financial statements may not be as accurate as they should be if the accounting software for financial services is not operating according to the principle of cost (Jasch, 2008) (Figure 1.7).

1.3.4. Principle of Consistency

The consistency principle is an accounting concept that enables a company to publish its accounting statements using the same accounting system procedures and standards. There are numerous benefits for those interested in financial statements if the accuracy hypothesis is used correctly and narrowly. That holds for the application of software for small business financial reporting. Utilizing software that adheres to the consistency principle will make your life easier (Wüstemann & Wüstemann, 2010).

1.3.5. Principle of Economic Entity

The dealer of a business corporation is subject to different legal obligations according to the business entity definition or business entity principle. This definition requires the corporation to distinguish all acquisitions from its shareholders, owners, and other companies. This suggests that the transactions shown in the entity accounts are the only ones the entity is responsible for (Maingot & Zeghal, 2006) (Figure 1.8).

Figure 1.8. Schematic of economic equity.

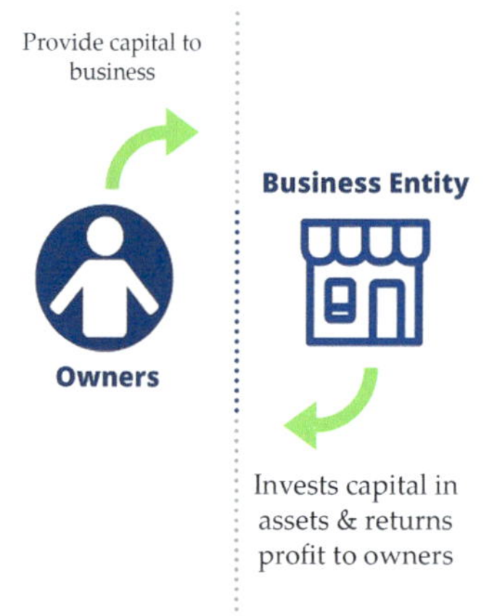

Source: Accounting, Creative Commons License.

1.3.6. Matching Principle

An accounting principle known as the matching theory controls how receipts and costs are reported and acknowledged in financial statements. The theory guarantees that the income statement accurately measures profits and liabilities for the period they were maintained (Geier, 1998). The same applies if you use accounting software for financial services. Net gains fairly reflect in the income statement when this principle is applied correctly. That is not because sales or expenses were overestimated (Zimmerman & Bloom, 2016).

1.3.7. Principle of Going Concern

If the financial reports are compiled on a going-concern basis, the entity can continue its operations shortly, usually within twelve months after the operation date. So, if a small business financial reporting software operates on the ongoing concern idea, that's a bonus (Zéman & Lentner, 2018). This principle assumes that the company will continue and complete its current plans using its assets as well continue to fulfill its future financial obligations.

KEYWORD

Financial report is a management tool used to efficiently communicate key financial information.

1.3.8. Principle of Full Disclosure

The Full Disclosure Principle requires the firm to include any related information in its financial report. The essential theory behind this approach is that users of an entity's financial statements can use them to make decisions. As a result, it is critical to use accounting software for financial services to ensure they have access to all required documentation. As a result, this idea ensures that the material presented in the entity's financial report follows accounting principles (Pounder, 2012).

1.4. IMPORTANCE OF FINANCIAL ACCOUNTING

Financial accounting completes several tasks in a firm and is critical for decision-making. Businesses could not operate if they could not record their finances through financial accounting. Here are some of the important ways financial accounting can help a business (Bhimani & Langfield-Smith, 2007):

1.4.1. External Communication

Financial accounting allows businesses to communicate their financial state to third parties, which is mandatory for completing business transactions. Companies require financial accounting to be eligible for loans and collaborate with suppliers (Dirsmith & Covaleski, 1983). Before starting a business with a firm, these external entities want to ensure it is in good standing. Companies can use financial accounting to provide these groups with a record of their finances, which decides their capital and ability to make payments (Gowthorpe & Amat, 1999).

1.4.2. Internal Communication

Businesses often use financial accounting for internal communication. Internal communication is about the personnel and financial staff of a corporation. Company employees must know how well the business is operating for several reasons. Knowing a company's financial status might make employees feel more secure. Understanding that the company is performing well means that no layoffs or downsizing should occur (Asif & Sargeant, 2000).

KEYWORD

Downsizing is the permanent reduction of a company's labor force through the elimination of unproductive workers or divisions.

This openness also makes employees feel more invested in the organization's growth. Understanding how well the company performs helps staff keep up the excellent job. A company's financial statement can reveal which departments are functioning well and which are struggling. Employees aware of this knowledge can significantly contribute to the company's improvement (Pincus et al., 2014). In some firms, meeting financial targets can result in bonuses, which is another reason employees should be aware of the company's financial situation. Employees can participate in stock-based or profit-sharing pay when financial accounting is used for internal communication (Dolphin, 2005).

1.4.3. Comparing Financial Reports

Financial accounting assists firms in evaluating their success in comparison to other businesses. Financial accounting is standardized, meaning various organizations' financial statements may be compared. This enables firms to compare their success to that of their competitors and identify areas for development. This form of comparison also allows organizations to identify investment options based on the success of other businesses (Tschopp & Huefner, 2015).

Comparing your firm to others in the same industry using financial accounting might provide more understanding than simply studying your unique report. Although your firm may appear to be thriving, a comparison to other companies may suggest plenty of potential for development and expansion in the industry. This might assist you in developing new strategies and setting new corporate objectives (Bens et al., 2011).

1.4.4. Recording Transactions

Financial accounting is also essential since it maintains a complete record of a company's transactions. This component of financial accounting, commonly known as bookkeeping, assists businesses in keeping track of their spending and remaining organized. These records may be requested during audits or when the company's spending and budgeting are reevaluated. Financial accounting is a constructive answer to these challenges, preventing businesses from losing vital information (Zaid, 2004) (Figure 1.9).

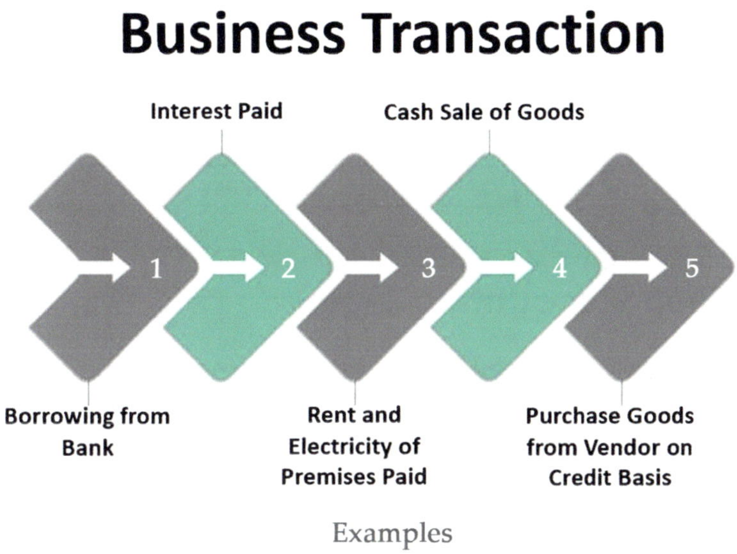

Figure 1.9. Picture of business transaction.

Source: Ashish Kumar Srivastav, Creative Commons License.

1.4.5. Filing Taxes and Abiding By-Laws

Financial accounting is crucial for a company's success, following rules, and avoiding legal problems. This relates to taxes for businesses in particular. When paying taxes, it is usually advantageous to organize all your financial data, but companies should always be mindful of their tax compliance. Certain expenses are tax deductible for a business, and some taxes must be paid earlier than others. Financial accounting assists firms in accurately and on time filing their taxes, avoiding needless audits and other legal complications (Su & Zheng, 2015).

1.4.6. Creating Budgets and Projections

Financial accounting is critical in helping businesses make informed decisions about their finances. It provides a clear picture of a company's financial standing, including its available cash and the allocation of funds to different areas of the business. This information is crucial in developing budgets and deciding which business areas may require additional funding (Schiff & Lewin, 1970).

Moreover, financial accounting also provides valuable insights into a company's future financial performance. Companies can make informed projections about their financial performance by examining past financial data in the coming year. This information can help companies identify opportunities and avoid repeating mistakes (Cardoş, 2014).

KEYWORD

Financial data refers to quantitative information that is used by organizations to make financial decisions.

1.5. TYPES OF FINANCIAL ACCOUNTING

1.5.1. Cash Accounting Method

Due to its simplicity, small businesses commonly use cash-based accounting. Rules-based on Generally Accepted Accounting Principles do not apply to the cash method approach (GAAP). When a financial transaction is genuinely accomplished, it is recorded using cash (Rayburn, 1986).

For instance, revenue is recorded when a payment is made, whereas costs are reported when a debt is paid off. Financial statements provided using a cash accounting method give details on the sources of funds used during the tax year, how they were used, and the cash balances as of the reporting date. Additional information on liabilities may be found in the notes to the financial statements (Penman, 2001).

Cash accounting can manage personal accounts up to a certain amount, but it is best suited for small businesses and one-person operations. For instance, the Internal Revenue Service (IRS) requires a company to use the accrual method of accounting if its annual revenues surpass $5 million. The system has a severe flaw in that it may give a deceptive impression of an entity's financial situation, mainly if certain operations, such as unpaid expenses, cash receipts, or pending receivables, are not recorded in the financial statements (Kwon, 1989) (Figure 1.10).

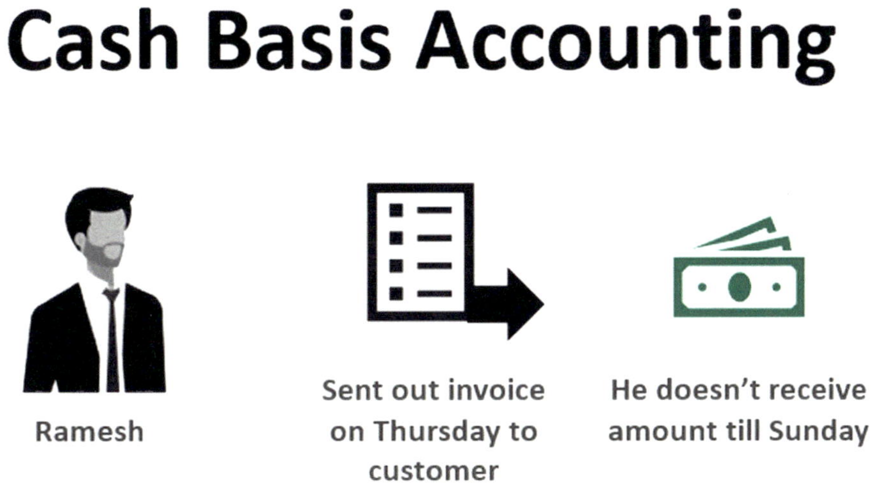

Figure 1.10. Image of cash accounting.

Source: Ashish Kumar Srivastav, Creative Commons License.

1.5.2. Accrual Accounting Method

The accrual method of accounting is predicated on the idea that revenue and expenditures should be coordinated in the same fiscal year. According to the matching principle, the criterion should consider the relationship between stated revenues and spending (Pina et al., 2009).

The accrual approach allows for a more precise assessment of a company's net income over time by recording transactions together in the same period and matching revenues and expenses. According to accrual accounting, revenues are only recorded when earned, and expenses are only recorded when incurred. The resulting invoice can be counted as revenue even if payment has not been received (Champoux, 2006).

Similarly, expenses are documented even if payment is delayed. If you choose the accrual approach and receive an advance payment, that money will not be counted as income until the following month. Delaying until the next tax year is not possible, though. Therefore, the advance payment must be included as income in the relevant financial statements and gross receipts for tax purposes (Christiaens & Rommel, 2008).

Did you Know?

According to the National Federation of Independent Business (NFIB), over 80% of small businesses in the United States use the cash accounting method.

1.6. FINANCIAL ACCOUNTING ADVANTAGES

Accounting is essential for any business since it reveals the proper financial health of the company. There is documentation for each year of business. That means we can evaluate how different periods fared in the books. The corporation can assess its financial standing relative to rival enterprises. Keeping accurate books is crucial for tax purposes, and the data contained therein could prove invaluable as evidence in a dispute (Felicia, 2014).

Accounting also helps prevent theft and fraud from occurring within an organization. The transfer is complete to the last penny. Similarly, a paper trail is left behind when fraudulent transactions occur. It's also worth noting that these documents are crucial for internal and external use. All sorts of choices, from those involving resources and their availability to those involving their most efficient deployment, rely on this information. From this document, financial backers, debt holders, and lenders can learn critical details about the company's performance and risks (Rewadikar, 2014).

KEYWORD

Debt is an obligation that requires one party, the debtor, to pay money borrowed or otherwise withheld from another party, the creditor.

1.7. DIFFERENCE BETWEEN FINANCIAL AND MANAGERIAL ACCOUNTING

Financial accounting and managerial accounting are two of the most often-used types of accounting in business. They share the same underlying tracks and have similar sounds, but they serve distinct purposes. Understanding the distinction between managerial and financial accounting helps decide which discipline to pursue (Richardson, 2002).

1.7.1. Audience

Financial Accounting: Both internal and external stakeholders, such as investors, lenders, and regulators, can use the data that financial accountants provide.

Managerial Accounting*:* Information is used internally to support management decisions and strategy development (Ahmed, 2022).

1.7.2. Governing Standards

Financial Accounting*:* Reports must adhere to legal standards like GAAP accounting.

Managerial Accounting: Because analyzes aren't for public view, the standards governing them are more flexible. They can use different rules and procedures to provide different perspectives on operational questions (Huy & Hien, 2010).

1.7.3. Timing

Financial Accounting: There is a predetermined order to statements. Whether it's a month, a quarter, or a year, they appear following the conclusion of each accounting period.

Managerial Accounting: Because analyzes are not meant for general consumption, the regulations governing them are laxer. To offer different points of view on relevant subjects, they can use various strategies and policies (Teki et al., 2012).

1.7.4. Focus

Financial Accounting: Statements give attention to past performance and provide information on recent activities.

Managerial Accounting: Reports could contain projections, including the economic effects of specific options (Hopper et al., 1992).

KEYWORD

Financial analyst is a professional, undertaking financial analysis for external or internal clients as a core feature of the job.

1.7.5. Level of Detail

Financial Accounting*:* Statements offer high-level summaries of the several categories in a company's financial records.

Managerial Accounting: Reports frequently provide more information on lower tiers of operations, including comparing the sales and costs of various products (Lamberton, 2005).

1.7.6. Career Opportunities

Financial Accounting: For seasoned professionals, common positions include controller, who oversees internal accounting, and financial analyst, who provides outside counsel to businesses and investors (Uyar et al., 2011).

Managerial Accounting: Typical positions include chief financial officer (CFO), responsible for a company's overall financial health, director of strategic planning, and data analytics manager (Samsuri et al., 2016).

1.7.7 Timeframe

Financial Accounting: It presents an analysis of the business firm based on past data and information.

Management Accounting: The analysis focuses on future strategies of the firm to achieve the financial goals.

ACTIVITY 1.1.

A small business owner has just started a new company and is trying to determine the best accounting method to use for the business. They have heard about the cash method and the accrual method, but they are not sure which one would be most appropriate for their business. The owner plans to sell products to customers and pay suppliers for the products as they are sold. Which accounting method would be best suited for this business, and why? Additionally, how would the chosen accounting method impact the financial statements of the business?What transactions would you record in the store's general ledger, and how would you classify them?

1.8. SUMMARY

- Financial accounting is producing and presenting financial accounts for decision-makers outside a company, such as investors, creditors, and regulators. Financial accounting aims to give these external stakeholders pertinent, trustworthy, and comparable information. Financial accounting is crucial because it provides external stakeholders with vital data supporting their decision-making. People can better grasp how financial information is used to make company choices by understanding the financial accounting principles, the distinctions between managerial and financial accounting, and the many types of financial accounting.

REVIEW QUESTIONS

1. What is the definition of financial accounting?
2. What is the purpose of financial accounting?
3. Who are the users of financial accounting information?
4. How does financial accounting differ from managerial accounting?
5. What are the different types of financial accounting?
6. Why is financial accounting important in business and society?
7. What are the key principles of financial accounting?

MULTIPLE CHOICE QUESTIONS

1. What is the main purpose of financial accounting?

a. To provide information to internal users

b. To provide information to external users

c. To assist in tax planning

d. To help in budgeting and financial planning

2. Which of the following is NOT a fundamental principle of financial accounting?

a. Objectivity

b. Consistency

c. Personal bias

d. Materiality

3. What is the main difference between managerial and financial accounting?

a. Managerial accounting provides information to internal users, while financial accounting provides information to external users.

b. Managerial accounting focuses on the future, while financial accounting focuses on the past.

c. Managerial accounting is mandatory, while financial accounting is optional.
d. Managerial accounting is based on historical cost, while financial accounting is based on market value.

4. **What is the primary focus of financial accounting?**
   a. To provide information to help make business decisions
   b. To comply with legal and regulatory requirements
   c. To provide a measure of the company's financial performance
   d. To provide information for tax purposes
5. **Which of the following is NOT a type of financial accounting?**
   a. Managerial Accounting
   b. Cost accounting
   c. Tax accounting
   d. Strategic Accounting
6. **Who are the primary users of financial accounting information?**
   a. Internal users such as management and employees
   b. External users such as investors, creditors, and regulators
   c. Consumers and customers
   d. All of the above
7. **Why is financial accounting important?**
   a. It provides information to help make business decisions
   b. It ensures the company complies with legal and regulatory requirements
   c. It provides a measure of the company's financial performance
   d. All of the above.

Answers to Multiple Choice Questions

1.	(b)	2.	(c)	3.	(a)	4.	(b)	5.	(d)
6.	(b)	7.	(d)						

REFERENCES

1. Ahmed, A. A. A., (2022). Perception of the audience of interests on the qualitative characteristics of financial reporting. *International Journal of Intellectual Property Management, 12*(3), 382–402.
2. Alexander, D., & Nobes, C., (2007). *Financial Accounting: An International Introduction* (Vol. 1, pp. 1–5). Pearson Education.

3. Ali, O. M., & Nesrine, A., (2015). Factors affecting auditor independence in Tunisia: The perceptions of financial analysts. *Journal of Finance and Accounting, 3*(3), 42–49.
4. Annand, D., (2008). Learning efficacy and cost-effectiveness of print versus e-book instructional material in an introductory financial accounting course. *Journal of Interactive Online Learning, 7*(2), 152–164.
5. Asif, S., & Sargeant, A., (2000). Modeling internal communications in the financial services sector. *European Journal of Marketing, 34*(3, 4), 299–318.
6. Balakrishnan, K., & Cohen, D. A., (2014). *Competition and Financial Accounting Misreporting*. Available at SSRN 2447882.
7. Barniv, R., Myring, M. J., & Thomas, W. B., (2005). The association between the legal and financial reporting environments and forecast performance of individual analysts. *Contemporary Accounting Research, 22*(4), 727–758.
8. Beattie, V., (2005). Moving the financial accounting research front forward: The U.K. contribution. *The British Accounting Review, 37*(1), 85–114.
9. Bens, D. A., Berger, P. G., & Monahan, S. J., (2011). Discretionary disclosure in financial reporting: An examination comparing internal firm data to externally reported segment data. *The Accounting Review, 86*(2), 417–449.
10. Bhattacharyya, A. K., (2012). *Financial Accounting for Business Managers* (Vol. 1, pp. 1–15). PHI Learning Pvt. Ltd.
11. Bhimani, A., & Langfield-Smith, K., (2007). Structure, formality and the importance of financial and non-financial information in strategy development and implementation. *Management Accounting Research, 18*(1), 3–31.
12. Boadway, R., (2006). Principles of cost-benefit analysis. *Public Policy Review, 2*(1), 1–44.
13. Brigham, E. F., & Houston, J. F., (2021). *Fundamentals of Financial Management: Concise* (Vol. 1, pp. 1–08). Cengage Learning.
14. Brorströim, B., (1998). Accrual accounting, politics and politicians. *Financial Accountability & Management, 14*(4), 319–333.
15. Brunnermeier, M., Crockett, A., Goodhart, C. A., Persaud, A., & Shin, H. S., (2009). *The Fundamental Principles of Financial Regulation* (Vol. 11). Geneva: ICMB, Internat. Center for Monetary and Banking Studies.
16. Cardoş, I. R., (2014). New trends in budgeting–a literature review. *SEA–Practical Application of Science, 2*(04), 483–489.
17. Champoux, M., (2006). *Accrual Accounting in New Zealand and Australia: Issues and Solutions* (No. 27, pp. 1–24). Briefing Paper.
18. Chandra, P., (2017). *Fundamentals of Financial Management* (Vol. 1, pp. 1–6). McGraw Hill Education.
19. Chiappetta, B., Shaw, K., & Wild, J., (2009). *Principles of Financial Accounting, 1*, 1–25.

20. Christiaens, J., & Rommel, J., (2008). Accrual accounting reforms: Only for businesslike (parts of) governments. *Financial Accountability & Management, 24*(1), 59–75.
21. Cloyd, C. B., (1995). The effects of financial accounting conformity on recommendations of tax preparers. *The Journal of the American Taxation Association, 17*(2), 50.
22. Dirsmith, M. W., & Covaleski, M. A., (1983). Strategy, external communication and environmental context. *Strategic Management Journal, 4*(2), 137–151.
23. Dolphin, R. R., (2005). Internal communications: Today's strategic imperative. *Journal of Marketing Communications, 11*(3), 171–190.
24. Dopuch, N., & Sunder, S., (1980). FASB's statements on objectives and elements of financial accounting: A review. *Accounting Review,* 1–21.
25. Duska, R. F., Duska, B. S., & Kury, K. W., (2018). *Accounting Ethics* (Vol. 1, pp. 1–20). John Wiley & Sons.
26. Dye, R. A., Glover, J. C., & Sunder, S., (2015). Financial engineering and the arms race between accounting standard setters and preparers. *Accounting Horizons, 29*(2), 265–295.
27. Felicia, S., (2014). Advantages and Disadvantages of applying evolved methods in management accounting practice. *Annals-Economy Series, 2*, 192–196.
28. Fogarty, T. J., Hussein, M. E., & Ketz, J. E., (1994). Political aspects of financial accounting standard setting in the USA. *Accounting, Auditing & Accountability Journal, 1*, 1–10.
29. Geier, D. A., (1998). The myth of the matching principle as a tax value. *Am. J. Tax Pol'y, 15*, 17.
30. Glover, J., (2014). Have academic accountants and financial accounting standard setters traded places? *Accounting, Economics and Law, 4*(1), 17–26.
31. Gordon, I. M., (2011). Lessons to be learned: An examination of Canadian and U.S. financial accounting and auditing textbooks for ethics/governance coverage. *Journal of Business Ethics, 101*, 29–47.
32. Gowthorpe, C., & Amat, O., (1999). External reporting of accounting and financial information via the internet in Spain. *European Accounting Review, 8*(2), 365–371.
33. Hackenbrack, K., & Nelson, M. W., (1996). Auditors' incentives and their application of financial accounting standards. *Accounting Review*, 43–59.
34. Hellman, N., (2008). Accounting conservatism under IFRS. *Accounting in Europe, 5*(2), 71–100.
35. Hines, R. D., (1991). The FASB's conceptual framework, financial accounting and the maintenance of the social world. *Accounting, Organizations and Society, 16*(4), 313–331.
36. Höglund, H., & Sundvik, D., (2016). Financial reporting quality and outsourcing of accounting tasks: Evidence from small private firms. *Advances in Accounting, 35*, 125–134.

37. Holmes, S., & Zimmer, I., (1994). The nature of the small firm: Understanding the motivations of growth and non-growth oriented owners. *Australian Journal of Management, 19*(1), 97–120.
38. Hopper, T., Kirkham, L., Scapens, R. W., & Turley, S., (1992). Does financial accounting dominate management accounting—A research note. *Management Accounting Research, 3*(4), 307–311.
39. Hopwood, A. G., (2000). Understanding financial accounting practice. *Accounting, Organizations and Society, 25*(8), 763–766.
40. Hussein, M. E., (1981). The innovative process in financial accounting standards setting. *Accounting, Organizations and Society, 6*(1), 27–37.
41. Huy, D. T. N., & Hien, D. T. N., (2010). The backbone of European corporate governance standards after financial crisis, corporate scandals and manipulation. *Economic and Business Review, 12*(4), 1.
42. Jasch, C. M., (2008). *Environmental and Material Flow Cost Accounting: Principles and Procedures* (Vol. 25). Springer Science & Business Media.
43. Kelton, A. S., & Pennington, R. R., (2012). Internet financial reporting: The effects of information presentation format and content differences on investor decision making. *Computers in Human Behavior, 28*(4), 1178–1185.
44. Kinney, Jr. W. R., (1994). Audit litigation research: Professional help is needed. *Accounting Horizons, 8*(2), 80.
45. Kirwan, F. P., (1964). Miscellaneous problems including whether to finance the contractor. *ABA Sec. Ins. Negl. & Comp. L. Proc.*, 70.
46. Krishnan, G., & Visvanathan, G., (2009). Do auditors price audit committee's expertise? The case of accounting versus nonaccounting financial experts. *Journal of Accounting, Auditing & Finance, 24*(1), 115–144.
47. Kwon, Y. K., (1989). Accrual versus cash-basis accounting methods: An agency-theoretic comparison. *Journal of Accounting and Public Policy, 8*(4), 267–281.
48. Lamberton, G., (2005). Sustainability accounting—A brief history and conceptual framework. In: *Accounting Forum* (Vol. 29, No. 1, pp. 7–26). Taylor & Francis.
49. Maingot, M., & Zeghal, D., (2006). Financial reporting of small business entities in Canada. *Journal of Small Business Management, 44*(4), 513–530.
50. Manzon, Jr. G. B., & Guo, J., (2006). *Demand for Information Enhancement: The Case of Chinese Firms*. Available at SSRN 895513.
51. McNally, G. M., Eng, L. H., & Hasseldine, C. R., (1982). Corporate financial reporting in New Zealand: An analysis of user preferences, corporate characteristics and disclosure practices for discretionary information. *Accounting and Business Research, 13*(49), 11–20.
52. Medley, P., (1997). Environmental accounting-what does it mean to professional accountants? *Accounting, Auditing & Accountability Journal, 10*(4), 594–600.

53. Melé, D., Rosanas, J. M., & Fontrodona, J., (2017). Ethics in finance and accounting: Editorial introduction. *Journal of Business Ethics, 140*, 609–613.
54. Meymandi, A. R., Rajabdoory, H., & Asoodeh, Z., (2015). The reasons of considering ethics in accounting job. *International Journal of Management, Accounting and Economics, 2*(2), 136–143.
55. Muda, S., Hussin, A. H., Johari, H., Sapari, J. M., & Jamil, N., (2013). The key contributing factors of non-accounting students' failure in the introduction to financial accounting course. *Procedia-Social and Behavioral Sciences, 90*, 712–719.
56. Muniandy, B., & Ali, M. J., (2012). Development of financial reporting environment in Malaysia. *Research in Accounting Regulation, 24*(2), 115–125.
57. Noor, N., Batool, I., & Arshad, H. M., (2020). Financial literacy, financial self-efficacy and financial account ownership behavior in Pakistan. *Cogent Economics & Finance, 8*(1), 1806479.
58. Peek, E., Cuijpers, R., & Buijink, W., (2010). Creditors' and shareholders' reporting demands in public versus private firms: Evidence from Europe. *Contemporary Accounting Research, 27*(1), 49–91.
59. Penman, S. H., (2001). On comparing cash flow and accrual accounting models for use in equity valuation: A response to Lundholm and O'Keefe (CAR, Summer 2001). *Contemporary Accounting Research, 18*(4), 681–692.
60. Pina, V., Torres, L., & Yetano, A., (2009). Accrual accounting in E.U. local governments: One method, several approaches. *European Accounting Review, 18*(4), 765–807.
61. Pincus, J. D., Rayfield, R. E., & Cozzens, M. D., (2014). The chief executive officer's internal communication role: A benchmark program of research. In: *Public Relations Research Annual* (pp. 1–35). Routledge.
62. Pounder, B., (2012). Full disclosure vs. effective disclosure: As a guiding principle for financial reporting, "full disclosure" is being overtaken by "effective disclosure." *Strategic Finance, 94*(2), 17–19.
63. Rayburn, J., (1986). The association of operating cash flow and accruals with security returns. *Journal of Accounting Research,* 112–133.
64. Rewadikar, B. H. A. W. A. N. A., (2014). Advantages of implementing green accounting. *Indian Research Journal, 1*(2), 1–7.
65. Richardson, A. J., (2002). Professional dominance: The relationship between financial accounting and managerial accounting, 1926–1986. *Accounting Historians Journal, 29*(2), 91–121.
66. Roslender, R., (1997). Accounting for the worth of employees: Is the discipline finally ready to respond to the challenge? *Journal of Human Resource Costing & Accounting, 2*(1), 9–25.
67. Saeed, S., Hamawandy, N. M., & Omar, R., (2020). Role of internal and external audit in public sector governance. A case study of Kurdistan regional government. *International Journal of Advanced Science and Technology, 29*(8), 1452–1462.

68. Salterio, S., (1996). The effects of precedents and client position on auditors' financial accounting policy judgment. *Accounting, Organizations and Society, 21*(5), 467–486.
69. Samsuri, A. S. B., Arifin, T. R. B. T., & Hussin, S. B., (2016). Perception of undergraduate accounting students towards professional accounting career. *International Journal of Academic Research in Accounting, Finance and Management Sciences, 6*(3), 78–88.
70. Satava, D., Caldwell, C., & Richards, L., (2006). Ethics and the auditing culture: Rethinking the foundation of accounting and auditing. *Journal of Business Ethics, 64*, 271–284.
71. Schiff, M., & Lewin, A. Y., (1970). The impact of people on budgets. *The Accounting Review, 45*(2), 259–268.
72. Schroeder, R. G., Clark, M. W., & Cathey, J. M., (2022). *Financial Accounting Theory and Analysis: Text and Cases* (Vol. 1, pp. 1–07). John Wiley & Sons.
73. Sian, S., & Roberts, C., (2009). U.K. small owner-managed businesses: Accounting and financial reporting needs. *Journal of Small Business and Enterprise Development, 16*(2), 289–305.
74. Sloan, R. G., (2001). Financial accounting and corporate governance: A discussion. *Journal of Accounting and Economics, 32*(1–3), 335–347.
75. Socea, A. D., (2012). Managerial decision-making and financial accounting information. *Procedia-Social and Behavioral Sciences, 58*, 47–55.
76. Strom, S. H., (1987). "Machines instead of clerks": Technology and the feminization of bookkeeping. *Computer Chips and Paper Clips: Technology and Women's Employment, Volume II: Case Studies and Policy Perspectives, 2*, 63.
77. Su, L. D., & Zheng, J., (2015). A study of the significance of tax planning for the enterprise's financial management. In: *Computing, Control, Information and Education Engineering. Proceedings of the 2015 2nd International Conference on Computer, Intelligent and Education Technology (CICET 2015)* (pp. 819–822).
78. Sugiarto, H. V. S., & Fachrurrozie, F., (2018). The determinant of accounting conservatism on manufacturing companies in Indonesia. *Accounting Analysis Journal, 7*(1), 1–9.
79. Tan, L., (2013). Creditor control rights, state of nature verification, and financial reporting conservatism. *Journal of Accounting and Economics, 55*(1), 1–22.
80. Teki, S., Grube, M., & Griffiths, T. D., (2012). A unified model of time perception accounts for duration-based and beat-based timing mechanisms. *Frontiers in Integrative Neuroscience, 5*, 90.
81. Tschopp, D., & Huefner, R. J., (2015). Comparing the evolution of CSR reporting to that of financial reporting. *Journal of Business Ethics, 127*, 565–577.
82. Tugas, F. C., (2012). Exploring a new element of fraud: A study on selected financial accounting fraud cases in the world. *American International Journal of Contemporary Research, 2*(6), 112–121.

83. Uyar, A., Gungormus, A. H., & Kuzey, C., (2011). Factors affecting students career choice in accounting: The case of a Turkish University. *American Journal of Business Education (AJBE), 4*(10), 29–38.
84. Wang, X., Cao, F., & Ye, K., (2018). Mandatory corporate social responsibility (CSR) reporting and financial reporting quality: Evidence from a quasi-natural experiment. *Journal of Business Ethics, 152*, 253–274.
85. Weidner, D. J., (1999). Synthetic leases: Structured finance, financial accounting and tax ownership. *J. Corp. L., 25*, 445.
86. Wüstemann, J., & Wüstemann, S., (2010). Why consistency of accounting standards matters: A contribution to the rules-versus-principles debate in financial reporting. *Abacus, 46*(1), 1–27.
87. Young, J. J., (2006). Making up users. *Accounting, Organizations and Society, 31*(6), 579–600.
88. Yu, T., Lin, Z., & Tang, Q., (2018). Blockchain: The introduction and its application in financial accounting. *Journal of Corporate Accounting & Finance, 29*(4), 37–47.
89. Zadek, S., (1998). Balancing performance, ethics, and accountability. *Journal of Business Ethics, 17*, 1421–1442.
90. Zaid, O. A., (2004). Accounting systems and recording procedures in the early Islamic state. *Accounting Historians Journal, 31*(2), 149–170.
91. Zéman, Z., & Lentner, C., (2018). The changing role of going concern assumption supporting management decisions after financial crisis. *Polish Journal of Management Studies, 18*(1), 428–441.
92. Zimmerman, A. B., & Bloom, R., (2016). The matching principle revisited. *Accounting Historians Journal, 43*(1), 79–119.

CHAPTER 2

ACCRUAL ACCOUNTING CONCEPT

UNIT INTRODUCTION

Accounting on an accrual basis is a conventional method accountants use to reconcile business documentation by comparing costs and revenues. A company's financial condition is more accurate using accrual accounting since it incorporates current and predicted future outflows and cash inflows. The period of transactions is not a computing concern since the accrual-based technique registers a transaction before such money is exchanged. A utility corporation, for example, offers services to all its consumers and bills people once per month (Ohlson et al., 1998). The utility provider keeps track of the costs of providing the monthly charge. It registers income when it issues the consumer bill only at the end of each month, even if the consumer has not yet paid. As a result, even if the consumer has not received the money, the accountant reports the costs and accrues income on the income statement for the month of services. By ensuring that there is a sufficient allowance or surplus cash set aside to cover all these expenditures, accrual-based accounts with sales returns, bad debts, or decreasing product value are often referred to as obsolescence (Beechy, 2007).

Modifications called accruals are frequently made by businesses before publishing their accounting information, including their statements for cash flow. Due to the potential economic risk, accrual accounting is typically not used by small enterprises. Companies frequently cover expenses while utilizing accrual accounting before related money is received (for instance, they funded the sales tax before they get their cash for sale) (Robinson, 1998). Because it accounts for both actual expenses spent and paid in addition to revenues collected and generated, the accrual accounting method gives a business the most accurate real financial picture possible. Because inventory is considered an asset by the IRS, organizations with inventory are typically required to utilize accrual-based accounting. Businesses frequently purchase inventory using credit and then pay for it. In other words, they register the acquisition once a purchase agreement is signed and update their financial records accordingly ((Bergmann et al., 2019; Azhar et al., 2022).

For instance, a business employing accrual-based accounting logs a transaction as quickly as it delivers an invoice to a consumer. The monthly average sales of the software company Technix Ltd are $10,000. The majority of these sales—about 60%—are cash; the remaining 40% are on credit. Credit transactions are treated as sales within accrual accounting, and also the profit such sales produce includes both credit and cash sales, which subtract costs and the price of products sold. Logan Allec, the founder of the company and CPA, says:

"It can require some time to get people to understand accrual accounting. People inquire about their company's performance last year, believing the answer can be found by glancing at their bank statements. People believe the amount they earned and invested (the cash basis) represents reality, yet the cash basis does not reflect how the business has been doing. Checking what this one produces and spends could be sufficient for simple, tiny firms, but something more complicated than a lemonade should consider adopting accrual accounting" (Figure 2.1).

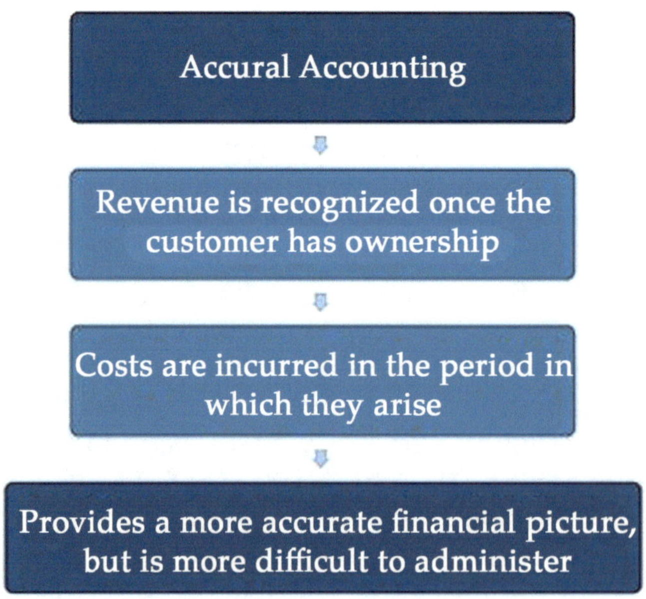

Figure 2.1. Illustration of accrual accounting process.

Source: Free management publications, Creative Commons License.

Learning Objectives

At the end of the chapter, the reader will be able to understand the following:

- The concept of accrual accounting
- The difference between accrual accounting and cash accounting
- The basics of adjustment entries
- The significance of different types of adjustment entries
- The concept of prepaid expenses
- The importance of unearned revenues
- The significance of GAAP and IFRS on the accrual principle

Key Terms

- Accrual Accounting
- Accrued Expenses
- Accrued Revenues
- Cash Accounting
- Generally Accepted Accounting Principles (GAAP)
- International Financial Reporting Standards (IFRS)
- Prepaid Expenses
- Unearned Revenues

2.1. ACCRUAL ACCOUNTING METHOD

The accrual accounting technique provides a more realistic view of a company's profitability, productivity, and general economic health at every given time. There is no delay in exchanging cash and expenditures under this accepted accounting procedure. Therefore, some organizations could find the accounting process overly complex without a proper accounting system (Pina et al., 2009).

KEYWORD

Profitability is a measure of an organization's profit relative to its expenses.

Businesses' accounting methods are displayed within their financial information. All those are high-level reports typically comprising a financial statement, a statement of income, and supporting notes. Whereas auditors may prepare both forms, they could only certify such statements when a corporation employs the accrual method of accounting. One disadvantage of an accrual accounting method is that it fails to provide an accurate picture of the company's cash flow in the statement of profits and losses. As a result, businesses must generate a CFS that reconciles the accrual loss and profit statements to available cash.

Accrual accounting alters how accountants or owners of small companies record their financial data and adds a layer to a company's accounting records. Clarifying any uncertainty surrounding revenue and expenses could reduce business instability. A company can be more flexible using accrual accounting by forecasting revenues and costs. Additionally, it helps analyze profitability and spot possibilities and possible problems faster and more precisely (Christiaens & Rommel, 2008).

2.2. PRINCIPLES OF ACCRUAL ACCOUNTING

Determining how much income and spending should be reported within a specific period can be challenging. Knowing the business operations of the company is necessary for accurate reports. The concept of revenue recognition and the correct amount are two main principles that serve as recommendations (Ellwood & Newberry, 2007).

Accrual-based accounting concepts come in two different varieties (Ouda, 2007).

2.2.1. Matching Principle

Following this rule, accountants report all receipts and outlay during the same reporting period, comparing them to determine the period's earnings and losses. When applying the matching principle, businesses must record the spending within the extended period, not necessarily whenever it occurred. Through accrual accounting, expenses are documented when a company is liable for them. Since the expense should be recorded within the period when it was incurred, it makes no difference when a corporation pays the expenditure (Zimmerman & Bloom, 2016).

If there were no facts, companies could recognize costs before or after the time they record income. It may be misleading when evaluating a company's financial standing at any one time. The scheduling of income taxes is a case in point. The revenue taxes can be excessive one month and too low the next if there is no proper expense-revenue balancing. Accountants typically classify expenses as variable costing when connecting or matching them to revenue is challenging. Rental and utilities, including administrative costs, are a few examples of all these costs. Accountants typically write off these expenses within the relevant period or treat them as incurred (Butler & Macey, 1996).

KEYWORD

Revenue is the total amount of income generated by the sale of goods and services related to the primary operations of the business.

The fundamental difference between accrual and cash basis accounting is the point at which expenditures and revenues are balanced. Accountants cannot provide an analysis of financial accounts without connecting the expenses to the income, as will be the case under the accrual accounting approach. Retail establishments are another excellent source for accrual accounting instances of expense reporting. The proprietor of a garden nursery shop invests $80,000 in soaking hoses. These horses sold for $170,000 during three months of storage. Through its costs of goods sold, the store recognizes and records the cost of getting and keeping the hoses when selling them. Within the same time frame as the $170,000 transaction, the business can equal the $80,000 expenditure (Fraenkel, 1969).

Business owners could classify their records using either the systematic and reasonable allocation or the instantaneous allocation when there is no apparent link between the expenditure and revenue. Payments are distributed systematically and rationally during an expense's helpful existence. For instance, a garden nursery could not link a new purchase of hose with a particular sales transaction if something did so to water its stock. The owner knows they cannot market the system again, even though it will continue to function well for roughly five years. Over those five years, the business will allocate a depreciation charge. Through this, the retailer can match and recognize the initial cost while spreading out any revenue from the water system as labor time saved—over its hose's usable duration (De Jonge & Dormann, 2006).

When a business cannot predict the cost-benefit of an expenditure in the future, it is classified as an urgent allocation. These fees may include commissions, debt, selling costs, and administration expenditures. When a corporation incurs these costs, an accountant promptly notes them inside the financial accounts for that period (Ullrich et al., 2007) (Figure 2.2).

Did you Know?

The International Financial Reporting Standard (IFRS) 2015, Accounting Rules Update No. 2014-09, and Revenue from Customer Contracts (Topic 606) provides comprehensive documentation of revenue recognition principle (ASC 606)

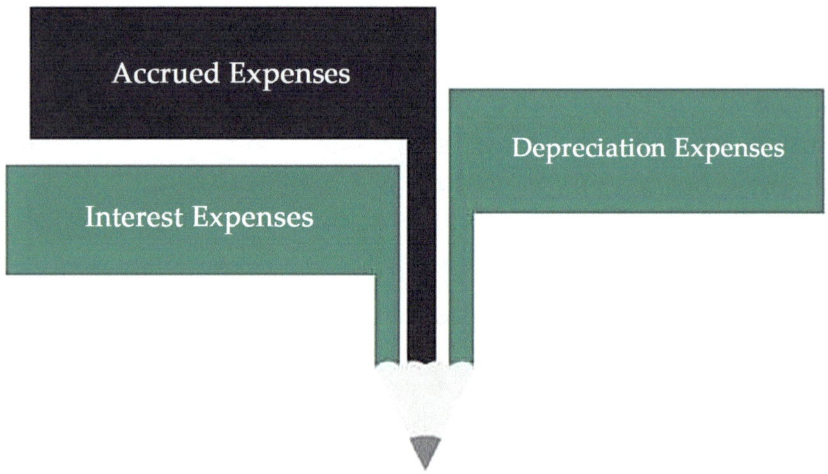

Figure 2.2. Schematic of types of expenses.

Source: Ashish Kumar Srivastav, Creative Commons License

2.2.2. Revenue Recognition Principle

The revenue detection principle "*GAAP*" covers standardized accounting as another process that explains the time frame and technique by which a company generates revenue; it gives auditors a more visible, apples-to-apples assessment of a company's economic position throughout industries (Wagenhofer, 2014).

Revenue is recorded whenever it is earned when payment is guaranteed under accrual-based accounting, and the accounting must occur during the same financial reporting period.

Whenever a purchaser and a seller sign a contract for the exchange of products and services with payment based upon that accrual basis concerning the accounting cycle, recognition is guaranteed. Periodicity is yet another essential component of the accrual system of accounting. The idea of periodicity is one that accountants use to modify their entries. According to this presumption, accounting involves discrete periods like months, quarters, and years. A business's revenue for a specific time heavily depends on these durations or periods. Without such periods, it would be impossible to assess a company's financial performance, let alone identify trends. While filing taxes, the IRS accepts fiscal years (any continuous 12 months that don't conclude in December) or calendar years (January 1 – December 31) (Dutta & Zhang, 2002).

KEYWORD

Buyback is when a corporation purchases its own shares in the stock market.

Retail serves as a great illustration of how to recognize revenue using accrual accounting. Using its retail locations, fashion brands market their products in clothes. When a consumer uses a credit card to buy an outfit in early November 15, the business processes the card immediately but doesn't get the cash payment before December. Because credit cards are claimed as money, the company treats them like cash. The accountant reports whenever the store recognizes and receives the money in November (Antle & Demski, 1989).

Whenever selling from inventory, accountants typically should recognize income now for sale. This rule must have certain limitations, such as the approach used to calculate the percentage completed. The exclusions are buyback contracts and refunds for transactions typically acknowledged at purchase (Zhang, 2005). Buyback contracts provide that the seller will purchase the item from them after selling it to a consumer. A seller-builder might promise to return a developing property from an occupant-buyer if the latter's business relocates in the first year of possession. To maintain the investment's appeal, it would be wiser for the supplier to buy back that property and resell it as it creates and sells new properties. Accountants respond by failing to record a sale on the business's accounts (Wüstemann & Kierzek, 2005).

When a consumer receives an item for a refund, they have completed a return. Many businesses find it challenging to predict how many returns they will accept in the future; therefore, they should limit the return term for each item. To deal with this, accountants estimate and subtract a projected rate of return for every period (Jones & Pagach, 2013) (Figure 2.3).

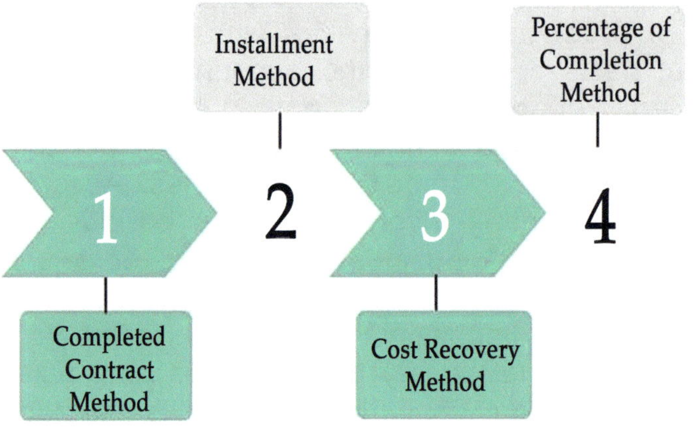

Figure 2.3. Illustration of principles of revenue recognition.

Source: Dheeraj Vaidya, Creative Commons License.

2.3. ACCRUAL VERSUS CASH BASIS OF ACCOUNTING

2.3.1. Accrual-Basis accounting

It indicates that even when no money is transferred, transactions that affect a business's financial statements are documented during the events. By employing the accrual basis, for example, companies must acknowledge revenues as soon as they are generated (the financial reporting concept), even though cash has not yet been received. Like the cash basis, the accrual method requires businesses to record expenses as they are incurred, regardless of whether money was paid. The cash basis is an alternative to an accrual basis (Yuliati et al., 2019).

2.3.2. Under Cash-Basis Accounting

After the money is received, does a company's revenue increase? After the payment is made, do they record expenses? According to generally accepted accounting rules, the accrual basis of accounting is illegal. Why? Because it violates the accrual accounting principle by failing to recognize revenue as it is realized. The matching principle is also broken because expenses are not recorded as incurred (Kwon, 1989). Comparing accrual-based versus cash-based data is shown in Table 2.1. Let's say that in 2009, Bright Colors paints a sizable structure. It spent $50,000 on salary and painting costs in 2009. It charges the client $80,000 but isn't paid until 2010. Bright Colors reports $80,000 in revenue for 2009 on an accrual basis because that is how it was earned (Rhodes & Smith, 2004).

Table 2.1. Comparison of Accrual Versus Cash-Based Data

	2009	2010
Activity	Purchased paint, painted building, paid employees	Received payment for work done in 2009
Accrual basis	Revenue $80,000 Expense 50,000 Net income $30,000	Revenue $ 0 Expense 0 Net income $0
Cash basis	Revenue $ 0 Expense 50,000 Net loss $ 50,000	Revenue $80,000 Expense 0 Net income $80,000

Source: Antle, R., & Demski, J. S., Creative Commons License.

The business balances the $50,000 in expenses with the $80,000 in revenue. Consequently, 2009's net earnings are $30,000 ($80,000, $50,000). The $30,000 in net earnings reported for 2009 shows how successful Bright Colors' efforts were throughout that time. Instead, Bright Paint should report $50,000 in costs in 2009 and $80,000 in revenues in 2010 under cash basis accounting. It might record a loss of $50,000 in 2009 and net earnings of $80,000 in 2010, as shown in Table 2.1. Because the corporation's financial results will be overstated for 2009 and 2010, it is evident that the cash-basis statistics are deceptive (Schapiro, 1974).

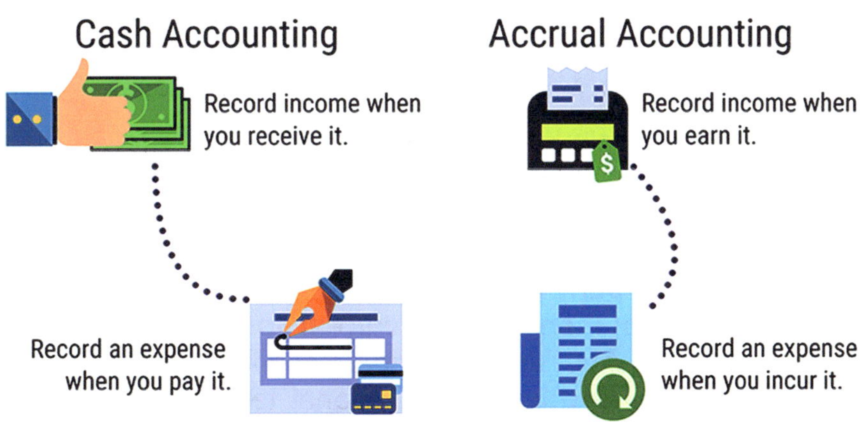

Figure 2.4. Image of difference between cash accounting and accrual accounting.

Source: Basis 365, Creative Commons License.

2.4. BASICS OF ADJUSTING ENTRIES

Adjusting entries are accounting journal entries which are made at the end of the accounting period once the trial balance is prepared. These entries are posted in the general ledger like any other accounting entry. Adjusting entries help to get adjusted revenues and expenses to the accounting period in which they are incurred. These entries are made on real time basis since invoices for the income and expenditure are raised under the accrual basis of accounting. The adjusting entry, therefore, witnesses that the money has been transferred in accounts. Further, it is also requirement under the accounting standards – such as the International Financial Reporting Standards (IFRS).

KEYWORD

Transaction Record in accounting is defined as a business occurrence that has a monetary effect on the financial records of a firm.

Companies create changing entries to ensure that revenues are reported when generated and that expenditures are recognized in the time spent. The accounts receivable (AR) and matching criteria are upheld by adjusting entries (Garrison, 1981). Because of the trial balance—the initial compilation of transaction records does not contain accurate and complete information, so adjusting inputs are required. It is valid for several reasons:

- Because doing so would not be productive, some occurrences are not documented daily. Examples include the utilization of resources and employees' receipt of payment (Manaf et al., 2011).
- Certain costs that expire over time instead of because of routine everyday transactions are not recorded within the accounting cycle. These include fees for using facilities and machinery, rent, and Insurance (Novita, 2022).
- There could be unrecorded objects—a utility bill that won't be collected until the following accounting cycle serves as an illustration.

Any time a business produces financial information, entries are necessary. The company examines the account with a trial balance to see if it is comprehensive and current for financial statement reasons. A balance sheet account and an account from the financial statements are included in each additional term (Vangermeersch, 1997) (Figure 2.5).

Source: Chegg, Creative Commons License.

Figure 2.5. Picture of adjusting entries.

2.5. TYPES OF ADJUSTING ENTRIES

Adjusting entries might be either accruals or deferred payments. Every one of these categories includes two subclasses, as shown in Illustration 4–3 on the following page.

2.5.1. Deferrals Entries

Prepaid Expenses: Cash payments made for expenditures that are then documented as assets before being utilized or consumed (Musselman, 1969).

Unearned Revenues: Money is received and documented as liabilities before earning income.

2.5.2. Accruals

Accrued Revenues: Earned revenue that has not remained documented or paid out in cash.

Accrued Expenses: Expenditures made but not documented or paid in cash (Dunn, 1960).

2.6. ADJUSTING ENTRIES FOR DEFERRALS

Defer is another word for postponed or delayed. Expenses or revenues which are deferred are those that are recorded at a time after the actual money exchange. By adjusting deferral entries, companies measure the portion of delayed items that have been spent as an expenditure or received as income during the current accounting year. Prepayments and unearned income are the two categories of deferrals (Ermaliza et al., 2022).

2.6.1. Prepaid Expenses

Prepaid expenses, often known as prepayments, are liabilities businesses record when paying for expenses, impacting many accounting periods. Whenever expenses are paid in advance, an assets account is raised (debited) to reflect the value or service the business will eventually get (Landman, 1950). Premium payments are frequently made for insurance, supplies, advertisement, and rent. Additionally, enterprises prepay for their purchases of machinery and buildings (Frankovic, 2000). Prepaid expenses include those that either run out with time (like rental and insured) or through use (e.g., supplies). This expenditure does not need to be entered daily, which is needless and impracticable. As a result, businesses wait to recognize such cost expiration dates until they have finished creating their financial statements. They create adjusting entries at every statement date to record the costs related to the current accounting cycle and display the balances in asset accounts (Hicks & Block, 1967).

Assets are exaggerated, and expenditures are undervalued before correction. A debit is recorded in an expense account, and a credit is recorded in an asset account due to an additional term for prepayable expenses (Rabinowitz, 1940) (Figure 2.6).

Figure 2.6. Illustration of prepaid expenses.

Source: CFI team, Creative Commons License.

2.6.1.1. Supplies

An asset account is increased (debited) when supplies like paper and envelopes are bought. The business uses supplies during the accounting cycle; companies recognize supply expenditure at the end of their accounting period instead of recording it as it is consumed. The firm counts the remaining stock at the end of each accounting period. Supply consumed (an expenditure) for that period is calculated as the difference between the unadjusted level inside the Supplies (assets) account and the actual price of supplies on hand (Naylor et al., 2000).

2.6.1.2. Insurance

Companies buy Insurance to shield themselves against losses brought on by fire, robbery, and other circumstances. Insurance premiums should be prepaid, frequently for several years. The asset or expense account Prepaid Insurance records the price of the Insurance (premium costs) paid in advance, like an increase (debit). Companies raise (debit) Insurance expenses and decrease (credit) Prepaid Insurance so that the financial statement date reflects the insurance cost that has lapsed during the period (Spence & Zeckhauser, 1978).

2.6.1.3. Depreciation

A business often possesses several long-lasting assets, including buildings, machinery, and automobiles. The asset's "*useful life*" is the time it will be used. A structure is regarded as an asset instead of a cost on the date it is acquired because it is anticipated to be used for several years. According to the cost principle, businesses must register these assets at cost. Companies distribute a part of this expense like an expense during every phase of the asset's usable life following the matching principle. Depreciation spreads an asset's cost throughout its service life (Jorgenson, 1996) (Figure 2.7).

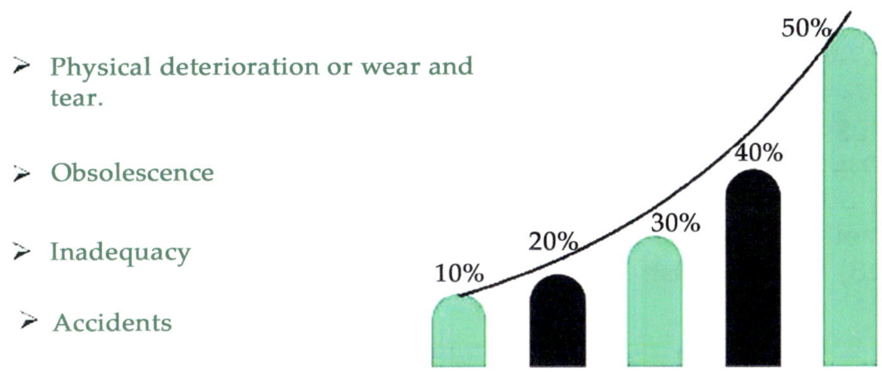

Figure 2.7. Illustration of types of depreciation.

Source: Wallstreetmojo Team, Creative Commons License.

2.6.1.4. Need for Modification

Lengthy prepayment of the usage of an asset is what buying long-lived assets entails. An adjustment input for depreciation is required to record the cost used during the time (an expense) and report any new price (assets) at the end of the period. Understanding that depreciation is just an allocation notion rather than a valuation idea is crucial. Depreciation, then, distributes the cost of an asset to the periods during which it is employed. Depreciation does not try to reflect the fundamental change in capital value (Hotelling, 1925).

2.6.2. Unearned Revenues

Companies increase (credit) a liabilities account named unearned revenues to record funds received while revenue is realized. Unearned income can come from renting magazines and newspapers and deposit accounts for future services. Before providing the flying service, airlines like United, American, with Delta, for example, regarded revenue through ticket sales as unearned revenue (Conrad & DeMeritt, 2013). Prepaid costs are the reverse of unearned revenues. Assuming similar accounting times, landlords, for instance, will have unearned rental revenue whenever a renter has paid rent in advance (Okon & Okon, 2021).

Remember

A prepayment on a single company's books is usually an unearned revenue item on the records of the business that received the advance payment.

A company boosts (credits) unearned (a liability) accounts whenever it gets paid for the services rendered to improve future periods and acknowledge the existing liability. After that, the business generates income by rendering services (Altamuro et al., 2005). Everyday entries during the accounting cycle are impractical because that is when the company generates revenue. Instead, we wait until after the correction procedure to recognize generated revenue. The business then creates an opening to show the obligation at the accounting cycle's conclusion and document the revenue collected during the period. Liabilities are frequently exaggerated, and revenues are undervalued before correction. Consequently, the debit to a liabilities account is increased by the additional term for unearned income, while the credit to something like a revenue account is decreased (Дегтеринская, 2018) (Figure 2.8).

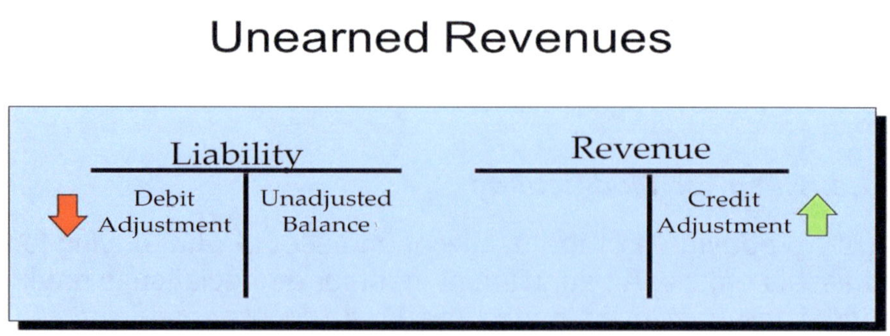

Figure 2.8. Schematic of difference between liability and revenue.

Source: Dictio Community, Creative Commons License.

2.7. ADJUSTING ENTRIES FOR ACCRUALS

Accruals make up the second group of adjusting entries. The revenue account (and the accompanying model of economics) or cost account (as well as the related liabilities account) are undervalued before accrual adjustments. As a result, a report on the income statement and balance sheet will be increased by the additional term for accruals (Malau et al., 2022).

2.7.1. Accrued Revenues

Accrued revenues have been earned but have not yet been reported as of the statement date. In the same way that interest revenue accumulates over the period, accrued revenues can do the same. Because generating interest does not require everyday transactions, those are not documented (Di Minin et al., 2016). Because doing so is frequently impractical, businesses do not consistently record interest income. Regarding fees and commissions, accrued revenues can also result from services that have been rendered but have not been paid or collected. Since only part of the entire service has been rendered and consumers will not be charged until it has been rendered, they may go unrecorded (Caylor, 2010).

KEYWORD

Capital is typically cash or liquid assets being held or obtained for expenditures.

The receivables balance sheet date and the revenue realized throughout the period are recorded inside an additional term. Capital and revenues are both understated before correction. Each adjusting entry for accumulated revenues causes an increase (a debit) to an asset's value and a rise (a credit) to an income statement. (Benson & Soriyan, 2018).

2.7.2. Accrued Expenses

Accrued costs have been incurred but have not yet been paid or reported as of the statement date. The most typical accumulated expenditures include interest, taxation, and salaries (Ngwenya, 2013).

Businesses make some adjustments for accounts payable (AP) to document the commitments that exist date of the balance sheet and record the expenditures relevant to the current accounting cycle. Liability and spending are both understated before correction. A debit is made to an expense report, and a credit is made to a liabilities account due to an adjusting entry regarding accrued expenses (Goller, 1950) (Figure 2.9).

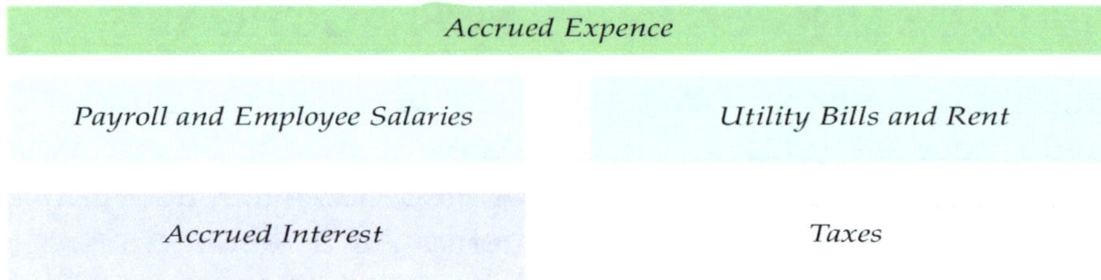

Figure 2.9. Image of accrued expenses.

Source: Wallstree prep, Creative Commons License.

2.8. ACCRUAL ACCOUNTING RATE OF RETURN FORMULA

The average year accounting profit is split by the original investment in the accrual accounting rate of return (ARR) formula. Managers use ARR to decide whether to move on to the next investment. They will move forward with a project if an ARR exceeds their hurdle rate (Fisher & McGowan, 1983) (Figure 2.10).

The accrual accounting rate of return considers the accounting rate of return calculation and applies the accrual method of accounting. In this situation, the income from the investment is recognized on the accrual basis i.e. when it is earned and not when it is received.

The minimal profit a business anticipates making when funding a project is known as the hurdle rate. Below is an illustration of an ARR estimate for a project with a $500,000 original investment. Accountants forecast the project will bring in $140,000 in yearly revenue over five years (Kelly & Tahir, 2009).

Figure 2.10. Picture of ARR.

Source: Madhuri Thakur, Creative Commons License.

ARR = (Average Annual Profit) / (Initial Investment)
ARR = $140,000/$500,000
ARR = 0.28, or 28%

Whether this rate is higher than the business's required rate of return (RRR), or hurdle rate, it can confidently pursue funding. Depending on how much investment risk they can tolerate, businesses have varied RRRs (Fritsche & Dugan, 1997). Although this technique is helpful for comparing projects, it cannot distinguish between investments with varying lifetime cash flows. Additionally, it doesn't consider the time value of money (TVM) or potential future earnings (Fritsche & Dugan, 2001) (Figure 2.11).

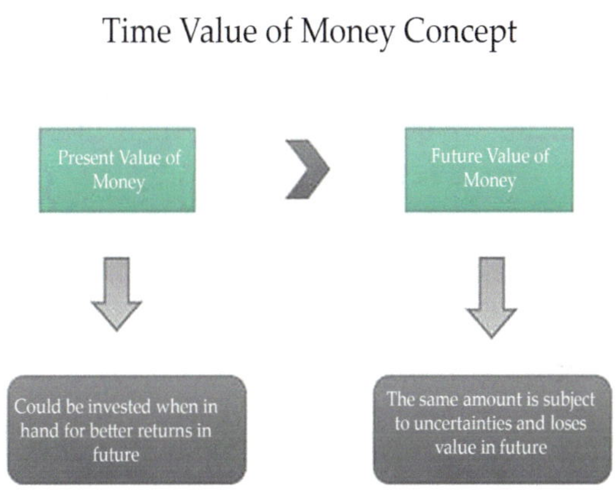

Figure 2.11. Illustration of types of the time value of money concept.

Source: Wallstreetmojo Team, Creative Commons License.

Suppose you have two projects, one generating more income in its early stages than the other in its latter stages, to help demonstrate this idea. Despite its ability to reinvest its revenues earlier, the project which generates money first would not have better worth (Fritsche & Dugan, 2009).

2.9. ACCRUAL ACCOUNTING INFLUENCE ON FINANCIAL STATEMENTS

Accrual-based accounting information offers a wider range of information than cash-based accounting records. They provide users with information on previous transactions involving cash transfers during the current period, the entity's assets, and upcoming activities like responsibilities to make cash payments or utilize the resources of other entities at the end of the reporting period. Compared to other accounting bases, the accrual basis offers information about previous transactions and other occurrences, which is particularly helpful for accountability and decision-making (Setiyawati et al., 2018).

Position financially, financial results, cash flow, adjustments in net investments, budget development, and notes are all included within a set of the accrual-basis income statement. Resources, liabilities, income, expenditures, ownership contributions, and distributions comprise accumulative financial information (Scott et al., 2003):

- Assets are the resources an entity currently controls because of a prior event.
- Liabilities are an entity's ongoing debt for resources expended as an outcome of an earlier occurrence.
- Other than those brought on by shareholder contributions, improvements in the entity's overall financial position are referred to as revenues (Newberry, 2014).
- In addition to those brought about by the owners' investments, expenditures are reductions inside the entity's net position financially.
- Owners' contributions represent inflows of assets from the owners that develop or grow an interest in the entity's awful financial situation (Ibrahim & Al-Matari, 2022).
- Owners' distributions are transfers of funds from the entity towards owners that increase or decrease an ownership stake within the entity's gross financial position.

KEYWORD

Financial position is the current balances of the recorded assets, liabilities, and equity of an organization.

An entity can only adhere to the accrual basis by reporting expenses over its financial results statement within the same time as the corresponding revenues using the accrual accounting method. Based on the accrual basis, financial transactions are recorded as soon as a cash flow occurs, or revenues and expenses are matched now of the transaction. Whether or not there were cash flows during that time, totals of expenditures and revenue are recognized in the statements through deduction (Riahi-Belkaoui, 1992).

On the income statement, expenditures have three different effects. A loss in cash will occur if the expenditure payment is made when the expense is incurred. If a cost is going to be paid in the future, AP will go up. Additionally, if a cost were prepaid, the number of prepaid charges would be reduced (Safkaur et al., 2019).

There are three different effects on revenues within the balance sheet, like how there are three distinct effects on expenses. The money would grow if the goods or services were paid in cash. Receivable accounts will rise if a service is provided on credit. Unearned earnings would be reduced if the consumer prepaid and the service was provided (Gamayuni, 2018).

The following adjustment entries are made at the end of each period using accrual-basis accounting due to the timing discrepancies in recognizing expenses and revenues.

- Accrued expenses and revenue are recorded using receivables and liabilities accounts before receiving or disbursing cash (Pollanen & Loiselle, 2012).
- When cash is collected or paid, deferred revenues and costs are recorded utilizing receivable or liabilities accounts (Hung, 2000).

The financial results and status of the company are more accurately portrayed using this strategy. The revenue statement shows only one hand, each of the revenue generated during the time and, on the other hand, each of the expenditures incurred to get the revenues, both on an accrual basis. Additionally, all earned resources are disclosed, and all incurred debts. The financial statement contains cash-basis data, which shows inflows and outflows of cash associated with the operational investment, including financing operations (Falkman & Tagesson, 2008).

TIPS

Revenues should be shown in the financial results statement whenever they are earned, frequently before clients pay with cash.

2.10. SHIFTING FROM CASH TO ACCRUAL ACCOUNTING IN THE PUBLIC SECTOR

The long-held belief that the cash-basics approach was ideal for public service accountancy and budgeting was supported by the high value of following rules and regulations. Moreover, due to various modifications and a rise in the difficulty of public sector activities all over the world, which are referred to as New Public Management (NPM) features, there has been a transformation in the orientation of budgeting and accounting processes within the public sector during the last thirty years from money to accruals (Peter, 2005).

The transition from the capital to accrual accounting within the public sector is crucial because it is intended to shift the focus from a strict scenario of cashed revenues and paid expenditures to performance-based accomplishments (Ouda, 2003).

The accrual-basics approach places a substantial premium on efficiency.

At multiple government levels (federal, provincial, and municipal), more nations have moved or are going onto accrual accounting over the past 30 years. However, today's governments are equally divided among cash-basis versus accrual-basis methods (Ofoegbu, 2014).

New Zealand and Australia have seen a considerable shift towards accrual-based accounting within the public sector since the late 1980s. By considering the investment opportunity cost and its use through time, the proponents claimed that it offers fresh and, arguably, superior information decision-making on balance between present and future investment. Eventually, the practice spread to other nations like the USA and the UK, where the management strategy significantly impacts. Around the world, there are numerous approaches to transition, ranging from a complete switch to accrual accounting (the New Zealand case in 1992) to progressive shifts in various regions (like in the example of the USA) or different levels of institutions and governments. Accounting information was implemented in the UK for local government accounts starting in the middle of the 19th century and for the National Health Service at the start of the 1990s. Then, in 1993, the national authority was asked to approve accrual-based accounting, which was put into practice (up until 2001) (Kuruppu et al., 2021).

KEYWORD

Accounting is the process of keeping track of all financial transactions within a business, such as any money coming in and money going out.

Governments now employ accounting systems in a growing number across Europe. According to PWC (2014), an accrual basis is currently used in 17 Eu countries and is being implemented in several others. The International Public Sector Accounting Standards are the foundation upon which the member states create nation-specific norms for accrual accounting in the public sector (IPSAS). Numerous pluralistic and diverse nations employ accrual at some or all government levels, intend to use accrual, or have already begun implementing accrual. However, the transition to an accrual base for financial accounting in the government sector has not been widely embraced; many nations are wary of accrual-based accounting and financial planning in the public sector (Guthrie, 1998).

For instance, the German national government gave up on its accrual-basis accounting and budget reform in 2010. Parliamentarian worries about losing control of the budgets and government budgets were the primary driver of this action. (Yusof & Jaafar, 2018).

In many nations, accrual-based accounting is the norm; however, status, and budget are different. Although if they utilize the accrual method for accounting, several states choose to use a cash basis for budgets or only use accruals for a small number of budgetary operations. According to the intricacy of accruals, the accruing plan is not widely used since it jeopardizes fiscal responsibility and impacts public funds' management. (Ahmed & Al-Kake, 2019).

KEYWORD

Budget is a spending plan based on income and expenses.

2.11. GAAP AND IFRS ON THE ACCRUAL PRINCIPLE

Two accounting standards govern the compilation of income statements: Generally Accepted Accounting Principles (GAAP) and International Financial Reporting Standards (IFRS). While IFRS is widely utilized worldwide, GAAP is primarily applied in the United States (Van & Vanstraelen, 2005).

ACTIVITY 2.1.

Imagine you own a small consulting business that provides services to clients. You complete a project for a client in December and send them an invoice for the work done in the amount of $10,000. However, the client does not pay the invoice until January of the following year. Under accrual-basis accounting, in which year should you recognize the revenue from the project and why?

The fundamental concepts of accrual accounting are the same for GAAP and IFRS. Revenues are recorded whenever generated instead of when payment is collected, and expenses are documented whenever incurred, regardless of how they are paid, according to accrual accounting (Liu et al., 2014).

The level of specificity and criteria for recognizing revenue is where GAAP and IFRS diverge most in this area. While IFRS offers a broader, principle-based method of recognizing revenue, GAAP offers more particular guidelines, especially industry-specific restrictions (Guillaume & Pierre, 2016). Both IFRS and GAAP aim to offer precise and transparent financial data that appropriately portrays a company's overall condition and condition. Therefore, IFRS, and GAAP may have different standards for reaching this objective (Bohusova & Nerudova, 2009).

2.12. SUMMARY

Accrual accounting is an accounting method that recognizes revenues and expenses when they are earned or incurred, regardless of when cash is exchanged. This differs from cash-based accounting, which only records revenues and expenses when cash is received or paid. The accrual accounting concept is based on the matching principle, which requires that revenues be matched with the costs incurred to generate them in the same accounting period.

In accrual accounting, revenue is recognized when earned, regardless of when it is received. This means that if a company completes a project for a client in December but does not receive payment until January of the following year, the revenue is still recognized in December. Similarly, expenses are recognized when they are incurred, even if the price is not made later.

The use of accrual accounting provides a more accurate picture of a company's financial health than cash basis accounting. It allows companies to track revenue and expenses in the same period, which provides a better understanding of profitability and cash flow. Additionally, accrual accounting is required by generally accepted accounting principles (GAAP) and International Financial Reporting Standards (IFRS) for public companies.

REVIEW QUESTIONS

1. What is the difference between accrual accounting and cash accounting?
2. Why do most businesses prefer the accrual accounting method?
3. What are the two types of accruals in accrual accounting?
4. How does the accrual accounting method help businesses better understand their financial position?
5. What are some examples of accruals that a business might record?
6. How do businesses use adjusting entries to record accruals?
7. What happens to a business's financial statements if they fail to record accruals?
8. How does the concept of revenue recognition relate to accrual accounting?
9. What is the purpose of the matching principle in accrual accounting?
10. Can a business use accrual accounting for tax purposes? Why or why not?

MULTIPLE CHOICE QUESTIONS

1. Which of the following best defines accrual accounting?

a. A system of accounting that recognizes transactions only when cash is exchanged

b. A system of accounting that recognizes transactions when revenues are earned, and expenses are incurred, regardless of when cash is exchanged

c. A system of accounting that recognizes transactions when cash is received and expenses are paid

d. A system of accounting that recognizes transactions when they are initially recorded in the ledger

2. **Which of the following is an example of an accrued expense?**
   a. Payment of an electricity bill
   b. Purchase of office supplies on credit
   c. Depreciation of office equipment
   d. Salaries owed to employees at the end of the month
3. **Accrued revenues refer to:**
   a. Revenues that have been earned but not yet billed or collected
   b. Revenues that have been billed but not yet collected
   c. Revenues that have not yet been earned
   d. Revenues that have been earned and collected
4. **Which financial statement is impacted by adjusting entries for accrued expenses and accrued revenues?**
   a. Income statement
   b. Balance sheet
   c. Cash flow statement
   d. Statement of retained earnings
5. **Which accounts would be credited in an adjusting entry for accrued salaries?**
   a. Salaries expense
   b. Salaries payable
   c. Cash
   d. Common stock
6. **Accrued expenses are recognized in the period:**
   a. In which the expense is incurred
   b. In which the expense is paid
   c. In which the expense is billed
   d. In which the expense is recorded in the ledger
7. **Which of the following is an example of an accrued revenue?**
   a. Rent collected in advance
   b. Interest received on a bank account
   c. Services rendered but not yet billed
   d. Inventory sold on credit

8. When a company records an adjusting entry for an accrued expense, which account is debited?

a. Cash

b. Prepaid expense

c. Expense

d. Liability

9. Which of the following financial statements is not directly impacted by accrual accounting?

a. Income statement

b. Balance sheet

c. Statement of cash flows

d. All of the above are impacted

10. Accrual accounting provides a more accurate picture of a company's financial health because it:

a. Allows the company to delay recognition of expenses and revenues

b. Recognizes transactions when cash is exchanged

c. Matches expenses with the revenues they help to generate

d. Does not require the use of adjusting entire

Answers to Multiple Choice Questions

1.	(b)	2.	(d)	3.	(a)	4.	(a)	5.	(b)
6.	(a)	7.	(c)	8.	(d)	9.	(c)	10.	(c)

REFERENCE

1. Ahmed, D. M., & Al-Kake, F., (2019). Application of accrual basis in the public sector and its role in providing useful information exploratory study of a sample of academic specialists in the Kurdistan Region of Iraq. *Qalaai Zanist Journal, 4*(1), 1012–1048.
2. Altamuro, J., Beatty, A. L., & Weber, J., (2005). The effects of accelerated revenue recognition on earnings management and earnings informativeness: Evidence from SEC staff accounting bulletin No. 101. *The Accounting Review, 80*(2), 373–401.
3. Antle, R., & Demski, J. S., (1989). Revenue recognition. *Contemporary Accounting Research, 5*(2), 423–451.
4. Azhar, Z., Alfan, E., Kishan, K., & Assanah, N. H., (2022). Accrual accounting at different levels of the public sector: A systematic literature review. *Australian Accounting Review, 32*(1), 36–62.

5. Beechy, T. H., (2007). Does full accrual accounting enhance accountability. *The Innovation Journal: The Public Sector Innovation Journal, 12*(3), 1–18.
6. Benson-Iyare, J. C., & Soriyan, H. A., (2018). *A Mathematical Model for Monitoring Laboratory Revenue Accrued from Tests* (Vol. 12, No. 13). Group.
7. Bergmann, A., Fuchs, S., & Schuler, C., (2019). A theoretical basis for public sector accrual accounting research: Current state and perspectives. *Public Money & Management, 39*(8), 560–570.
8. Bohusova, H., & Nerudova, D., (2009). US GAAP and IFRS convergence in the area of revenue recognition. *Economics and Management*, (14), 12–19.
9. Butler, H. N., & Macey, J. R., (1996). Externalities and the matching principle: The case for reallocating environmental regulatory authority. *Yale L & Pol'y. Rev., 14*, 23.
10. Caylor, M. L., (2010). Strategic revenue recognition to achieve earnings benchmarks. *Journal of Accounting and Public Policy, 29*(1), 82–95.
11. Christiaens, J., & Rommel, J., (2008). Accrual accounting reforms: Only for businesslike (parts of) governments. *Financial Accountability & Management, 24*(1), 59–75.
12. Conrad, C. R., & DeMeritt, J. H., (2013). Constrained by the bank and the ballot: Unearned revenue, democracy, and state incentives to repress. *Journal of Peace Research, 50*(1), 105–119.
13. De Jonge, J., & Dormann, C., (2006). Stressors, resources, and strain at work: A longitudinal test of the triple-match principle. *Journal of Applied Psychology, 91*(6), 1359.
14. Di Minin, E., Leader-Williams, N., & Bradshaw, C. J., (2016). Banning trophy hunting will exacerbate biodiversity loss. *Trends in Ecology & Evolution, 31*(2), 99–102.
15. Dunn, C. L., (1960). Teaching of adjusting and reversing entries in the elementary accounting courses. *The Accounting Review, 35*(1), 135–137.
16. Dutta, S., & Zhang, X. J., (2002). Revenue recognition in a multiperiod agency setting. *Journal of Accounting Research, 40*(1), 67–83.
17. Ellwood, S., & Newberry, S., (2007). Public sector accrual accounting: Institutionalizing neo-liberal principles? *Accounting, Auditing & Accountability Journal, 20*(4), 549–573.
18. Ermaliza, R., Lubis, S., & Muda, I., (2022). Prepare adjusting entries for deferrals cases. *Journal of Positive School Psychology, 6*(3), 2355–2360.
19. Falkman, P., & Tagesson, T., (2008). Accrual accounting does not necessarily mean accrual accounting: Factors that counteract compliance with accounting standards in Swedish municipal accounting. *Scandinavian Journal of Management, 24*(3), 271–283.
20. Fisher, F. M., & McGowan, J. J., (1983). On the misuse of accounting rates of return to infer monopoly profits. *The American Economic Review, 73*(1), 82–97.
21. Fraenkel, L. E., (1969). On the method of matched asymptotic expansions: Part I: A matching principle. In: *Mathematical Proceedings of the Cambridge Philosophical*

Society (Vol. 65, No. 1, pp. 209–231). Cambridge University Press.

22. Frankovic, J., (2000). The income tax treatment of prepaid expenses and similar costs: A time value analysis. *Can. Tax J., 48*, 1371.
23. Fritsche, S. R., & Dugan, M. T., (1997). A simulation-based investigation of errors in accounting-based surrogates for internal rate of return. *Journal of Business Finance & Accounting, 24*(6), 781–802.
24. Fritsche, S. R., & Dugan, M. T., (2001). Evaluating models of the relationship between accounting profitability measures and internal rate of return. In: *Allied Academies International Conference. Academy of Accounting and Financial Studies. Proceedings* (Vol. 6, No. 1, p. 151). Jordan Whitney Enterprises, Inc.
25. Fritsche, S. R., & Dugan, M. T., (2009). Evaluating models of the relationship between accounting profitability measures and internal rate of return. *Journal of Applied Business Research (JABR), 25*(2).
26. Gamayuni, R. R., (2018). The effect of internal audit function effectiveness and implementation of accrual based government accounting standard on financial reporting quality. *Review of Integrative Business and Economics Research, 7*(1), 46–58.
27. Garrison, L. L., (1981). Adjusting entries: An overview. *The Journal of Business Education, 56*(5), 176–178.
28. Goller, M. S., (1950). Teaching accrued expenses. *The Journal of Business Education, 26*(3), 117–118.
29. Guillaume, O., & Pierre, D., (2016). The convergence of US GAAP with IFRS: A comparative analysis of principles-based and rules-based accounting standards. *Scholedge International Journal of Business Policy & Governance, 3*(5), 63–72.
30. Guthrie, J., (1998). Application of accrual accounting in the Australian public sector–rhetoric or reality. *Financial Accountability & Management, 14*(1), 1–19.
31. Hicks, E. L., & Block, M., (1967). Four basic distinctions between prepaid expenses and deferred charges. *New York Certified Public Accountant (pre-1986), 37*(000004), 298.
32. Hotelling, H., (1925). A general mathematical theory of depreciation. *Journal of the American Statistical Association, 20*(151), 340–353.
33. Hung, M., (2000). Accounting standards and value relevance of financial statements: An international analysis. *Journal of Accounting and Economics, 30*(3), 401–420.
34. Ibrahim, T. K. T., & Al-Matari, E. M., (2022). The effect of governance rules application controls and the accrual basis application controls on quality of financial reporting: Applying to Jouf university. *Sustainability, 14*(5), 2831.
35. Jones, J. P., & Pagach, D., (2013). The next step for revenue recognition. *The CPA Journal, 83*(10), 30.
36. Jorgenson, D. W., (1996). Empirical studies of depreciation. *Economic Inquiry, 34*(1), 24–42.

37. Kelly, G., & Tahir, M. I., (2009). Time series and cross-sectional dynamics of accounting rate of return and the prediction of cash flow per ordinary share. *Accounting, Accountability & Performance, 15*(2), 1–39.

38. Kuruppu, C., Adhikari, P., & Van, H. J., (2021). Editorial–a plea for changing directions of public sector accounting research in emerging economies. *Journal of Accounting in Emerging Economies, 11*(5), 677–690.

39. Kwon, Y. K., (1989). Accrual versus cash-basis accounting methods: An agency-theoretic comparison. *Journal of Accounting and Public Policy, 8*(4), 267–281.

40. Landman, J. H., (1950). *Depreciable Assets are Prepaid Expenses* (Vol. 20, No. 000009, p. 546). New York Certified Public Accountant (pre-1986).

41. Liu, C., Yip, Y. C., Yao, L. J., & Chan, S. H., (2014). Differences in earnings management between firms using US GAAP and IAS/IFRS. *Review of Accounting and Finance, 13*(2), 134–155.

42. Malau, A., Teguh, M., & Muda, I., (2022). The accrual basis of accounting and the reasons for adjusting entries. *Journal of Positive School Psychology, 6*(3), 2401–2404.

43. Manaf, N. A. A., Ishak, Z., & Hussin, W. N. W., (2011). Application of problem based learning (PBL) in a course on financial accounting principles. *Malaysian Journal of Learning and Instruction, 8*, 21–47.

44. Musselman, V. A., (1969). The theory of adjusting entries. *The Journal of Business Education, 45*(2), 56–57.

45. Naylor, R. L., Goldburg, R. J., Primavera, J. H., Kautsky, N., Beveridge, M. C., Clay, J., & Troell, M., (2000). Effect of aquaculture on world fish supplies. *Nature, 405*(6790), 1017–1024.

46. Newberry, S., (2014). The use of accrual accounting in New Zealand's central government: Second thoughts. *Accounting, Economics and Law, 4*(3), 283–297.

47. Ngwenya, F., (2013). Accrued expenses, provisions and contingent liabilities explained. *Professional Accountant, 2013*(2), 22, 23.

48. Novita, S. K., (2022). Efforts to improve student understanding on the basic competency of making adjustment journal through working papers. *Indonesian Journal of Education Teaching and Learning (IJETL), 2*(1), 51–58.

49. Ofoegbu, G. N., (2014). New public management and accrual accounting basis for transparency and accountability in the Nigerian public sector. *IOSR Journal of Business and Management, 16*(7), 104–113.

50. Ohlson, J. A., & Zhang, X. J., (1998). Accrual accounting and equity valuation. *Journal of Accounting Research, 36*, 85–111.

51. Okon, E. B., & Okon, N. S., (2021). Sources of state revenue and state effectiveness: The Nigerian experience. *International Journal of Financial Research, 12*(1), 111–122.

52. Ouda, H. A., (2003). Accrual accounting in the government sector. *Public Fund Digest, 3*(2), 52–73.

53. Ouda, H. A., (2007). Accrual accounting principles and postulations in the public sector: Rhetoric or reality. *Accounting and Performance Management Perspectives in Business and Public Sector Organizations,* 258.
54. Peter, V. D. H. M., (2005). From cash to accrual budgeting and accounting in the public sector: The Dutch experience. *Public Budgeting & Finance, 25*(1), 32–45.
55. Pina, V., Torres, L., & Yetano, A., (2009). Accrual accounting in EU local governments: One method, several approaches. *European Accounting Review, 18*(4), 765–807.
56. Pollanen, R., & Loiselle-Lapointe, K., (2012). Accounting reform in the government of Canada: Exploratory evidence on accrual accounting adoption and impact. *Financial Accountability & Management, 28*(4), 359–377.
57. Rabinowitz, S. I., (1940). Treatment of prepaid expenses on the cash basis of accounting. *The Accounting Review, 15*(4), 474–484.
58. Rhodes, K., & Smith, A., (2004). Using games to teach basics: Learn to love learning accounting. *Academy of Educational Leadership Journal, 8*(3), 67–75.
59. Riahi-Belkaoui, A., (1992). Accrual accounting, modified cash basis of accounting and the loan decision: An experiment in functional fixation. *Managerial Finance, 18*(5), 3–13.
60. Robinson, M., (1998). Accrual accounting and the efficiency of the core public sector. *Financial Accountability & Management, 14*(1), 21–37.
61. Safkaur, O., Afiah, N. N., Poulus, S., & Dahlan, M., (2019). The effect of quality financial reporting on good governance. *International Journal of Economics and Financial Issues, 9*(3), 277.
62. Schapiro, D., (1974). Prepayments and distortion of income under cash basis tax accounting. *Tax L. Rev., 30*, 117.
63. Scott, J. E., McKinnon, J. L., & Harrison, G. L., (2003). Cash to accrual and cash to accrual: A case study of financial reporting in two NSW hospitals 1857 to post-1975. *Accounting, Auditing & Accountability Journal, 16*(1), 104–140.
64. Setiyawati, H., Iskandar, D., & Basar, Y. S., (2018). The quality of financial reporting through increasing the competence of internal accountants and accrual basis. *International Journal of Economics, Business and Management Studies, 5*(1), 31–40.
65. Spence, M., & Zeckhauser, R., (1978). Insurance, information, and individual action. In: *Uncertainty in Economics* (pp. 333–343). Academic Press.
66. Ullrich, J., Wieseke, J., Christ, O., Schulze, M., & Van, D. R., (2007). The identity-matching principle: Corporate and organizational identification in a franchising system. *British Journal of Management, 18*, S29–S44.
67. Van, T. B., & Vanstraelen, A., (2005). Earnings management under German GAAP versus IFRS. *European Accounting Review, 14*(1), 155–180.
68. Vangermeersch, R. G., (1997). Dropping debits and credits in elementary accounting: A huge disservice to students. *Issues in Accounting Education, 12*(2), 581.

69. Wagenhofer, A., (2014). The role of revenue recognition in performance reporting. *Accounting and Business Research, 44*(4), 349–379.
70. Wüstemann, J., & Kierzek, S., (2005). Revenue recognition under IFRS revisited: Conceptual models, current proposals and practical consequences. *Accounting in Europe, 2*(1), 69–106.
71. Yuliati, R., Yuliansyah, Y., & Adelina, Y. E., (2019). The implementation of accrual basis accounting by Indonesia's local governments. *International Review of Public Administration, 24*(2), 67–80.
72. Yusof, N. S., & Jaafar, H., (2018). The implementation of accrual-based accounting in Malaysian public sector: Opportunities and challenges. *International Business Education Journal, 11*(1), 49–62.
73. Zhang, Y., (2005). Revenue recognition timing and attributes of reported revenue: The case of software industry's adoption of SOP 91-1. *Journal of Accounting and Economics, 39*(3), 535–561.
74. Zimmerman, A. B., & Bloom, R., (2016). The matching principle revisited. *Accounting Historians Journal, 43*(1), 79–119.
75. Degterinskaya, M., (2018). Unearned revenue. In: The Modern Specialist-Professional: Theory and Practice (Vol. 1, pp. 168–171).

CHAPTER 3

FUNDAMENTALS OF FINANCIAL STATEMENT

UNIT INTRODUCTION

Financial statements represent a company's commercial activities and economic performance formally documented within a given period. Government agencies, accounting organizations, and others commonly conduct financial account assessments to verify their accuracy and meet taxation, financing, or investment requirements. The balance sheet, operating income, cash flow statements (CFS), and statement of profit and loss are mainly used for businesses operating for profit. Not-for-profit companies make use of a collection of financial statements that are comparable but different (Danzi & Boom, 1998). Analysts and investors rely significantly on the company's financial information when analyzing a company's earnings and trying to estimate how the company's stock price will move in the future. Each annual company survey, which includes the company's financial statements, is considered one of the most significant sources of accurate and verified financial information.

The income financial statement, the balance sheet, the cash flow report, and the cash flow statement are the three critical reports included in a financial statement. There is not one standard format for all income statements. General Accounting Principles are the standards used by companies in the United States. In contrast, International Financial Reporting Standards (IFRS) are the regulations often utilized by companies in other countries. In addition, each agency within the United States federal government follows its unique guidelines for financial statements (Greer, 1943).

The balance sheets are the fundamental and official annual reports used by the management of a business to communicate banking details to its owners and numerous external users, such as investors, tax officials, the government, workers, and other parties. The three financial statements referred to here are the cash flow (positioning statement) as it exists after an accounting cycle, the statement of financial position for a corporation, and the statement of cash flow (Mohanram, 2005).

Learning Objectives

At the end of this chapter, the reader will be able to understand:

- The nature of the financial statement
- The objectives of the financial statement
- The concept of a balance sheet
- The importance of income statement and cash flow statement
- The idea of a nonprofit financial statement
- The limitations of financial statement

Key Terms

- Cash Flow Statement
- Financial Statement
- Income Statement
- Nonprofit Financial Statement
- Revenue
- Shareholder's Equity

3.1. NATURE OF FINANCIAL STATEMENTS

Continuing income statements are based mostly on chronologically documented facts regarding activities presented in monetary values for a specific period. These financial statements show the financial status as of a particular date and the financial outcomes realized during that time. Monetary statements are "statements delivered to provide a process for dealing with a report on growth by the management and deal with the state of the company's investment and also the result achieved during the analyzed period" by the American Institute of Certified Public Accountants. These are based on verifiable facts, accounting methods, and subjective opinions (Mohamed & Handley, 2014).

Remember

Shareholders, economic experts, and creditors examine a business's financial statements to determine how healthy the company's finances are and how much potential revenue the company has.

The following points explain the nature of the income statement:

3.1.1. Recorded Facts

Details in the form of expense data collected in books of accounts serve as the foundation for creating financial statements. The foundation for recording transactions is the actual price or historical cost. Cash in hand, money in the bank, AR, capital assets, etc., are just a few examples of accounts whose figures are taken from the data entered in the books of accounts. All assets bought at various points in time and at different prices are combined and represented as costs. These financial statements need not reflect the company's current financial situation because they are not based on actual values (Froelich et al., 2000).

3.1.2. Accounting Conventions

Financial statements are created using accounting procedures. Inventory is valued according to the custom of the market price or cost price, which is the lowest. The asset valuation at cost minus depreciation approach is applied for balance sheet reasons. When interacting with little objects like pens, pencils, postage stamps, etc., the conventions of physicality are observed. Even though they constitute assets by nature, these goods are considered expenses during the year they are purchased. Instead of using the idea of price or market price, whatever is lower, the stationery is rated at cost. Accounting norms make financial statements straightforward, comparable, and accurate (Yamey, 2014).

3.1.3. Postulates

Postulates, like the viable business postulate, the financial accounting postulate, and the realization postulate, are the foundations upon which financial statements are constructed. The possible business hypothesis posits that the business is considered viable and endures longer. As a result, the resources are displayed using historical cost data. The money-measuring hypothesis holds that its cash value will not change over time. The assets bought at various times will be represented at a price paid for them even though there has been a significant change in buying power of money. Although the sale price could be paid over the years, when generating a statement of profits and losses, income is added to sales in the year the transaction was undertaken. A realization postulate is the name of the assumption (Ahmed, 1994).

3.1.4. Personal Judgments

Financial statements frequently contain details and figures dependent on the authors' estimates, judgments, and personal opinions. Capital assets' usable economic life is considered when calculating depreciation. Estimated and individual assessments are used to make provisions for doubtful debts. When valuing inventory, the lower market value or cost is used. Many personal decisions must be based on various factors when determining stock or inventory market prices. When creating financial statements, individual judgments, estimates, and opinions are used to avoid the danger of overstating assets, liabilities, earnings, and expenditures while keeping in mind the tradition of conservatism (Maines & McDaniel, 2000).

Figure 3.1. Illustration of nature of financial statement.

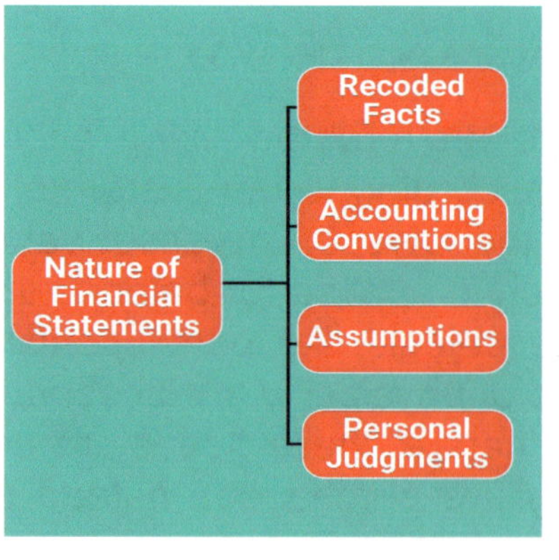

Source: Topper.com, Creative Commons License.

Financial statements, created by the following financial reporting, conventions, financing decisions, accounting rules, and legal obligations, are thus summarized reports of facts that have been documented (Phillips, 1999) (Figure 3.1).

3.2. OBJECTIVES OF FINANCIAL STATEMENTS

Financial information is the fundamental data source for investors and all other stakeholders to analyze and understand every business's profitability and financial position, They offer data on the company's performance regarding assets and liabilities, which serve as the foundation for making decisions. Therefore, the main objective of financial reports is to support users' judgment. The following are some of the specific goals (Figure 3.2):

3.2.1. Economic Resources and Obligations

It provides information about economic resources and obligations of a business. Shareholders and other interested stakeholders who may have limited control, ability, or resources to gather data can rely on them to deliver adequate, trustworthy, and timely information on the financial resources and liabilities of a business firm (Lennard, 2007).

KEYWORD

Financial data refers to quantitative information that is used by organizations to make financial decisions.

3.2.2. Earning Capacity of the Business

It provides information about the earning capacity of the business. They must offer useful financial data that can be used to accurately estimate, contrast, and assess the commercial firm's earning potential (Zeff, 2016).

3.2.3. Information about Cash Flows

They must offer details that help investors and creditors forecast, compare, and assess anticipated cash flows in terms of their quantity, time, and associated uncertainties.

3.2.4. Judge the Effectiveness of Management

They provide data that can be used to assess management's capacity to successfully employ a company's resources (Govindarajan, 1980).

3.2.5. Activities of Business Affecting Society

It provides information about activities of business affecting society. The corporate organization's operations that impact society may be identified, characterized, or assessed, and are significant in its social surroundings, must be reported.

3.2.6. Disclosing Accounting Policies

Understand such statements better; these reports must include the essential accounting principles, procedures, and modifications implemented throughout the year (Sprouse, 1974).

Figure 3.2. Schematic of objectives of financial statement.

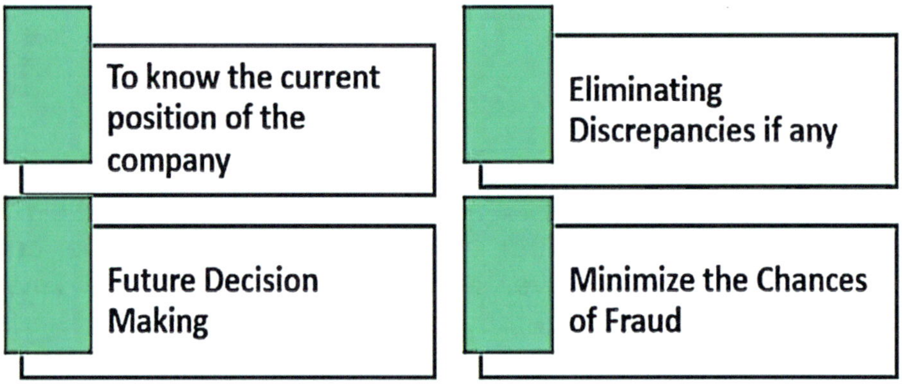

Source: Ashish Kumar Srivastav, Creative Commons License.

3.3. TYPES OF FINANCIAL STATEMENTS

A small-business owner should understand these four sorts of financial statements and the information they include for investing or creditors willing to lend cash to your company (Tomilina & Kurilova, 2020) (Figure 3.3).

These financial records, individually, and collectively, offer a lot of information to a potential investor or creditor that could significantly impact your business's capacity to generate the required funds (Ashtiani & Raahemi, 2021).

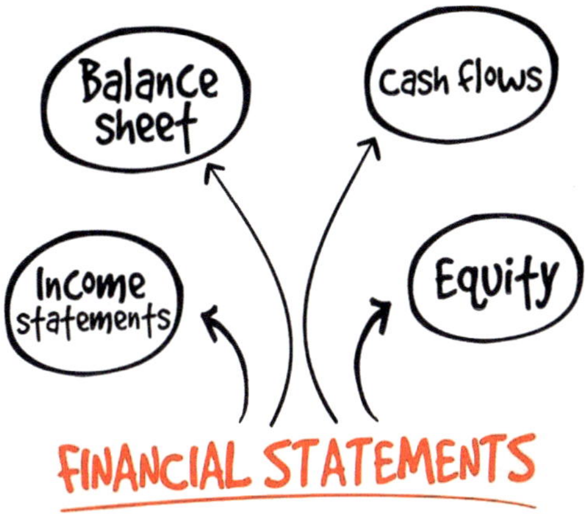

Source: Belle Wong, J.D., Creative Commons License.

Figure 3.3. Picture of types of financial statement.

3.4. BALANCE SHEET

A balance sheet represents a company's assets, liabilities and investors' resources. By examining the time at the top of a balance sheet, that frequently the end of a reporting period, one could understand the time period for which the Balance sheet has been prepared. The following are the components of a balance sheet (Adrian & Shin, 2011).

KEYWORD

Reporting period is the span of time covered by a set of financial statements.

3.4.1. Assets

The different types of assets are illustrated as follows:

- Cash and its substitutes, including Treasuries and bank certificates, are considered liquid assets.
- Receivables are the amount customers still owe the company for selling its products and services (Ahn et al., 2009).
- A company's account is its supply of supplies it believes in selling often. An account might include over goods, incomplete works in development, and natural resources that have not been processed.
- Scheduled costs are those that have been prepaid on their deadlines. Because their value makes sure yet improved, these expenses are reported as an asset; if they did, the company would potentially be eligible for a return (Michalisin et al., 1997).

- A company owns houses, machinery, and equipment as capital assets for long-term advantage. These comprise buildings used for manufacturing and substantial machinery for material management.
- Investing are possessions kept for future potential growth. They are not used in activities but are only retained for capital expansion.
- Trademarks, patents, trademarks, and numerous other intellectual capitals provide significant economic (and usually long-term) benefits for the firm even while they cannot be personally touched (Brynjolfsson, 1994).

3.4.2. Liabilities

Various kinds of liabilities are explained below:

KEYWORD

Dividend is a distribution of profits by a corporation to its shareholders.

- Payables are the bills needed for a company's everyday operations. Utility bills, leasing accounts, and contracts to buy raw materials are examples of this document.
- Payable payments are amounts owing to workers for time worked.
- Payables, and certified treasury bills, include all the details of official debt agreements, along with the payment schedule and amount (Sharpe & Tint, 1990).
- Dividend payments due are payments proclaimed to be paid to shareholders but have not yet been received.
- Long-term debt includes mortgage loans, sink bond money, and other debts with protracted complete payment deadlines. Remember that the short-term portion of the loan is shown as a current obligation (Catão & Milesi, 2014).

3.4.3. Shareholders' Equity

Shareholders' equity is explained below:

- Capital is equal to a business share, less all total liabilities. The amount which would be returned to shareholders after all the company's assets were liquidated, and each of its obligations were paid is known as shareholders' capital, sometimes known as stockholders' capital.
- Retained earnings are a part of investors' equity and refer to the fraction of net earnings which was not given to dividends to shareholders (Becker, 1987).

3.4.4. Example of a Balance Sheet

Lower is a portion of the ExxonMobil Corporation (XOM) income statements as of December 31, 2021, for the financial year 2021.

- Total assets remained at $338.9 billion.
- Total liabilities remained at $163.2 billion.
- Total equity remained at $175.7 billion
- Total liabilities and equity were $338.9 billion, which equals the total assets for the period.

3.5. INCOME STATEMENT (THEN WHAT IS THE INCOME STATEMENT?)

Contrary to the income statement, the financial statements cover a year for an annual income statement and a fourth for quarterly reports. The accounting information includes a summary of all sales, expenses, and net results, especially per-share earnings (Penman, 2009).

Author to redefine the Income statement for better clarity and understanding

KEYWORD

Income statement is a financial statement that shows you the company's income and expenditures.

3.5.1. Revenue

Managing income is produced through the sale of products or services. Operating cash flow is what an automaker would get from making and selling cars. The main business lines of a corporation generate operating income (McGill & Van Ryzin, 1999).

Non-operating income is the income earned by non-core company activities. These revenues are unconnected to the primary objective of the business. Non-operating income examples include:

- Interest received on cash in the bank.
- Rental revenue from a property
- Income from strategic partnerships like royalty payment receipts
- Income after an ad display placed on the company's property.

Additional income is the money earned through other activities. Earnings from the sale of long-term assets such as real estate, vehicles, or a subsidiary may also be considered supplementary income (Jones & Butler, 1988).

3.5.2. Expenses

When a company participates in its primary activity, it spends a lot of money to make money. Expenses include selling, administrative, and general (SG&A), depreciation or amortization, development, and research (R&D) (Swaminathan & Weintrop, 1991).

Workers 'wages, sales commissions, utility, energy, and travel expenditures are a few examples of regular expenses, and loan or interest payments are costs related to a supplementary activity. Expenses for loss on asset sales are also recorded. The income statement's primary purpose is to provide data on profit or the financial results of corporate activities. However, if contrasted several times, it may also be a valuable tool for showing when increasing transactions or income. Investors might also examine how well a company firm controls expenses to determine whether reducing its sales costs should enhance profit over time (Doyle et al., 2003) (Figure 3.4).

Figure 3.4. Illustration of the formula of expenses.

Source: Fourweek MBA, Creative Commons License.

3.5.3. Example of an Income Statement

The excerpts below are from the income statement of ExxonMobil Company as of December 31, 2021.

- Total revenue remained at $276.7 billion.
- Total costs remained at $254.4 billion.
- Net income or profit remained at $23 billion.

3.6. CASH FLOW STATEMENT

The cash flow statement (CFS) measures the efficiency with which a company generates money to pay a debt, operational expenses, and expenditures. The CFS, financial statements, and balance sheet are improved (Hertenstein & McKinnon, 1997).

Due to the CFS, shareholders may get knowledge about how a company functions, where its funding originates from, and the way it spends the money. The CFS also provides data on a company's financial condition (Kwok, 2002).

There is no set formula for calculating a CFS. Instead, it is divided into three sections that describe the cash flow for all the many ways a corporation spends its money. The three components of CFS are listed below (V. Kousenidis, 2006).

KEYWORD

Lease payments are monthly fees paid for the right to use an asset under the terms of a contract between the lessor who owns it and the lessee who will use it.

3.6.1. Operating Activities

The continuous activities of the CFS incorporate all income and costs from running the business and marketing its goods or services. Cash flow from processes includes adjustments to receivables, money accounts, repayment, inventory, and payable accounts; this list of actions includes salaries, income taxes on earnings, interest charges, lease payments, and cash proceeds from selling products or services (Martani et al., 2009).

3.6.2. Investing Activities

Investment interests are any beginnings and work out of capital obtained from a corporation's assets, often throughout a company's long term. Each payment attached to a merger or purchase involving the purchase or sale of an asset, lending money to or borrowing it from providers, including customer loans, falls under this classification (Jones, 2001).

Furthermore, assets of long-term assets like industrial real estate, technology, and equipment are included in this section (PPE). In all other words, changes to assets, machinery, or investments are connected to investment income (Klychova et al., 2019).

Did you Know?

According to a report published by the Financial Executives Research Foundation (FERF) in 2018, a survey of financial executives found that 92% of companies in the United States prepare a cash flow statement.

3.6.3. Financing Activities

Payments to investors and funds received from investors and banks make up the financing budget. Financing operations include loans, leasing, dividend payments, stock holdings, stock issues, and stock repurchases.

The income and balance sheets are resolved by the statements of cash flows in three essential business operations (Wang et al., 2018) (Figure 3.5).

3.6.4. Example of a Cash Flow Statement

Below is a portion of the CFS for ExxonMobil Corporation's fiscal year 2021 as of December 31. Each CFS's three components and their respective results are precise.

- Operating activities produced a $48 billion positive cash flow.
- Investing activities have a negative cash flow or $10,2 billion in cash outflows for the quarter. Most cash outflows went toward acquiring new real estate, machinery, and equipment, showing that the company made some fresh investments in stable assets.
- Financing activities had a negative cash flow of $35.4 billion in cash outflows throughout the quarter. Many cash outflows were from dividend payments and short-term debt reduction.

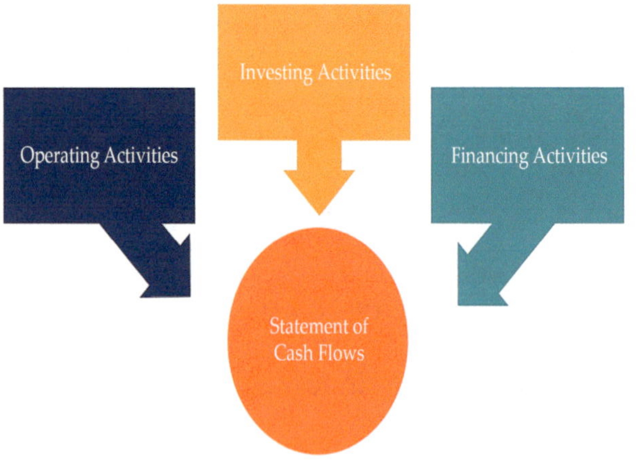

Figure 3.5. Image of components of the statement of cash flow.

Source: CFI Team, Creative Commons License.

3.7. COMPREHENSIVE INCOME STATEMENT

Expected net revenue is shown in a statement of overall revenue, a typically underused financial statement that also considers fluctuations in other comprehensive revenue (OCI). Additional income flows encompass all unrealized gains and losses not represented in the income statement. Profits and expenses which have not yet been declared following accounting rules are included in financial statements. It also shows the entire fluctuating income of the firm (Lin et al., 2018).

KEYWORD

Net revenue is the dollar value of the total sales made by a company after certain expenses are deducted.

The following are some transactions that appear on the comprehensive income statement.:

- Net revenue (from the statement of revenue).
- Losses or profits from unrealized investments in debt securities
- Profits or losses that derivatives have not yet realized.
- Translational adjustments that weren't made because of foreign currency.
- Detail loss or profit from unrealized pension program investments (Linsmeier et al., 1997).

In the example below, ExxonMobil had an unrecognized income of over $2 billion. Whenever extra, fully assessed, is considered, ExxonMobil reports nearly $26 billion in total revenue compared to approximately $23.5 billion in net profitability (Bhamornsiri & Wiggins, 2001) (Figure 3.6).

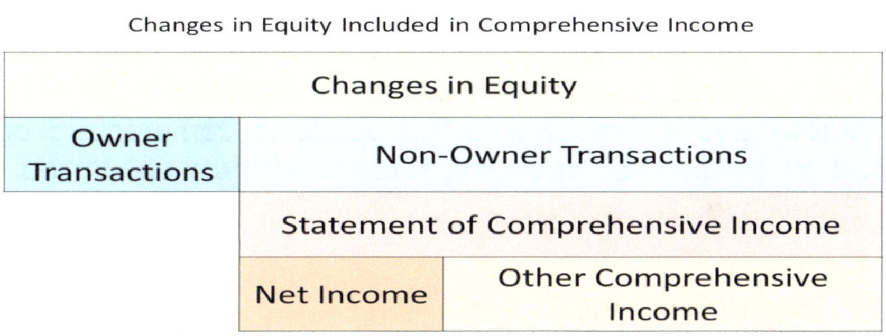

Figure 3.6. Schematic of comprehensive income statement.

Source: Michael Brown, Creative Commons License.

3.8. NONPROFIT FINANCIAL STATEMENTS

Nonprofit organizations record transfers of money using a similar financial statement set. Based on differences, there are also differences between the revenue statements used by a for-profit company like this one and an utterly nonprofit corporation. Below is the financial statement that a nonprofit organization often uses (Keating & Frumkin, 2003).

3.8.1. Statement of Financial Position

It is a statement of assets, liabilities, and capital of a business at a particular point in time, comprising of the balance of income and expenditure over the preceding period It is equal to a for-benefit company's balance sheet. The fundamental difference between nonprofit and for-profit businesses is that the latter do not possess equity interests; instead, "net assets" refer to any remaining funds after all resources have been exhausted and responsibilities have been fully fulfilled (Ashburne, 1962).

3.8.2. Statement of Activities

It is analogous to a financial statement from a business. It tracks the company's development, along with contributions, fundraising, and revenue from events, and increases substantially to get things done (Mook & Quarter, 2006).

TIPS

When analyzing financial statements, it is important to compare reports from several periods to identify patterns and to evaluate how a company's performance stacks against its competitors within the same industry.

3.8.3. Statement of Functional Expenses

Operational costs are reported for every entity function (often broken down into organizational, program, or fundraising expenditures). Such knowledge is provided to the public to comprehend better the portion of business spending that may be directly linked to a goal (Froelich et al., 2000).

3.8.4. Statement of Cash Flow

It can be described as a financial statement that provides aggregate data related to all cash inflows that a company receives from its ongoing operations and external investment sources. Also, it comprises of all cash outflows that pay for business activities and investments during a given period. It is equivalent to a commercial organization's cash-flow statement. While the accounts provided might vary according to a nonprofit group's particular features, the statement is separated into functioning, investment, and supporting activities (Broome, 2004). An outside auditor's responsibility is to measure whether an entity's economic reports have been made following generally accepted accounting standards and if any material errors would jeopardize the accuracy of the findings. (Miao et al., 2016).

3.9. LIMITATIONS OF FINANCIAL STATEMENTS

Even though economic statements provide a surplus of data about a company, they have limits. Investors typically draw different assumptions about a company's financial progress due to the ambiguity inside a statement (Ballwieser, 2004). For example, although other investors may favor stock purchasing, certain investors prefer investing their money in long-term resources. The level of debt a company has could be acceptable to one investor but problematic for another (Faello, 2015).

ACTIVITY 3.1.

ABC Inc. is a manufacturing company that produces and sells furniture. The company recently purchased a new factory for $2 million, and financed the purchase with a loan from a bank. The loan has an interest rate of 5% and a term of 10 years. How would the purchase of the new factory affect the balance sheet of ABC Inc.?

Finally, and not least, the knowledge needed to produce financial accounts affects their correctness. Several times, it has been demonstrated that misleading financial statements have been made due to incorrect economic transactions or inadequate oversight. Even though reviewing audited financial documents, consumers must have some faith in the integrity of the reports and the information supplied (Paton, 1928).

The following limitations of financial statements can be explained

- Only Interim Reports
- Do not Give Exact Position
- Historical Costs
- Impact of Non-Monetary Factors Ignored, and
- No precision.

3.10. SUMMARY

- The chapter on Fundamentals of financial statements provides an overview of the nature and objectives of financial statements, including the concept of a balance sheet, income statement, and CFS. The chapter also highlights the significance of nonprofit financial statements and the limitations of financial statements in terms of providing a complete picture of an organization's financial health. The chapter emphasizes the importance of understanding financial statements in evaluating an organization's financial performance and making informed decisions.

REVIEW QUESTIONS

1. What is the nature of financial statements, and what are their main components?
2. What are the objectives of financial statements, and how do they help businesses make informed decisions?
3. How does the balance sheet concept help us understand a company's financial position, and what are its key components?
4. What is the importance of the income and CFSs in financial reporting, and how are they different?
5. What are some unique considerations when creating financial statements for nonprofit organizations, and how do they differ from for-profit businesses?
6. What are some of the limitations of financial statements, and how can investors and analysts overcome these limitations to make more informed decisions?

MULTIPLE CHOICE QUESTIONS

1. Which of the following is a primary objective of financial statements?

a. To provide information about the company's profitability
b. To disclose the company's financial position
c. To communicate the company's plans
d. To promote the company's products and services

2. What is the primary purpose of a balance sheet?

a. To show the company's revenue and expenses for a specific period
b. To provide information on the company's cash flows
c. To report the company's financial position at a particular point in time
d. To explain the company's management

3. Which financial statement shows a company's profitability over a specific period?

a. Balance sheet

b. Income statement

c. Cash flow statement

d. Nonprofit financial statement

4. What is the purpose of a nonprofit financial statement?

a. To report a nonprofit organization's revenue and expenses

b. To show the financial position of a nonprofit organization

c. To disclose a nonprofit organization's plans

d. To communicate a nonprofit organization's management strategy

5. What are the limitations of financial statements?

a. They only provide historical information

b. They may not reflect the company's actual financial position

c. They do not account for non-financial factors

d. All of the above

Answers to Multiple Choice Questions

1. (b) 2. (b) 3. (b) 4. (a) 5. (d)

REFERENCE

1. Adrian, T., & Shin, H. S., (2011). Financial intermediary balance sheet management. *Annu. Rev. Financ. Econ., 3*(1), 289–307.
2. Ahmed, E. A., (1994). Accounting postulates and principles from an Islamic perspective. *Review of Islamic Economics, 3*(2), 1–18.
3. Ahn, D. H., Conrad, J., & Dittmar, R. F., (2009). Basis assets. *The Review of Financial Studies, 22*(12), 5133–5174.
4. Ashburne, J. G., (1962). A forward-looking statement of financial position. *The Accounting Review, 37*(3), 475.
5. Ashtiani, M. N., & Raahemi, B., (2021). Intelligent fraud detection in financial statements using machine learning and data mining: A systematic literature review. *IEEE Access, 10*, 72504–72525.
6. Ballwieser, W., (2004). The limitations of financial reporting. *The Economics and Politics of Accounting*, 58–77.
7. Becker, B. E., (1987). Concession bargaining: The impact on shareholders' equity. *ILR Review, 40*(2), 268–279.

8. Bhamornsiri, S., & Wiggins, C., (2001). Comprehensive income disclosures. *The CPA Journal, 71*(10), 54.
9. Boyd, T., & Cortese-Danile, T. M., (2000). Using the cash flow statement to improve credit analysis. *Com. Lending Rev., 16*, 55.
10. Broome, O. W., (2004). Statement of cash flows: Time for change! *Financial Analysts Journal, 60*(2), 16–22.
11. Brynjolfsson, E., (1994). Information assets, technology and organization. *Management Science, 40*(12), 1645–1662.
12. Castillo, E. A., (2016). Beyond the balance sheet. *Journal of Nonprofit Education and Leadership, 6*(3), 287–303.
13. Catão, L. A., & Milesi-Ferretti, G. M., (2014). External liabilities and crises. *Journal of International Economics, 94*(1), 18–32.
14. Danzi, J. T., & Boom, M. L., (1998). Fundamentals of financial statement analysis for academic physician managers. *Academic Medicine: Journal of the Association of American Medical Colleges, 73*(4), 363–369.
15. Doyle, J. T., Lundholm, R. J., & Soliman, M. T., (2003). The predictive value of expenses excluded from pro forma earnings. *Review of Accounting Studies, 8*, 145–174.
16. Faello, J., (2015). Understanding the limitations of financial ratios. *Academy of Accounting and Financial Studies Journal, 19*(3), 75.
17. Froelich, K. A., Knoepfle, T. W., & Pollak, T. H., (2000). Financial measures in nonprofit organization research: Comparing IRS 990 return and audited financial statement data. *Nonprofit and Voluntary Sector Quarterly, 29*(2), 232–254.
18. Govindarajan, V., (1980). The objectives of financial statements: An empirical study of the use of cash flow and earnings by security analysts. *Accounting, Organizations and Society, 5*(4), 383–392.
19. Greer, H. C., (1943). Structural fundamentals of financial statements. *The Accounting Review, 18*(3), 193–205.
20. Hertenstein, J. H., & McKinnon, S. M., (1997). Solving the puzzle of the cash flow statement. *Business Horizons, 40*(1), 69–77.
21. Jones, G. R., & Butler, J. E., (1988). Costs, revenue, and business-level strategy. *Academy of Management Review, 13*(2), 202–213.
22. Jones, J. P., (2001). The implications of firms' investment opportunities for the valuation of cash flows from investing activities. *Advances in Accounting, 18*, 169–193.
23. Keating, E. K., & Frumkin, P., (2003). Reengineering nonprofit financial accountability: Toward a more reliable foundation for regulation. *Public Administration Review, 63*(1), 3–15.
24. Klychova, G., Zakirova, A., Mannapova, R., Pinina, K., & Ryazanova, Y., (2019). Assessment of the efficiency of investing activities of organizations. In: *E3S Web of Conferences* (Vol. 110, p. 02075). EDP Sciences.

25. Kousenidis, D. V., (2006). A free cash flow version of the cash flow statement: A note. *Managerial Finance, 32*(8), 645–653.
26. Kwok, H., (2002). The effect of cash flow statement format on lenders' decisions. *The International Journal of Accounting, 37*(3), 347–362.
27. Lennard, A., (2007). Stewardship and the objectives of financial statements: A comment on IASB's preliminary views on an improved conceptual framework for financial reporting: The objective of financial reporting and qualitative characteristics of decision-useful financial reporting information. *Accounting in Europe, 4*(1), 51–66.
28. Lin, S., Martinez, D., Wang, C., & Yang, Y. W., (2018). Is other comprehensive income reported in the income statement more value relevant? The role of financial statement presentation. *Journal of Accounting, Auditing & Finance, 33*(4), 624–646.
29. Linsmeier, T. J., Gribble, J., Jennings, R. G., & Lang, M. H., (1997). An issues paper on comprehensive income. *Accounting Horizons, 11*(2), 120.
30. Maines, L. A., & McDaniel, L. S., (2000). Effects of comprehensive-income characteristics on nonprofessional investors' judgments: The role of financial-statement presentation format. *The Accounting Review, 75*(2), 179–207.
31. Martani, D., Khairurizka, R., & Khairurizka, R. J. C. B. R., (2009). The effect of financial ratios, firm size, and cash flow from operating activities in the interim report to the stock return. *Chinese Business Review, 8*(6), 44–55.
32. McGill, J. I., & Van, R. G. J., (1999). Revenue management: Research overview and prospects. *Transportation Science, 33*(2), 233–256.
33. Miao, B., Teoh, S. H., & Zhu, Z., (2016). Limited attention, statement of cash flow disclosure, and the valuation of accruals. *Review of Accounting Studies, 21*, 473–515.
34. Michalisin, M. D., Smith, R. D., & Kline, D. M., (1997). In search of strategic assets. *The International Journal of Organizational Analysis, 5*(4), 360–387.
35. Mohamed, N., & Handley-Schachelor, M., (2014). Financial statement fraud risk mechanisms and strategies: The case studies of Malaysian commercial companies. *Procedia-Social and Behavioral Sciences, 145*, 321–329.
36. Mohanram, P. S., (2005). Separating winners from losers among low book-to-market stocks using financial statement analysis. *Review of Accounting Studies, 10*, 133–170.
37. Mook, L., & Quarter, J., (2006). Accounting for the social economy: The socioeconomic impact statement. *Annals of Public and Cooperative Economics, 77*(2), 247–269.
38. Paton, W. A., (1928). Limitations of financial and operating ratios. *Accounting Review*, 252–260.
39. Penman, S. H., (2009). Accounting for intangible assets: There is also an income statement. *Abacus, 45*(3), 358–371.
40. Phillips, F., (1999). Auditor attention to and judgments of aggressive financial reporting. *Journal of Accounting Research, 37*(1), 167–189.
41. Sharpe, W. F., & Tint, L. G., (1990). Liabilities-a new approach. *Journal of Portfolio Management, 16*(2), 5–10.

42. So, S., & Smith, M., (2009). Value-relevance of presenting changes in fair value of investment properties in the income statement: Evidence from Hong Kong. *Accounting and Business Research, 39*(2), 103–118.
43. Sprouse, R. T., (1974). Discussion of opportunities and implications of the report on objectives of financial statements. *Journal of Accounting Research,* 25–28.
44. Swaminathan, S., & Weintrop, J., (1991). The information content of earnings, revenues, and expenses. *Journal of Accounting Research, 29*(2), 418–427.
45. Tomilina, E. P., & Kurilova, K. D., (2020). *Types of Financial Statements* (p. 190). ББК 72 С56.
46. Wang, T. S., Lin, Y. M., Werner, E. M., & Chang, H., (2018). The relationship between external financing activities and earnings management: Evidence from enterprise risk management. *International Review of Economics & Finance, 58*, 312–329.
47. Yamey, B. S., (2014). The development of company accounting conventions. In: *Evolution of Corporate Financial Reporting (RLE Accounting)* (pp. 243–252). Routledge.
48. Zeff, S. A., (2016). The trueblood study group on the objectives of financial statements (1971–73): A historical study. *Journal of Accounting and Public Policy, 35*(2), 134–161.

CHAPTER 4

CASH FLOW WITHIN A COMPANY

UNIT INTRODUCTION

Cash flow shows the net amount of cash and cash equivalents (CCE) flowing into and out of a corporation. Money received indicates cash inflows, and cash consumption means cash outflows. Essential to a company's capacity to create shareholder value is its potential to produce positive cash flows and, more particularly, to optimize its long-term free cash flow (FCF). FCF is the cash flow produced by a company's everyday activities less cash outlays for capital expenditures (CapEx) (Merrill & Edwards, 1996) (Figure 4.1)).

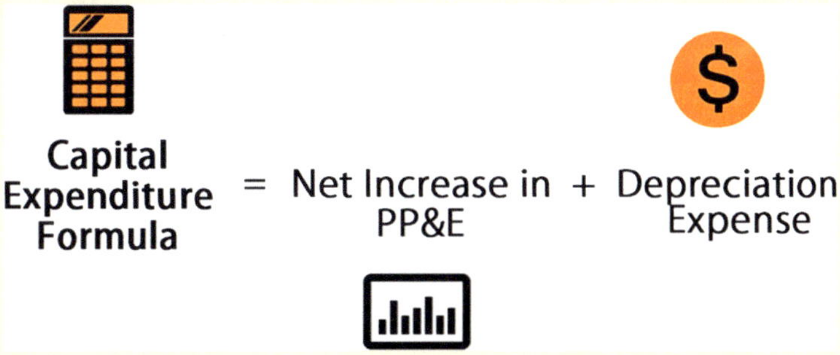

Figure 4.1. Illustration of the formula of capital expenditure.

Source: Mary Girsch-Bock, Creative Commons License.

Expand PP&E as Property, Plant and Equipment

The money made through sales is considered the company's income, while the money spent goes toward the company's expenses. They may offer products on credit with the anticipation of receiving the amount owed later and getting money through interest payments, deposits, fees, and licensing agreements. Evaluating the stability, time keeping, and irregularity of cash flows, in addition to determining where cash flows begin and where they ultimately lead, is one of the most important financial reporting objectives. To properly evaluate a company's liquidity, adaptability, and overall financial performance, it is essential to have this information (Jones et al., 1995).

A healthy cash flow indicates that a company's liquid assets are increasing, which enables it to meet its commitments, invest in the growth of the business, distribute profits to shareholders, pay operating expenses, and provide a shield against the possibility of future financial difficulties. Companies in better financial shape are better able to capitalize on profitable investment opportunities. They are also in a better position to benefit during depressions because they can avoid the effects of economic turmoil (Sayari & Mugan, 2013).

The cash flow statement (CFS) is a fundamental financial statement that shows a company's sources and expenditures of cash over a specific period. This statement can be utilized to analyze cash flows. It can be used by corporate management, industry specialists, and investors to evaluate a company's potential to create cash to pay off its debts and cover the costs of its operations. The CFS, together with the balance sheet and income statement, is one of the three most essential financial statements published by a firm. Cash flow could be negative whenever a company's disbursements exceed its inflows (King, 1987).

There are three essential components of financial statements:

1. The balance sheet provides a snapshot of an organization's assets and liabilities.
2. The income statement reflects the firm's profitability within a given period.
3. The CFS serves as the company's checkbook and unifies the other two financial statements. It details the firm's cash transactions (outflows and inflows) for the time in question. It demonstrates if all revenues reflected on the financial statements have been received (Plewa & Friedlob, 1995).

Yet, the cash flow may not reflect the company's expenditures directly. This is because not all corporate expenses are paid immediately. Even though the corporation might incur obligations, any payouts towards such duties are not recorded as cash outflows until the transaction occurs (Kenley, 2003).

The bottom line should be the first to notice on the CFS. This is expected to represent the net change in CCE. The bottom line displays the difference in the company's cash reserves and cash equivalents (immediately convertible assets) over the previous period. On the balance sheet, CCE can be found under current assets. If you subtract the current

CCE from the CCE of the prior year or quarter, you should obtain the identification number that appears at the bottom of the statement of cash flows (Jury, 2012).

Learning Objectives

At the end of the chapter, the reader will be able to understand:

- The importance of cash flow
- The concept of cash flow from operations (CFO), cash flow from investing (CFI), cash flow from financing (CFF)
- The concept of price-to-cash flows ratio
- The method to calculate cash flow
- The difference between cash flow and profit

Remember

CFO metrics outflows and inflows of cash from the sale of products or services as well as other operational activities, like the account receivable collection and the billing of accounts payable.

Key Terms

- Cash Flow
- Cash Flow from Financing (CFF)
- Cash Flow from Investing (CFI)
- Cash Flow from Operations (CFO)
- Debt Service Coverage Ratio (DSCR)
- Free Cash Flow
- Unlevered Free Cash Flow (UFCF)

4.1. IMPORTANCE OF CASH FLOW

Cash flow is an essential accounting indicator showing the cash flow out of and into a company's accounts. It offers valuable insight into a company's capacity to generate and utilize cash and its brief financial stability.

The significance of cash flow is evident in several key ways:

4.1.1. Solvency

Positive cash flow is crucial to a company's solvency because it allows it to cover its expenses and fulfill its duties. Negative cash flow places a company at risk of insolvency or other financial challenges (Eisdorfer, 2007).

4.1.2. Growth

Good cash flow enables a business to invest in new chances, including expanding its activities or gaining new assets, that could contribute to its lengthy profitability and growth.

4.1.3. Liquidity

Cash flow gives a measure of a company's liquidity or its capacity to cover payments, invest in new prospects, or respond to unforeseen expenses.

4.1.4. Debt Management

KEYWORD

creditworthiness is a measure of how well you've handled your credit and debt obligations.

Investors and lenders use a company's cash flow to evaluate its creditworthiness and if it represents a good investment opportunity. The ability of a company to produce positive cash flow is crucial to its capacity to obtain financing and repay debt (Scott, 2007).

4.1.5. Financial Planning

Cash flow is an essential financial planning tool, enabling businesses to forecast their future cash requirements and make well-informed investment and spending choices.

Cash flow is a vital measurement that provides critical insight into an organization's financial performance, consistency, and growth potential. Long-term success is more probable for businesses that track their cash flow and use this data to make educated financial decisions (Kent & Bu, 2020).

4.2. TYPES OF CASH FLOW

4.2.1. Cash Flows from Operations (CFO)

Cash Flows from Operations (CFO) is a financial metric that calculates the money produced or consumed by a company's primary continuing operations. It is a crucial element of a firm's CFS, which gives data on how a business is trying to generate and use cash.

This metric gives a more precise depiction of the operating performance of a business as it eliminates non-operating products, including investment opportunities, financing activities, and taxation (Nwaeze et al., 2006).

Figure 4.2. Flow diagram of cash flow analysis.

A positive CFO suggests that a company's operating activities generate sufficient cash to pay its expenditures and invest in the business. Conversely, a negative CFO indicates that a company's functional operations consume more money than they generate, suggesting financial difficulties and the requirement for financing or expense metrics. Investors and analysts frequently use CFO to evaluate a company's financial health and its capacity to produce future cash flows. It is also a significant determinant of a firm's creditworthiness and ability to repay debt (Brown & Christensen, 2014).

Cash flows from operations (CFO) is a vital measurement for investors and businesses to evaluate a company's financial condition and capacity to generate money from its core activities. Especially in comparison to other measures such as net income, it gives a more precise depiction of a company's performance (Drtina & Largay, 1985).

Did you Know?

According to a study by US Bank, 82% of businesses fail due to cash flow issues.

4.2.2. Cash Flows from Investing (CFI)

The term "CFI," also known as "investing cash flow," refers to the total amount of money earned or lost as a result of various investment-related activities carried out throughout a given time frame (Jones, 2001). Buying speculative assets, purchasing securities, and selling securities or assets are the three primary activities that makeup investing activities. A negative CFI operations is not always a red flag because it could result from significant investments in the company's long-term health, including development and research. In these cases, the negative cash flow is a good sign (R&D) (Martani & Dini, 2010).

Figure 4.3. Image of the formula of price-to-cash flow.

4.2.3. Cash Flows from Financing (CFF)

The term "cash flows from financing," also known as "financing cash flow," shows the net cash flows utilized to fund a business's operations and capital expenditures. The issuing of debt and equity and the dividend payments are all examples of actions that fall under the financing category. Investors can evaluate a company's financial strength and the efficiency with which it manages its working capital using the cash flow generated from its financing activities (Liman & Mohammed, 2018) (Figure 4.2).

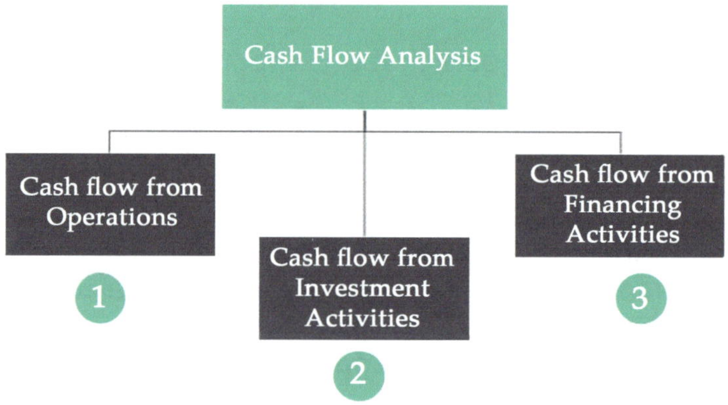

Source: Roshan Waingankar, Creative Commons License.

4.3. PRICE-TO-CASH FLOWS RATIO

The price-to-cash-flow (P/CF) ratio is a stock multiple that compares its value to its ability to operate cash flow per share. This ratio utilizes operating cash flow, which also helps to add back to net income non-cash expenditures like amortization and amortization (Rostan & Rostan, 2012). P/CF is particularly beneficial for valuing stocks with positive cash flow that are not profitable due to significant non-cash charges. Cash flow refers to incoming and outgoing cash. A positive cash flow signifies an increase in incoming funds, whereas a negative cash flow implies an increase in outgoing funds. The latter is not necessarily negative, as it may indicate that you are investing in growth. Yet, if your spending gets excessive, you cannot save for a rainy day or pay your creditors or suppliers. Whether you are operating a company or a home, it is essential to maintain a healthy cash flow (Sehgal & Pandey, 2009) (Figure 4.3).

Figure 4.4. Picture of the formula of free cash flow.

$$\text{Price-to-Cask Flow (P/CF) Ratio} = \frac{\text{Market Capitalization}}{\text{Cask Flow From Operations}}$$

Source: Wall street prep, Creative Commons License.

4.4. METHODS TO CALCULATE CASH FLOWS

Using the CFS in combination with other financial statements can assist experts and investors in determining various metrics and ratios that can be utilized to make educated choices and suggestions (Fernandez, 2007).

TIPS

The greater a company's free cash flow, the greater its cash on hand. This entire cash could be reinvested in the company's performance or distributed as a dividend.

4.4.1. Debt Service Coverage Ratio (DSCR)

Even profitable businesses can struggle if their activities do not generate sufficient cash flow to remain liquid. This can occur if a company's profits are tied down by exceptional accounts receivable (AR) and overstocked assets or if excessive capital expenditures are incurred (CapEx) (Hermawan et al., 2020).

Therefore, investors, and creditors want to see if the company has sufficient CCE to settle its short-term liabilities. Analysts evaluate the DSCR to determine if a company can pay its current liabilities with cash produced from operations (DSCR).

Debt Service Coverage Ratio = Net Operating Income / Debt Obligations (or Debt Service)

Total debt service / obligation = Interest payments + Principal payments + Sinking funds

But liquidity only provides limited insight. A company may be flush with cash since it is paying back its potential for future growth by trying to sell off its lengthy assets or incurring unsustainable debt levels (Polato & Beltrame, 2019).

4.4.2. Free Cash Flow

Free cash flow (FCF) is the cash remaining after a business pays its operational costs and capital expenditures. It is the money remaining after paying expenses such as salary, rent, and taxes. Companies may utilize FCF as they see fit (Richardson, 2006) (Figure 4.4).

Understanding how to determine and evaluate FCF assists a corporation with its cash management while providing investors with financial insight, permitting them to make more informed investment choices.

FCF is crucial because it indicates a company's cash generation efficiency. It evaluates the accessible liquidity to investors.

Eventually, this would boost the company's value, resulting in a growing investor portfolio (Lang et al., 1991). Evaluating the firm's FCF can be difficult due to the formula's length and the need for solid analytic abilities.

The following is the equation:

A formula for the company's free cash flow

Free Cash Flow to the Firm = Net Income + Non-cash Charges (for example – depreciation and amortization) + Interest (1-Tax Rate) – Capital Expenditures (fixed capital such as equipment) – Working Capital Expenditures

Or,

Free Cash Flow = Operating Cash Flow – CapitalEx

The result is the free cash flow obtainable to the company's debt and equity holders.

Table 4.1. The Walmart Statement of Cash Flows for the Fiscal Year

Source: Quick Books, Creative Commons License.

4.4.3. Unlevered Free Cash Flow (UFCF)

When calculating the total FCF of the company, the UFCF metric should be used. This is a firm's cash flow that does not include interest payments, and it reflects how much cash the company has before considering its financial commitments. The differential between levered and UFCF tells if a corporation has an unhealthy level of debt or whether its debt load is manageable (Boussabaine & Elhag, 1999).

4.5. EXAMPLE OF CASH FLOW

The Walmart statement of cash flows for the fiscal year that ended January 31, 2019 is reproduced (Table 4.1). All the figures in Table 4.1 are in millions of United States dollars (Song & Qi, 2013).

Walmart Statement of Cash Flows (2019)	
Cash flows from operating activities:	
Consolidated net income	7,179
(Income) loss from discontinued operations, net of income taxes	—
Income from continuing operations	7,179
Adjustments to reconcile consolidated net income to net cash provided by operating activities:	
Unrealized (gains) and losses	3,516
(Gains) and losses for disposal of business operations	4,850
Depreciation and amortization	10,678
Deferred income taxes	(499)
Other operating activities	1,734
Changes in certain assets and liabilities:	
Receivables, net	(368)
Inventories	(1,311)
Accounts payable	1,831
Accrued liabilities	183
Accrued income taxes	(40)
Net cash provided by operating activities	27,753
Cash flows from investing activities:	
Payments for property and equipment	(10,344)
Proceeds from the disposal of property and equipment	519
Proceeds from the disposal of certain operations	876
Payments for business acquisitions, net of cash acquired	(14,656)
Other investing activities	(431)
Net cash used in investing activities	(24,036)
Cash flows from financing activities:	
The net change in short-term borrowings	(53)
Proceeds from the issuance of long-term debt	15,872
Payments of long-term debt	(3,784)
Dividends paid	(6,102)
Purchase of company stock	(7,410)
Dividends paid to noncontrolling interest	(431)
Other financing activities	(629)
Net cash used in financing activities	(2,537)

Effect of exchange rates on cash and cash equivalents	(438)
Net increase (decrease) in cash and cash equivalents	742
Cash and cash equivalents at the beginning of the year	7,014
Cash and cash equivalents at the end of the year	7,756

Source: Bodenhorn, Creative Commons License.

The term "cash and cash equivalents (CCE) at the end of the year" appears in the last line of the CFS and the first line under current assets in the balance sheet. Both terms refer to the same financial asset category. The bottom line, which is referred to as "income from continuing operations" on the income statement, is identical to the first number that appears on the CFS, which is referred to as "consolidated net income" (Mackevičius & Senkus, 2006).

KEYWORD

Liquid assets are assets that can easily be exchanged for cash.

Since the CFS only matters liquid assets in the shape of CCE, it tries to adapt to operating revenue to determine the net effect in cash. This is done to meet the requirements of generally accepted accounting principles (GAAP). The purpose of including amortization and depreciation expense on the income statement is to provide a more accurate depiction of the gradual decline in the value of assets throughout their useful lives. On the other hand, the operating cash flows take into account only the money transfers that affect cash; thus, these changes are turned around (Ruback, 2002).

In addition, the net change in assets that are not cash, such as AR and inventories, is not included in operating income. For instance, there is a reduction of $368 million in net receivables when operating income is calculated. As a result, we can deduce that the amount of money owed to creditors increased by 368 million dollars compared to the previous year (Penman, 2001).

If the cash had been received by the end of the year, then this increase in revenue would have been reflected in the operating income as additional revenue. To demonstrate the positive effect that sales had on net cash flow throughout the year, it was necessary to subtract from the growing amount of receivables. To arrive at the figure for cash flow from operating activities, the same removal process must be performed for current liabilities (da Costa Moraes et al., 2015).

The section of the CFS that accounts for CFI activities considers investments in property, plant, and equipment (PP&E), as well as acquisitions of other businesses. In the section titled "cash flow from financing (CFF) activities," you will find accounting for the proceeds from the issuance of long-term debt, the repayment of the debt, and dividends paid out (Turtle et al., 1994).

The most important thing to take away from this is that Walmart had a positive cash flow (an increase of $742 million). This suggests that it has kept cash on hand at the business and added to its deposits to protect itself against brief liabilities and future market fluctuations.

ACTIVITY 4.1.

Suppose you own a small business that manufactures and sells handcrafted furniture. You have recently noticed that although your sales have been increasing steadily, your cash balance has been decreasing. You are concerned about this trend and want to understand why it is happening.

What steps would you take to analyze your cash flow and identify the factors contributing to the decrease in your cash balance? What strategies could you implement to improve your cash flow and ensure the financial stability of your business?

4.6. CASH FLOW VS. PROFIT

Cash flow and profit are two crucial accounting and corporate finance concepts, yet they are distinct (Lee, 1985).

Profit, often referred to as net income, measures a business's profitability. It is the amount of cash a firm receives after subtracting all its expenses, such as the cost of the products sold, operational expenses, and taxes. Profit indicates a company's financial condition and profitability, as it reveals the amount of money retained after covering expenses (Bodenhorn, 1964).

In contrast, cash flow measures the money from and to a business's accounts. It consists of cash inflows from sales, investments, and loans and cash outflows from operating costs, capital spending, and debt servicing. Cash flow is an essential indicator of a business's ability to earn and utilize cash and its quick economic stability (Foerster et al., 2017).

Profit measures a company's profitability, whereas cash flow reflects its ability to earn and utilize cash. Although they are related, profits, and cash flow are not identical; a corporation may earn a high profit but negative cash flow, or conversely. A business must have good profit and positive cash flow to be economically viable and profitable over a lengthy period (Foerster et al., 2017).

4.7. DIFFERENCE BETWEEN CASH FLOWS AND REVENUES

Cash flow and profit are two crucial financial terms in accounting and business. They are connected, yet they are not identical.

Revenue is the income a business makes via its operations and sales. It represents the sum of money a company makes before deducting expenses. The top-line success of a firm is measured by its revenue, which is used to compute its gross profit (Lev et al., 2010).

Cash flow, in contrast, is the amount of cash that a business generates or spends during a specified period. The money flows from and to accounting records, including inflows from sales and investment earnings and outflows from operating costs and capital spending.

Cash flow is a measure of the cash that flows into and out of a firm's accounts, whereas revenue is a measure of the top-line success of a corporation. A corporation might have high sales but negative cash flow if it has more cash outflows than cash inflows, indicating it may have difficulty paying its payments shortly (Atwood et al., 2011) (Figure 4.5).

Figure 4.5. Depiction of difference between revenue and cashflow.

Source: Alex Lewis,_Creative Commons License.

4.8. SUMMARY

- Cash flow within a company refers to the amount of cash that flows in and out of business over a specific period. Free cash flow (FCF) is a critical measurement of cash flow that evaluates a company's cash generation efficiency. It is the cash remaining after a business pays for operational costs and capital expenditures. FCF helps corporations to manage their cash and assists investors in making informed investment choices. The greater a company's FCF, the greater its cash on hand, which could be reinvested in its performance or distributed as a dividend, ultimately increasing its value and resulting in a growing investment portfolio. While calculating FCF can be challenging, it provides significant insights into a company's financial health, making it a vital metric for investors and companies.

REVIEW QUESTIONS

1. What is free cash flow, and why is it essential for a company?
2. How can a company improve its free cash flow?
3. What are the key factors that impact a company's cash flow?
4. How can a company use its free cash flow to create shareholder value?
5. What risks are associated with relying solely on free cash flow to measure a company's financial health?

MULTIPLE CHOICE QUESTIONS

1. What is free cash flow?

a. The cash a company generates after paying its expenses and investments.
b. The cash a company generates before paying its expenses and investments.
c. The cash a company generates only from its investments.
d. The cash a company generates from its sales revenue.

2. What does free cash flow indicate about a company?

a. Its cash generation efficiency.
b. Its net income.
c. Its total assets.
d. It's accounts payable.

3. How can a company utilize its free cash flow?

a. To pay its operational costs.
b. To pay its taxes.
c. To invest in new projects.
d. To pay its debt.

4. **What does a high free cash flow signify about a company?**
   a. It has low liquidity.
   b. It has high liquidity.
   c. It has low profitability.
   d. It has high profitability.
5. **What could a company do with its excess free cash flow?**
   a. Use it for share buybacks.
   b. Invest in new projects.
   c. Increase employee salaries.
   d. Pay off its short-term debts.
6. **Why is free cash flow considered an important metric?**
   a. It indicates a company's ability to pay off its debt.
   b. It indicates a company's profitability.
   c. It indicates a company's efficiency in generating cash.
   d. It indicates a company's total assets.
7. **What is the formula for calculating free cash flow?**
   a. Net income minus dividends.
   b. Operating cash flow minus capital expenditures.
   c. Revenue minus expenses.
   d. Gross profit minus operating expenses.

Answers to Multiple Choice Questions

1.	(a)	2.	(a)	3.	(c)	4.	(b)	5.	(a)
6.	(c)	7.	(c)						

REFERENCES

1. Ali, U., Ormal, L., & Ahmad, F., (2018). Impact of free cash flow on profitability of the firms in automobile sector of Germany. *Journal of Economics and Management Sciences, 1*(1), 57–67.
2. Almeida, H., Campello, M., & Weisbach, M. S., (2004). The cash flow sensitivity of cash. *The Journal of Finance, 59*(4), 1777–1804.
3. Atwood, T. J., Drake, M. S., Myers, J. N., & Myers, L. A., (2011). Do earnings reported under IFRS tell us more about future earnings and cash flows? *Journal of Accounting and Public Policy, 30*(2), 103–121.

4. Bodenhorn, D., (1964). A cash-flow concept of profit. *The Journal of Finance, 19*(1), 16–31.
5. Boussabaine, A. H., & Elhag, T., (1999). Applying fuzzy techniques to cash flow analysis. *Construction Management & Economics, 17*(6), 745–755.
6. Bowen, R. M., Burgstahler, D., & Daley, L. A., (1986). Evidence on the relationships between earnings and various measures of cash flow. *Accounting Review*, 713–725.
7. Brown, N. C., & Christensen, T. E., (2014). The quality of street cash flow from operations. *Review of Accounting Studies, 19*, 913–954.
8. Da Costa, M. M. B., Nagano, M. S., & Sobreiro, V. A., (2015). Stochastic cash flow management models: A literature review since the 1980s. *Decision Models in Engineering and Management*, 11–28.
9. Dechow, P. M., Kothari, S. P., & Watts, R. L., (1998). The relation between earnings and cash flows. *Journal of Accounting and Economics, 25*(2), 133–168.
10. Drtina, R. E., & Largay, III. J. A., (1985). Pitfalls in calculating cash flow from operations. *Accounting Review*, 314–326.
11. Eisdorfer, A., (2007). The importance of cash-flow news for financially distressed firms. *Financial Management, 36*(3), 33–48.
12. Fernandez, P., (2007). Valuing companies by cash flow discounting: Ten methods and nine theories. *Managerial Finance, 33*(11), 853–876.
13. Foerster, S., Tsagarelis, J., & Wang, G., (2017). Are cash flows better stock return predictors than profits? *Financial Analysts Journal, 73*(1), 73–99.
14. Graham, C., & Knight, J., (2000). Cash flows vs. earnings in the valuation of equity REITs. *Journal of Real Estate Portfolio Management, 6*(1), 17–25.
15. Hermawan, I., Sinaga, B. M., & Andati, T., (2020). External factors with government and company policies that have an impact on the debt service coverage ratio of coal companies. *Jurnal Aplikasi Manajemen, 18*(2), 371–382.
16. Jensen, M. C., (1986). Agency costs of free cash flow, corporate finance, and takeovers. *The American Economic Review, 76*(2), 323–329.
17. Jones, J. P., (2001). The implications of firms' investment opportunities for the valuation of cash flows from investing activities. *Advances in Accounting, 18*, 169–193.
18. Jones, S., Romano, C. A., & Smyrnios, K. X., (1995). An evaluation of the decision usefulness of cash flow statements by Australian reporting entities. *Accounting and Business Research, 25*(98), 115–129.
19. Jury, T., (2012). *Cash Flow Analysis and Forecasting: The Definitive Guide to Understanding and Using Published Cash Flow Data* (Vol. 1, pp. 1–15). John Wiley & Sons.
20. Kenley, R., (2003). *Financing Construction: Cash Flows and Cash Farming* (Vol. 1, pp. 1–10). Routledge.

21. Kent, R. A., & Bu, D., (2020). The importance of cash flow disclosure and cost of capital. *Accounting & Finance, 60*, 877–908.
22. King, M. A., (1987). The cash flow corporate income tax. In: *The Effects of Taxation on Capital Accumulation* (pp. 377–400). University of Chicago Press.
23. Lang, L. H., Stulz, R., & Walkling, R. A., (1991). A test of the free cash flow hypothesis: The case of bidder returns. *Journal of Financial Economics, 29*(2), 315–335.
24. Lee, T. A., (1985). Cash flow accounting, profit and performance measurement: A response to a challenge. *Accounting and Business Research, 15*(58), 93–97.
25. Lev, B., Li, S., & Sougiannis, T., (2010). The usefulness of accounting estimates for predicting cash flows and earnings. *Review of Accounting Studies, 15*, 779–807.
26. Liman, M., & Mohammed, A., (2018). Operating cash flow and corporate financial performance of listed conglomerate companies in Nigeria. *Journal of Humanities and Social Science, 23*(2), 1–11.
27. Mackevičius, J., & Senkus, K., (2006). The system of formation and evaluation of the information of cash flows. *Journal of Business Economics and Management, 7*(4), 171–182.
28. Martani, D., & Dini, N., (2010). The influence of operating cash flow and investment cash flow to the accounting conservatism measurement. *Chinese Business Review, 9*(6), 1.
29. Merrill, P. R., & Edwards, C. R., (1996). Cash-flow taxation of financial services. *National Tax Journal, 49*(3), 487–500.
30. Nwaeze, E. T., Yang, S. S., & Yin, Q. J., (2006). Accounting information and CEO compensation: The role of cash flow from operations in the presence of earnings. *Contemporary Accounting Research, 23*(1), 227–265.
31. Penman, S. H., (2001). On comparing cash flow and accrual accounting models for use in equity valuation: A response to Lundholm and O'Keefe (CAR, Summer 2001). *Contemporary Accounting Research, 18*(4), 681–692.
32. Plewa, Jr. F. J., & Friedlob, G. T., (1995). *Understanding Cash Flow* (Vol. 1, pp. 1–05). John Wiley & Sons.
33. Polato, M., & Beltrame, F., (2019). Bank's asset quality review using debt service coverage ratio: An empirical investigation across European firms. *Frontier Topics in Banking: Investigating New Trends and Recent Developments in the Financial Industry*, 225–244.
34. Richardson, S., (2006). Over-investment of free cash flow. *Review of Accounting Studies, 11*, 159–189.
35. Rostan, P., & Rostan, A., (2012). Assessing the predictive power of customer satisfaction for financial and market performances: Price-to-earnings ratio is a better predictor overall. *International Review of Management and Marketing, 2*(1), 59–74.
36. Ruback, R. S., (2002). Capital cash flows: A simple approach to valuing risky cash flows. *Financial Management,* 85–103.

37. Sayari, N., & Mugan, F. N. C. S., (2013). Cash flow statement as an evidence for financial distress. *Universal Journal of Accounting and Finance, 1*(3), 95–103.
38. Scott, S., (2007). The importance of cash flow analysis for small businesses. *Com. Lending Rev., 22*, 37.
39. Sehgal, S., & Pandey, A., (2009). The behavior of price multiples in India (1990–2007). *Asian Academy of Management Journal of Accounting & Finance, 5*(1).
40. Song, X., & Qi, C., (2013). Enterprise valuation based on UFCF discount model take Changyu a as an example. In: *2nd International Conference on Science and Social Research (ICSSR 2013)* (pp. 784–787). Atlantis Press.
41. Turtle, H., Bector, C. R., & Gill, A., (1994). Using fuzzy logic in corporate finance: An example of a global cash flow netting problem. *Managerial Finance, 1*, 1–25.

CHAPTER 5

ASSETS, LIABILITIES, AND DEPRECIATION

UNIT INTRODUCTION

A company's assets are some resources that own and have measurable financial value. They can be tangible assets like physical facilities or intangible assets like trademarks and exclusive rights. Assets are significant to a company's overall financial stability. They stand in for the assets of a business that must increase its income level and size. They protect creditors and lenders; assets are essential in luring investment and securing finance. A source of liquidity that could be utilized to meet its obligations and keep activities running can be provided by assets. It is another way that assets can assist a business in weathering the effects of financial declines.

A person or company is liable when it owes money or fulfills other responsibilities to third parties. There are financial or source obligations that a business must pay back to its creditors, lender, or workers, among other parties. The time necessary to pay back a debt affects the type of liability sustained, whether long-term or short-term, for example, debt, mortgages, unpaid amounts on credit cards, and other forms of exceptional debt of all liabilities. Together with equity and assets, liabilities are an essential element that should be included in the income statement of a business. A snapshot of a business's financial situation at a particular time can be obtained from the balance sheet, which details the business resources, obligations, and equity. Financial analysts and investors can better understand a business's economic commitments and capacity to repay its debts by analyzing its liabilities (Sigidov et al., 2016).

Businesses need to practice efficient management of their liabilities to preserve their economic stability and avoid a financial crisis. It requires always keeping a close eye on obligations, prioritizing debt repayment, and ensuring a healthy cash flow. Every business's capacity to successfully manage its liabilities can allow it to maintain a strong financial position, supporting its development and success over the long run (Sahminan, 2007).

Distributing the value of a material and the cost of a tangible asset during the asset's use is known as devaluation, an accounting rule. An asset's value consumed is equivalent to its depreciation. It enables businesses to generate money from assets they control by allowing customers to pay for those assets over a predetermined time (Simon, 1959). The initial cost of ownership is significantly lowered because businesses do not have an account with them entirely in the year that assets are owned. Depreciation can substantially impact a company's bottom line if not accurately accounted for. In addition, businesses can write off the value of long-term investments on their tax returns and financial statements. One can compare depreciation to amortization, the process of accounting for value change that takes place over time using intangible resources (Liao, 2016).

Learning Objectives

At the end of this chapter, the reader will be able to understand

1. The concept of assets, liabilities, and depreciation
2. The importance of tangible and intangible asses
3. Working on financial and derivative assets
4. The main properties of assets
5. The method to determine assets
6. The concept of current and noncurrent liabilities
7. The importance of different types of depreciation
8. The critical difference between liabilities and assets

Key Terms

1. Current Liabilities
2. Depreciation
3. Double Declining Balance (DDB)
4. Exchange Traded Funds (ETFs)
5. Fixed Assets
6. Mutual Funds
7. Real Estate Investment Trust (RELTs)
8. Standard Cost Method
9. Sum-of-the-Year Digits (SYD)
10. Trademark

5.1. ASSETS

An asset is a valuable resource, like a business, under a company's authority and may be used to generate financial gains. A rare resource that possesses the potential to help the economy by increasing cash inflows or reducing cash outflows is referred to as a financial resource. Accessibility to others or companies cannot be represented as an asset. Additionally, a right or another access may be legally valid, meaning a company may use financial resources as it finds fit. Any owner may restrict or prohibit their use from the date of a business's financial statements. A business must have a right to an asset to be counted as an asset (Ahn et al., 2009).

Remember

A business needs to have efficient management of its assets to maximize the worth of such assets and ensure the company's long-term economic stability and growth.

The asset is a word commonly used to describe someone who is a valuable addition to their community. But what exactly do financial analysts understand by assets within commercial accounting? An asset is anything of value that even a business expects will be useful in the future. The main element of a business's net worth is its assets. While giving loans, lenders could also consider a company's assets. That article solely discusses company-owned assets; it does not discuss right-of-use resources (i.e., leased assets) (Michalisin et al., 1997).

The International Financial Reporting Standards (IFRS) explain an asset as

"A resource that the company currently controls like a result of previous occurrences from which it expects to receive future financial gains." In other words, the ability to create income or transform an item into cash makes it valuable. They may be concrete objects like machinery or immaterial things like intellectual property—one of a company's most essential income statements, economic reports, and lists of assets (Gupta & Lehmann, 2003) (Figure 5.1).

Figure 5.1. Image of assets.

Source: SorWikiFinancepedia, Creative Commons License.

5.2. TYPES OF ASSETS

Various factors can be used to categorize assets. The proper classification for businesses is essential for financial monitoring and assessing the company's financial position. According to IFRS, assets are commonly assessed based on their present state's predicted future cash flows (Driver et al., 2006).

5.2.1. Tangible Assets

Assets with actual purchasing worth are considered measurable business assets. A company uses these assets to run, manufacture products and services, or make money. Long-term versus short-term tangible assets are both possible. They typically fit into two subgroups (Francl, 2013):

- Financial capital
- Physical equipment, systems, and infrastructure

These are some examples of tangible assets:

- Cash equivalents and cash
- Business premises, property, or land
- Company automobiles
- Equipment and machinery
- IT apparatus
- Investments (Harc, 2015).
- Any debts you may have.
- Stock in hand and any confirmed orders worth

Non-physical assets like reputation, brand recognition, including intellectual property are also possible for businesses. We refer to them as intangible assets.

A business's core is made up of tangible assets. These are typically not for sale to clients, yet they constitute a significant portion of the value of your business. One can use physical resources:

- To offer services or goods
- To contribute to your business' cashflow
- To generate money for emergency
- To achieve your professional aims and objectives.

KEYWORD

Brand recognition is the extent to which a consumer can correctly identify a particular product or service just by viewing the product or service's logo, tag line, packaging or advertising campaign.

- As insurance for loans

Learn more about the evaluation of business assets (Thum et al., 2019).

You must manage and monitor the whole of your company's tangible assets if you want to get the most out of them. You must include all assets in your income statement on an accrual basis. You could be eligible to depreciate some assets or split their cost across their useful lifetime if they lose value with time. See all the information on asset depreciation.

You can keep track of the company's tangible assets' position, amount, status, and maintenance need with the help of an achieving effective asset tracking system. It might also aid in preventing asset stealing—more information on utilizing resources in a business (Greco et al., 2013).

Your actual goods could be in danger of damage or loss in addition to theft. You might want to get insurance or take other safety precautions for your belongings. Learn more about safeguarding corporate assets (Chukwu & Egbuhuzor, 2017) (Figure 5.1).

5.2.1.1. Current Assets

- Cash and its equivalent, including certificates of deposits including treasury bills.
- Securities can be traded, including stocks, bonds, and other protections.
- Sales made to clients on credit that is payable within a short period are known as accounts receivable (AR).
- Inventory is a business's stock of supplies and products that can be sold (Cheatham, 1989).

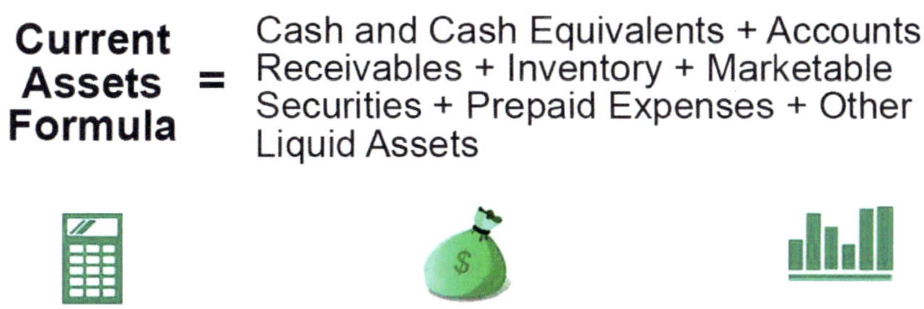

Figure 5.2. Picture of the formula of current assets.

Source: Ashish Kumar Srivastav, Creative Commons License.

5.2.1.2. Fixed Assets

A fixed asset is utilized in a business' activities over a longer time frame and is not expected to be traded or transformed into cash within the following year. Fixed assets, usually referred to as "properties, plant, and equipment" (PP&E), are significant contributors to the long-term value of a company (Raximova, 2020) (Figure 5.3).

Figure 5.3. Depiction of fixed assets.

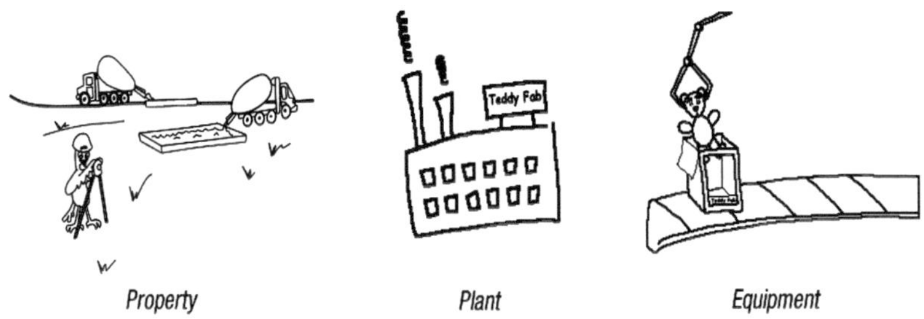

Source: Play accounting, Creative Commons License.

Typical illustrations of fixed assets include:

- **Buildings and Real Estate:** These resources include the real estate and buildings a business uses for its activities. These can be utilized in the business's production process or to produce cash (via rent or leasing, for example).

Equipment: Equipment refers to apparatus, machinery, and automobiles a business employs to manufacture things and provide services. Heavy manufacturing equipment, electronics, and other technologies are all examples of equipment (GOLOVETSKY et al., 2019).

- **Furniture and Fixtures**: Tables, chairs, and other objects used for a business' activities are included under fixtures and furniture. These can be utilized in buildings like offices, shops, and others.
- **Infrastructure:** Roadways, bridges, as well as pipelines are examples of infrastructure assets that are essential to a business's operations (Biryukov et al., 2019).

On a balance sheet, a company's fixed assets are typically listed and evaluated only at acquisition cost less than the accumulating loss. Degradation is an accounting system that distributes a fixed asset or expense account throughout its estimated usefulness and aids businesses in matching the value of existing assets with their revenue-generating potential. As they supply the resources required for manufacturing and revenue creation, tangible costs are crucial to a company's activities. These are frequently regarded as vital signs of a company's long-term growth and stability potential and can be used as collateral to acquire financing or investments (Aleskerova et al., 2018).

Did you Know?

In 2019, the top 5 global brands with the highest brand value were Apple, Google, Amazon, Microsoft, and Coca-Cola, all of which rely heavily on intangible assets for their success.

5.2.2. Intangible Assets

The absence of biological material is an intangible asset's defining feature. You can't see or feel it. These are typically long-term and derive value from your company's contractual or intellectual property rights (Erik, 1997).

Intangible assets include, for example:

- your character
- brand
- knowledge and skills
- business secrets
- secret processes and formulas
- research conclusions
- intellectual property (copyrights, projects, exclusive rights, and trademarks)
- customer supplier and employee relationships
- generosity
- contracts
- franchise rights
- license rights
- domain names
- commercial software and processes
- competent and skilled workforce (Kaplan & Norton, 2004).

Intangible assets can be produced by:

- Contracts – like lease agreements, service arrangements, use rights, etc.
- Technology – including software, secret recipes, patents, etc.
- Customers – customer databases and lists, open orders, backlogs in production, etc.

- Marketing – domain names, brand perception, trademarks, etc., (Gu & Lev, 2011).

Intangible assets are frequently challenging to measure and track because they typically lack physical characteristics. However, these can give your company a significant commercial benefit and competitive edge.

TIPS

However, it's crucial to remember that tangible resources may also be susceptible to depreciation or obsolescence, and they could eventually need expensive upkeep and replacement. Their fixed assets remain meaningful contributors to their overall value; businesses must constantly manage and track their physical assets

You must only include intangible assets in your business's balance sheet for accountancy and valuation reasons if:

- You have purchased them for a price.
- They have individual value.
- They have a useful lifespan.

They should show up as long-term assets on your company's balance sheet. Valued following the acquisition price and, if necessary, the amortization or depreciation plan. See much information on asset depreciation (Barth et al., 2001).

Internally generated assets frequently lack reportable costs. Thus, you should not include them in your business's balance sheet. Learn more about the evaluation of business assets. Even though certain intangible assets might not appear on that income statement, it is still essential to assess the company resources and develop a productive approach to managing them. View more information on managing funds in a firm (Teece, 1998).

5.2.3. Financial Asset

Financial assets are a form of investment that can be purchased and sold through the financial system. Such assets are frequently utilized to increase wealth and diversify portfolios because they are made to produce income or increase value over time (Corbet et al., 2019).

Some typical forms of financial assets are:

5.2.3.1. Stocks

Stocks allow the owner to participate in the company's value and represent the ownership of the company. A company sells a part of its ownership to shareholders, who subsequently become stockholders when its problems are solved. Dividends from stocks can be a reliable source of income, and as a business expands and makes more money, the value of its shares could rise (Ang et al., 2005).

5.2.3.2. Bonds

Companies, towns, and governments all issue bonds as a form of debt security. In essence, if an investor purchases a bond, individuals are lending money to an issuer in exchange for regular interest charges and the eventual repayment of their initial investment (the bond's face amount). Compared to stocks, bonds are usually considered lower-risk investments, yet they provide smaller returns (Campbell & Viceira, 2001).

5.2.3.3. Mutual Funds

Mutual funds are financial assets that aggregate numerous investors' funds to buy various bonds, stocks, and other securities. Financial professionals representing the interests of a collective fund's investors operate mutual funds. Mutual funds provide a straightforward approach for investors to obtain exposure to various financial assets without buying and maintaining individual stocks (Glode, 2011).

5.2.3.4. Exchange-Traded Funds (ETFs)

Mutual and ETFs are comparable, but ETFs trade on stock markets like regular stocks. ETFs offer a handy alternative to mutual funds, frequently charging cheaper charges while still allowing clients to invest in a broad range of financial assets (Gastineau, 2001).

5.2.3.5. Real Estate Investment Trusts (REITs)

Apartment complexes, office towers, and shopping malls are a few examples of the real estate assets that REITs, or property investment trusts, hold, and manage. Investors find REITs to be an appealing source of revenue since they are obligated to pay out a significant amount of their earnings as dividends to shareholders.

There are various financial assets; these are only a few more popular ones. Investing is critical to comprehend the features, dangers, and how every financial asset fits into your strategy (Haslam et al., 2015).

KEYWORD

Brand recognition is the extent to which a consumer can correctly identify a particular product or service just by viewing the product or service's logo, tag line, packaging or advertising campaign.

5.2.4. Derivative Assets

Financial assets, known as derivative assets, derives its value from an underlying asset, like a bond, commodity, stock, or currency.

Traders and investors utilize derivatives to control risk, predict price changes, and protect against damage in all other investments (Rubinstein, 1987).

Typical derivative asset classes include the following:

5.2.4.1. Futures

Futures are agreements that require the purchaser to acquire an underlying security (such as a commodity or financial assets) once at a specified price later. Traders and investors utilize futures to predict price changes or as a hedge versus price volatility (Lang, 1995).

5.2.4.2. Options

Options are agreements that grant the owner the opportunity, however not the obligation, to purchase or dispose of an underlying value at a specified price. Traders and investors use choices to make predictions about price changes or as hedging versus losses in other investments (Ross, 1976).

5.2.4.3. Swaps

Swaps are agreements between two parties to trade cash flows depending on changes in the price of an underlying asset. Financial institutions and businesses frequently utilize swaps to control risk and profit from favorable interest rates or currency changes (Stulz, 2010).

5.2.4.4. Forwards

Forward agreements bind the buyer to acquire the underlying security at the agreed-upon price later. Although forwards and futures are comparable, forwards are tailored for investors and cannot be exchanged on trades (Reeds & Shepp, 1990) (Figure 5.4).

Figure 5.4. Illustration of types of derivative assets.

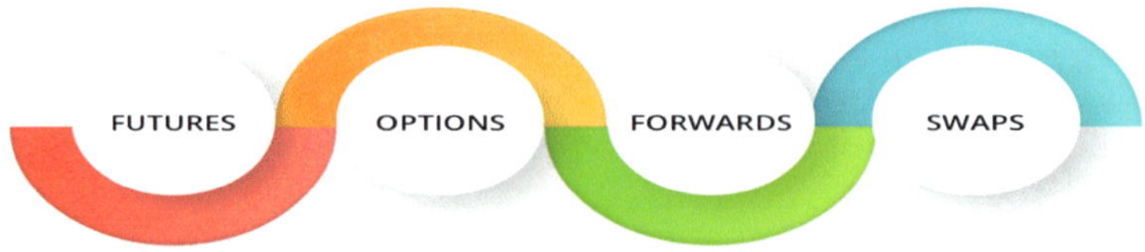

Source: Club Financial, Creative Commons License.

5.2.4.5. Contracts for Difference (CFDs)

Using CFDs, investors can speculate on fundamental market changes for securities without holding the underlying asset. Because CFDs are exchanged on leverage, investors can take a significant stake with a small amount of money (Brown et al., 2010).

Incorrect usage of derivative assets may result in significant losses due to their complexity and volatility. As a result, investors, and traders should understand the dangers and workings of derivative assets before investing. Additionally, investors might be required to obtain a license or registration to exchange some derivatives assets.

Inside a portfolio, derivatives assets could be useful for controlling risk and optimizing returns, and it's crucial to be aware of their risks and utilize them carefully. Make wise choices and be successful while trading in derivatives; it is essential to have a solid knowledge of the base asset, the derivative's workings, and the market environment (Spodniak et al., 2014) (Figure 5.5).

Figure 5.5. Illustration of contract for differences (CFD).

Source: IG team, Creative Commons License.

5.3. EXAMPLES OF ASSETS

Businesses may need a wide range of assets to operate at their peak efficiency. They consist of the following:

5.3.1. Cash and Cash Equivalents

It contains actual money, checking accounts, and quickly converted short-term investments. Existence of the most liquid assets, cash equivalents are utilized to cover immediate liabilities and control cash flow (Mikkelson & Partch, 2003).

5.3.2. Accounts Receivable

AR is the term used to describe money that consumers owe a business for products or services which have been provided but have yet to be compensated. ARs are regarded as a current asset since companies usually anticipate receiving payment for them in a few months or weeks (Mian & Smith, 1992).

5.3.3. Inventory

Inventory describes a business's unfinished products, work-in-progress, and natural resources for sale. Inventories are regarded as current assets since companies anticipate selling them within one year. Inventory value may be impacted by manufacturing costs, demands, and obsolescence (Seigworth & Gregg, 2010).

KEYWORD

Inventory value shows how much unsold inventory is worth at the end of a company's accounting period.

5.3.4. Property, Plant, and Equipment (PPE)

PPE stands for long-term tangible assets, including machinery, property, and structures used to generate services and goods. PPE is included on a corporation's balance sheet and is amortized over time to show its eroding worth (Hlaing & Pourjalali, 2012).

5.3.5. Patents

Patents are legislative monopolies that grant a business the sole authority to create and market a specific good or method for a predetermined time. Patents may be a valuable intangible asset and give businesses a competitive edge (Allison et al., 2003).

5.3.6. Trademarks

Trademarks are images, words, or logos that set one company's goods or services from those offered by other businesses.

Trademarks are intangible assets that protect a company's brand recognition (Mendonça et al., 2004).

5.3.7. Goodwill

The worth of a business brand and its connections with clients, partners, and staff are referred to as goodwill. Goodwill is regarded as intangible and is often developed from acquisitions, purchases, or internal growth (McCroskey & Teven, 1999).

5.3.8. Investments

A business's assets to generate revenue or capital growth are investments. Securities such as shares, bonds, property investment, including private equity are examples of investments.

These are a few illustrations of the various varieties of assets which a business could possess. The value and makeup of its assets may vary significantly based on elements, including a company's size, sector, and business plan (Farbey et al., 1992) (Figure 5.6).

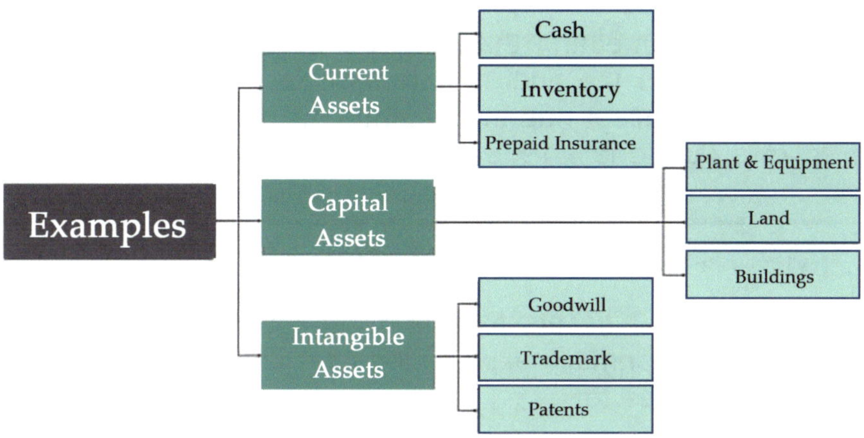

Figure 5.6. Schematic of examples of different assets.

Source: Dheeraj Vaidya, Creative Commons License.

5.4. THREE KEY PROPERTIES OF ASSETS

A thing needs to possess three characteristics to be regarded as an asset:

5.4.1. Ownership

Any asset must initially be owned or under the authority of a company. That restricts access to an asset and allows the business to convert it into cash or even a cash value. Not all assets with a right to use are convertible. It's common for lease agreements to prohibit the lease from being sold or transferred. The ownership attribute is crucial when contrasting an asset's colloquial and technical meanings. Companies frequently claim that their workers are their "biggest asset," however, from an accounting standpoint, they have little real control over employees as they can quickly leave for another position (Honoré, 2013).

5.4.2. Economic Value

An asset should secondly have a financial benefit. Most investments, except for a few right-of-use assets like rental contracts, could be transferred and converted into cash. Assets may help business growth and expansion (Pearce, 2001).

KEYWORD

Cash value refers to an investment component in life insurance that grows tax-free over the course of the policy's life.

5.4.3. Resource

A resource, or something that may be used to create long-term financial benefit, is the final requirement for an asset. It typically indicates that its asset has the potential to provide positive future cash inflows (Mahoney, 1995).

5.5. IMPORTANCE OF ASSETS

The significance of assets to a firm cannot be overstated. Here are a few of the primary explanations for its appeal. The assets helps in a business to;

- generate revenue
- increase your business' value
- help the running of your business

5.5.1. Account for All Assets

This method allows businesses to easily maintain track of most of their liquid and fixed assets. The position of its assets, how they were used, and if any modifications have been made will all be known to the firm's owners. Additionally, it assesses any obligations, short or long-term (Waggle & Englis, 2000).

5.5.2. Ensures Accurate Amortization Rates

Because items are routinely checked, the asset management approach ensures that assets are appropriately documented inside the financial accounts (Kopriva, 2000).

5.5.3. Aids in Identifying and Managing Risks

Asset management includes identifying and managing hazards connected to the use and ownership of certain assets. It suggests that a business will always be prepared to handle any risks that could arise (Bedard & Graham, 2002).

KEYWORD

Ownership is the state or fact of legal possession and control over property, which may be any asset, tangible or intangible.

5.5.4. Eliminates Fictitious Assets from the Inventory

In certain instances, assets that have been stolen, lost, or destroyed have been wrongly recorded, mostly on books. That used a strategic asset administration approach; the company's ownership will be informed of lost assets and deleted from the books (Peloubet, 1950).

5.6. METHODS TO VALUE THE ASSETS

Businesses display their assets on an income statement along with the values connected with them. They arrange the assets according to product cost, expected liquidity, and how soon they can turn them into cash. Various techniques using the amount you purchased and today's market rates can be used to estimate an asset's value. The above are two methods for determining an asset's worth (Chen et al., 2022).

5.6.1. Standard Cost Method

The standard cost technique does not include actual costs; projected or predicted costs are used. It enables valuations that are quicker, more accurate, and so more accurate. Accountants keep close tabs on any differences between expected and actual costs. The stages of valuing an asset that uses the standard cost technique are as follows (Kaka & Price, 1993):

5.6.1.1. Determine Product Cost

Products possess standard costs, estimates of what a business typically costs for every item.

5.6.1.2. Multiply

Once you have the cost of the item, you may multiply it by the number of units to get the value of the assets (Figure 5.7).

$$\frac{\text{Value}}{\text{Metric}} = \text{Multiple}$$

Figure 5.7. Pictorial representation of formula of multiple.

Source: Mercer Capital, Creative Commons License.

KEYWORD

Standard cost refers to the cost management beliefs that should be incurred to produce goods or services under anticipated conditions.

For example, a producer makes toys for kids. The cost of producing each of the five types of toys produced by the company is $2, $2.12, $1.99, $2.08, and $2.10. The business may decide to account because of its inventory by utilizing a uniform per-item price of $2.06 rather than determining the worth of inventory using every slightly varied cost. If the business has 450,000 toys in stock, the asset value is $2.06 times that of $927,000 (Jacobs et al., 1978).

5.6.2. Market Value Method

This technique establishes an asset's actual market value. Analyzing buy-sell agreements for comparable assets is a part of the process. The calculations are based on a significant amount of publicly available and accessible data, which is the main benefit of the market price method. The actions you can take to use this technique are as follows (Drake, 1992):

5.6.2.1. Determine Comparable

Businesses might investigate their rivals to find out who has resources comparable to each other regarding expansion rate, size, categorization, and profitability (Vanderwalde et al., 2018).

5.6.2.2. Gather Financial Information

The accounting statements of the companies can be used to learn more about them and to assess if their pricing schemes are lucrative for you.

5.6.2.3. Compare Data

After reviewing the data, you can establish the average market worth of a service or product to assist you in choosing the price to sell your products.

For example, a 45-day-old, 1,000-square-foot apartment with one bedroom or one bathroom is discovered by an investment business looking to purchase a rental property. The list price is $200 per square foot, or $200,000; it needs only modest modifications and is in a populated place, and it contains a dryer and washer hookups but still no appliances or view. This company conducts market value research to identify three comparable units, compares their pricing, and evaluates each unit's position, view, quality, and facilities. This investigation leads the company to propose a $150,000 offer, which even the seller accepts (Pavlo et al., 2009).

KEYWORD

Liabilities are the debts that a business owes to third-party creditors.

5.7. CONCEPT OF LIABILITIES

A liability generally is an agreement between two parties that have not been fulfilled or paid for; a financial liability is a responsibility within the field of accounting; however, it is more characterized explicitly by past commercial transactions, occurrences, sales, exchanges of items or services, or any other activity that will generate income in the future. Noncurrent liabilities are typically viewed as long-term obligations because they are anticipated to last more than a year (12 months or greater).

Based on their temporality, liabilities are classed as noncurrent or current. It can be a future responsibility to provide services to everyone (a short- or long-term loan from a bank, a person, or another entity) or a prior deal that left an unresolved duty. The most significant liabilities, such as payables and bonds due, are typically the most prevalent. Most businesses will include these two items on their income statement since they represent a component of continuous current or long-term activities (Denk et al., 2012).

Since they are employed to finance projects and significant expansions, liabilities are a crucial business component. They could also improve the effectiveness of business-to-company interactions. For instance, a wine distributor will not request payment while delivering a wine case to a restaurant. Instead, it sends a bill to a restaurant to facilitate payment and expedite the drop-off process. An obligation is an unpaid balance the restaurant owes its wine provider (Sharpe & Tint, 1990).

In contrast, the wine provider views the cash it owes as an asset. Liability can also relate to a person's or a company's legal responsibility. For instance, many companies get liability insurance if a client or worker brings a claim against them for carelessness.

Other Definitions of Liability: Liability may relate to any amount of cash or service owing to another person and integrated experience to being accountable for anything. Tax responsibility, for instance, can apply to the federal revenue tax a homeowner owes or the real estate taxes he pays to the municipal authorities. Before sending the money to a county, city, or statewide, a retailer that receives sales tax from the client has a sales tax liability on its records. In a civil action, one's prospective damages are another example of liability (Ramachandran & Pant, 2010) (Figure 5.8).

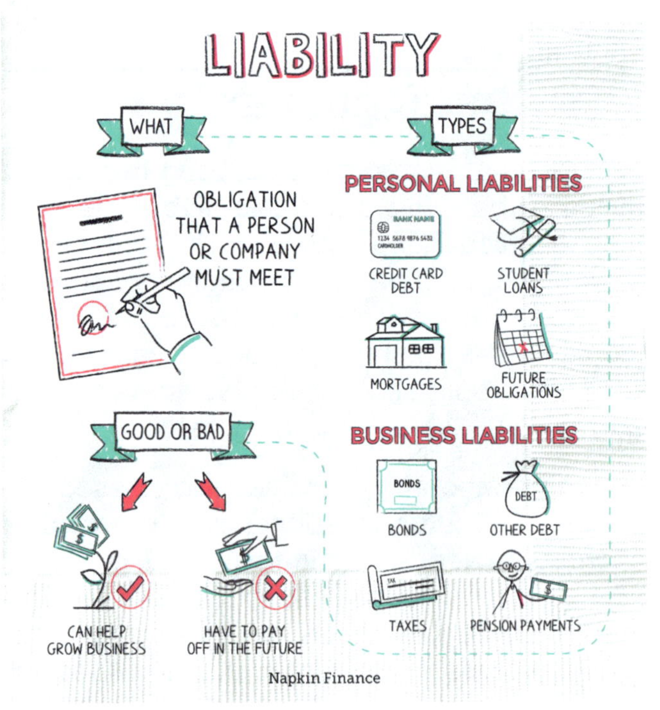

Figure 5.8. Illustration of liabilities.

Source: Napkin Finance, Creative Commons License.

5.8. TYPES OF LIABILITIES

Businesses divide their responsibilities into present and long-term obligations. Long-term obligations must be paid over a more extended period than current assets. A 15-year mortgage, for instance, that even a company is taking out is a good illustration of long-term debt. The short-term liabilities part of the balance sheet shows the mortgage due this year because they constitute the current element of long-term debt (Sakhno et al., 2020).

5.8.1. Current (Near-Term) Liabilities

Investors generally want to verify that even a company can pay its year-ahead current liabilities using cash. Payroll costs and payables, which comprise money owing to vendors, standard utilities, and resources as necessary, are a few instances of short-term liabilities. Other illustrations include (Thompson et al., 2020):

KEYWORD

Wages are the amount of money that is regularly paid to them for the work that they do.

5.8.1.1. Wages Payable

The sum of the accruing wages that staff members have worked for but have yet to receive. Most businesses pay their workers every two weeks; therefore, this responsibility constantly changes (Clemens & Strain, 2022).

5.8.1.2. Interest Payable

Businesses frequently utilize the money to fund short-term purchases of services and goods. It refers to the interest paid on short-term credit sales (Teng et al., 2005).

5.8.1.3. Dividends Payable

It is the sum owed to investors after the payout was announced by businesses that have issued shares to investors and then paid a dividend. This responsibility often arises four to five times a year during these two weeks until the dividend payment is made.

5.8.1.4. Unearned Revenues

A business must provide customers with goods and services after receiving payment in advance. Once goods or services are supplied, this sum will be decreased by an offsetting statement (Conrad & DeMeritt, 2013).

5.8.1.5. Liabilities of Discontinued Operations

Most individuals pass over this special liability but should examine it more carefully. Businesses must consider the economic effect of any operations, divisions, or entities that are up for sale or have previously been sold. It also includes the financial consequences of a line of products that are now being discontinued or were just done so (Gornik & Shoaf, 2004) (Figure 5.9).

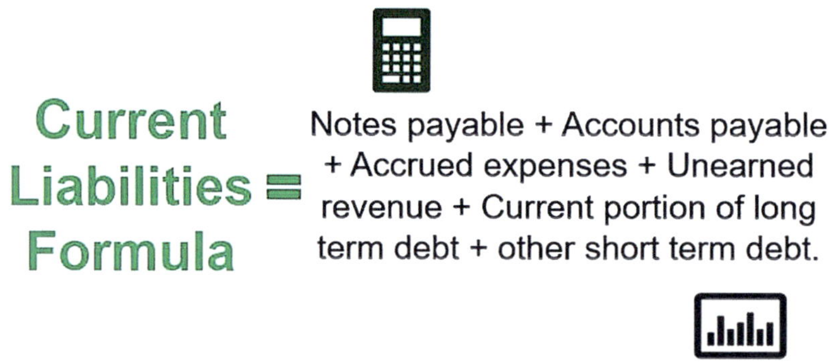

Figure 5.9. Picture of current liabilities.

Source: Ashish Kumar Srivastav, Creative Commons License.

5.8.2. Noncurrent (Long-Term) Liabilities

Given the name, it should be clear that any debt not near falls within noncurrent liabilities, which are obligations anticipated to be paid in a year or longer. Again, using AT&T as an example, the number of goods listed at your typical corporation might only include one or two. Bonds payable, commonly called long-term debt, are typically the most significant liability and appear at the top of the priority list.

Businesses of all sizes borrow money from the parties that buy their bonds to finance a portion of their continuous long-term activities. As the bonds are issued, reach maturity, or are asked to return by an issuer, that line item constantly changes (Sitorus et al., 2021).

Analysts must see if long-term obligations may be settled with assets acquired from upcoming revenues or financing deals. Companies have other long-term liabilities besides loans and bonds. Long-term liabilities can also include commitments for rent, deferred taxes, salaries, and pensions. Other illustrations include:

5.8.2.1. Warranty Liability

Certain liabilities must be assessed because AP is not always accurate. That estimates the time and cost required to fix things after a warranty is accepted. Most automobiles have lengthy warranties that may be expensive, a frequent liability within the automotive sector (Kim & Kim, 2018).

5.8.2.2. Contingent Liability Evaluation

A contingent obligation is a responsibility that might materialize based on how a future outcome plays out.

5.8.2.3. Deferred Credits

Based on the particulars of the transactions, it is a broad category that may well be listed as noncurrent or current. Such credits are revenue that has been received but has not yet been shown as received on the financial statements. Customer loans, deferred income, or a transaction wherein credits are paid but are not regarded as revenue may all fall under this category. This category is lowered by the revenue produced and added to a company's revenue stream once money is no longer postponed (Herring & Jacobs, 1977).

KEYWORD

Compensation is the remuneration awarded to an employee in exchange for their services or individual contributions to your business.

5.8.2.4. Post-Employment Benefits

These retirement-related benefits that an employee or family member could be eligible for are recorded as a lengthy liability as they are incurred. It accounts for one-half of overall noncurrent debt within the AT&T example, which is next only with long-term debt. That liability should not be disregarded due to the constantly rising healthcare costs with employee compensation (Noja & Caran, 2015).

5.8.2.5. Unamortized Investment Tax Credits (UTC)

It refers to the difference between an asset's historical cost and depreciation. Although it is simply a preliminary estimate of the asset's fair market value, any unamortized component is a liability. It gives an analyst basic information about how extreme or conservative a company's depreciating practices are (Olson, 1985).

5.9. DIFFERENCE BETWEEN LIABILITIES AND ASSETS

In finance and accounting, liabilities versus assets are two different ideas that characterize a company's financial condition. Liabilities are debts a corporation owes to third parties, whereas assets are things a firm owns, which is the critical distinction between them (An et al., 2022).

A company's liabilities are the obligations or debts it owes certain other parties, including leases, bonds, and payable accounts. The business will eventually have to pay back such items.

Contrarily, assets such a firm possesses that are valuable, including money, assets, property investment, stock, and equipment, are considered its assets. All those are goods that the business can sell to recover debts or utilize to generate income.

A business's liabilities must typically be lower than the assets, implying a positive total value. It is a sign of stability and strength in the economy. However, a business could be in financial trouble with a negative net value and more obligations than assets (Guenther & Sansing, 2000) (Figure 5.10).

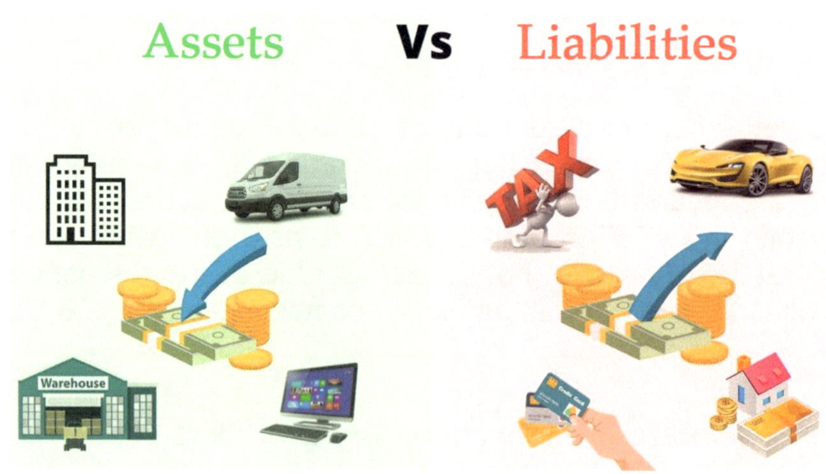

Figure 5.10. Image of difference between assets and liabilities.

Source: Education leaves, Creative Commons License.

5.10. LIABILITIES VS. EXPENSES

Any expense is a business's operational cost faced to produce income. Expenses are tied to revenue, contrasting liabilities and assets, shown on an organization's financial statements. In essence, net income is determined by subtracting the costs. Net income is defined as revenues and fewer expenses.

For example, if a business has been making losses for the last three years and its expenses have exceeded its revenues, this may indicate insufficient economic security (Beatty & Welch, 1996).

Liability and costs should never be conflated. The first appears on a business's balance sheet, whereas the second does so on its financial statements. Liabilities are the commitments and debts a firm owes, whereas costs are the expenses associated with running a business. Cash payments for expenses can be made immediately, but delaying the payment may result in liability (Bakar, 2018).

5.11. EXAMPLE OF LIABILITIES

Let us look at a real example utilizing AT&T's 2020 financial statement to illustrate how to grasp a company's liabilities. Just on the balance sheet, present, and short-term liabilities are segregated from long-term and noncurrent liabilities (Arend, 2004).

Within current liabilities, AT&T identifies its bank debt with a maturity of less than one year. For one business of this size, operational capital is frequently employed for ongoing expenses rather than long-term debt financing major purchases (Ritchie & Macdonald, 2009).

Liabilities are often handled at cost rather than market price and, as they are classified, can indeed be presented in preferred order under generally accepted accounting principles (GAAP). Regarding current liabilities, the AT&T example has a comparatively high debt amount. Smaller businesses will have more current financial obligations, other line items, including accounts payable (AP), and different future liabilities, including wages.

Since they cover daily operations, AP often has the greatest balances. Services, natural resources, office equipment, and all other services and goods for which no note being issued may be included in AP. AP is comparable to a pile of unpaid bills because most businesses need not pay for products and services when purchased (Censi et al., 2019).

KEYWORD

Noncurrent liabilities, also known as long-term liabilities, are obligations listed on the balance sheet not due for more than a year.

5.12 METHODS TO CALCULATE LIABILITIES

Establishing a company's liabilities is very simple since most accounting nowadays is managed by software that automatically creates income reports instead of paper and pen. These liabilities must all be available on the balance sheet if you have not made any errors in company bookkeeping. It would be done manually by adding each liability in the company ledger accounts and totaling it on the company income statement. However, additional calculations could consider liabilities to assess them to ensure your money isn't continually going toward paying down debts. It is called credits accounting (Yang et al., 2017).

KEYWORD

Bookkeeping is the process of recording your company's financial transactions into organized accounts on a daily basis.

Following are some typical calculations used by accountants for credit accounting and also an explanation of their significance:

5.12.1. Debt Ratio

The debt ratio is unquestionably the most crucial calculation in credit accounting. It determines how leveraged—or burdened with debt—your company is by comparing your total liabilities with your assets (Byrd & Mizruchi, 2005).

The debt ratio equation is:

Debt ratio = Total Debt / Total assets

Considering the financial statement example, (which example) the debt ratio for Annie's Pottery Palace would look like follows:

Debt ratio = \$7,000 / \$22,000 = 31.8%

Generally, the smaller your company's debt ratio, the less indebted it is and the better it can pay off its loans. Higher amounts indicate greater leverage and greater liability risk.

Although standard debt-to-income ratios differ considerably by business, you are safe if your ratio is 40% or below. Lenders and investors may believe your company has excessive debt when your debt-to-income ratio is 60% or greater (Smyth & Hsing, 1995).

5.12.2. Long-Term Debt Ratio

The only difference between this ratio and the debt ratio is that it does not include current liabilities in the calculation (Gramlich et al., 2001).

The long-term debt ratio equation is:

Long-term debt ratio = Long-term liabilities / Total assets

Therefore, the long-term debt ratio for a corporation with $4,000 in long-term obligations and $20,000 in net capital would be:

Long-term debt ratio = $4,000 / $20,000

Long-term debt ratio = 20%

We utilize the long-term debt ratio to determine the percentage of your company supported by long-term liabilities. In general, you would like this quantity to decrease with time. If it increases, it may indicate that your company is increasingly dependent on debt (D'Mello et al., 2018).

KEYWORD

Debt ratio refers to a financial ratio that measures the extent of a company's leverage.

5.12.3. Debt to Capital Ratio

Prospective lenders or investors commonly measure the debt to total capital to evaluate your company's viability (Hein, 2006).

The loan-to-capital ratio's equation is:

Debt to capital ratio = Total debt / Total Debt + Shareholders equity

Debt to capital ratio = $7,000 / $7,000 + $15,000

Debt to capital ratio = $7,000 / $22,000

Debt to capital ratio = 31.8%

Investors and lenders frequently use this ratio to contrast your business with rival companies. A corporation with a reduced tax-to-capital ratio is typically a safer investment than one with a greater ratio, which denotes a riskier wager (Falk & Steiger, 2018).

5.13. DEPRECIATION

Machines and equipment are costly assets. Businesses can use amortization to extend out the expense of an asset rather than collect the entire cost in the first year and to match corresponding revenues and expenses in a single reporting year. It enables a business to pay off an asset's worth over time, particularly its useful life.

Businesses constantly depreciate their assets to transfer costs from their financial statements to their respective financial statements. Whenever a company purchases an asset, it registers the transaction as a credit to decrease cash (or increasing AP) that appears on the income statement and a debit to raise an asset account upon that balance sheet. Neither journal item impacts the financial statements listing revenues and costs (Jorgenson, 1996).

An accountant records depreciation with all capitalized assets that have not been completely depreciated after an accounting cycle. Each entry in the journal includes a:

- The debit for the depreciation expense is carried over to the financial statements.
- Credit to the balance sheets reported accumulated depreciation.

KEYWORD

Taxable income refers to the base upon which an income tax system imposes tax.

As mentioned, businesses can use depreciation for accounting and tax reasons. As a result, their taxable income will be lower because they can deduct the asset or expense account from their taxes. However, the internal revenue service (IRS) mandates that businesses spread the cost of depreciating assets over the years. Whether businesses may deduct expenses is also governed by IRS regulations (Preinreich, 1938).

Because it would not involve a cash outflow, depreciation is regarded as a non-cash charge. Whenever an asset is bought, the cumulative cash outlay may be paid at once, but the costs are recorded in stages for accounting purposes. It is so because assets assist the business over a long period. However, depreciation costs still lower a company's financial performance, which is advantageous for taxation (Li & Hall, 2020).

Following the generally accepted accounting principles (GAAP) matching principle, expenditure should be linked to the exact period when the relevant revenues are generated. That is a concept of accrual accounting. Depreciation aids in connecting an asset's cost to its long-term value. In all other words, the asset utilized annually and creates income also has an extra expense associated with using it.

The depreciation rate is the annual total amount of depreciation expressed as a percentage. When the yearly depreciation was $15,000, all depreciation throughout the asset's anticipated lifespan was $100,000; as an illustration, This is (Lonvaud, 1999).

Depreciation is allowed for buildings and other structures but not for land.

5.13.1. Threshold Amounts

Various businesses may establish cutoff points when depreciating a tangible asset or pieces of plant, property, and equipment (PP&E). For instance, a small business might show a $500 cutoff point above which it depreciates an asset. In contrast hand, a bigger company can establish a $10,000 cap below which all transactions are instantly expensed (Klančar et al., 2015).

5.13.2. Accumulated Depreciation

In contra assets account, depreciation expense has a natural balance of a credit which lowers the value of the total asset. Every asset's accumulated depreciation is the amount of depreciation it has experienced up to that point. Carrying value, as previously mentioned, is the sum of the investment account and accrued depreciation. The carrying amount on the income statement once all depreciation is compensated for is also known as salvage value. This value is used till the asset is disposed of or sold (Simon, 1959). It is predicated on what a business expects to get in return for an asset when its useful life is over. The expected salvage value of an item plays a significant role in determining depreciation. According to different asset classes, the IRS releases depreciation plans that specify how many years an asset could be written down for tax reasons (Sohn, 2009) (Figure 5.11).

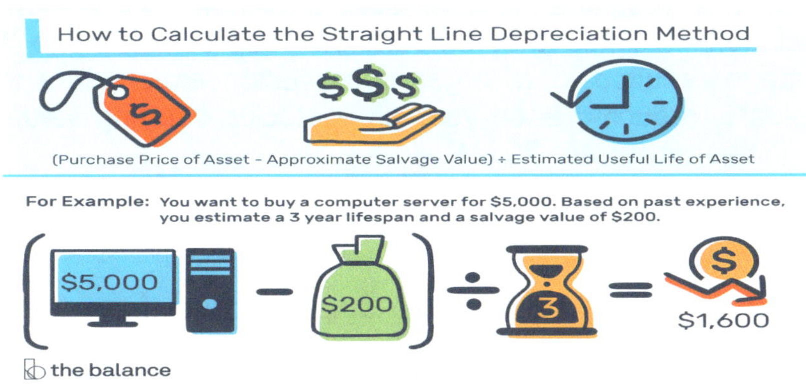

Figure 5.11. Schematic of an example of accumulated depreciation.

Source: Alicia Tuovila, Creative Commons License.

5.14. TYPES OF DEPRECIATION

Accountants typically devalue financial capital as well as other earnings assets using a variety of techniques. These include the following: unit of productivity, sum-of-the-years' numbers, straight edge, decreasing balance, with double balance. Below, we have outlined some fundamental ideas (Sigidov et al., 2016).

5.14.1. Straight-Line

The most straightforward method for keeping track of depreciation is the straight-line technique. Throughout the asset's overall useful life, until the point at which the real asset has been depreciated towards its salvage value, it records an identical accumulated depreciation yearly (York, 1966).

Suppose that a business spends $5,000 to purchase a machine. A salvage value of $1,000 as well as a service life of 5 years, is chosen by the corporation. The depreciable value, given these suppositions, is $4,000 ($5,000 cost – $1,000 salvage value).

The accumulated depreciation is divided by the total years to determine the yearly depreciation that uses the straight-line technique. In this instance, it equals $800 annually ($4,000 / 5). The consequence is a 20% depreciation rate ($800 / $4,000) (Bartlett, 1949).

KEYWORD

Depreciable value of the asset is the combined cost of purchase and installation of an asset that can be depreciated minus its salvage value.

5.14.2. Declining Balance

An accelerated depreciation approach is the decreasing balance method. The machine is depreciated annually at straight-line depreciation % times that amount still depreciable. The same percentage resulted in a larger depreciation expenditure in the early years, reducing each year as a stock's carrying value was larger (Sheehan et al., 2014).

Declining Balance Depreciation = (Net Book Value – Salvage Value) x (1 / Useful Life) x Depreciation Rate

According to the straight-line examples above, the cost is $800 in the beginning ($4,000 of accumulated depreciation x 20%), $640 within the next year ($4,000 – $800) x 20%), and so forth. The system costs $5,000, has a salvage value of $1,000, a five-year life, and is therefore depreciated at 20% yearly (Greene, 1963).

5.14.3. Double-Declining Balance (DDB)

Another technique for accelerating depreciation is the DDB technique. That rate is added to the depreciation expense basis, which is the asset's book value, over the remaining estimated life of an asset, multiplying the asset's service life by its reciprocal and by two. As a result, it moves roughly twice as quickly as the declining balance technique.

DDB = (Net Book Value – Salvage Value) x (2 / Useful Life) x Depreciation Rate

A five-year-old asset, for instance, has a typical value of 1/5, or 20%. The asset's latest book value is reduced by twice the depreciation rate or 40%. Even though the ratio doesn't change, the dollar value would diminish over time (Matsumoto, 1982).

5.14.4. Sum-of-the-Years Digits (SYD)

Accelerated depreciation is also possible using the sum-of-the-years' digits (SYD) approach. Start by adding up all the asset's projected lifespan digits.

For instance, the basis of an asset with such a five-year life would be 1 + 2 + 3 + 4 + 5 = 15, or the total of the digits 1 through 5. 5/15 of the accumulated depreciation base will be written off during the first year of depreciation. Just 4/15 of the accumulated depreciation base will be depreciated within the following year. It occurs until the final 1/15 of a base is depreciated over five years (Feinschreiber, 1968).

Both the dropping DDB and balance computations use the rate of depreciation.

KEYWORD

Depreciation refers to an accounting method used to allocate the cost of a tangible or physical asset over its useful life.

5.14.5. Units of Production

An overall estimate of units that the asset will create throughout its service life is needed for this procedure. The depreciation cost is then computed annually based on the volume of production units. Depending on the depreciable amount of production, this approach also calculates depreciation costs (Lewontin, 1970) (Figure 5.12).

Figure 5.12. Illustration of types of depreciation.

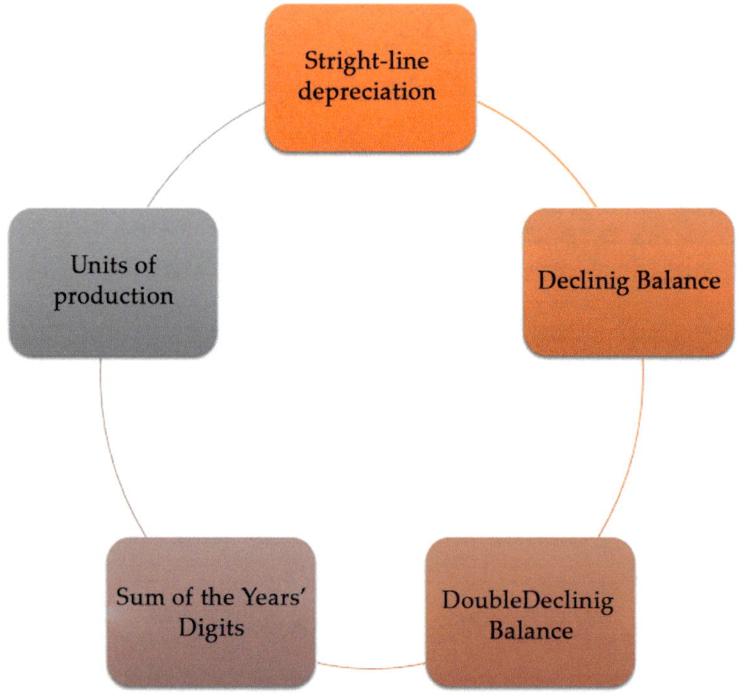

Source: Deskera, Creative Commons License.

5.15. EXAMPLE OF DEPRECIATION

Here is a fictional illustration of depreciation in action. But be aware that some systems of accounting permit multiple methods of depreciation. Let's say a business purchases a $50,000 piece of machinery. It could spend the total cost within the first year or write off from the asset's worth throughout its 10-year service life. It explains why company owners prefer depreciation. Most business owners merely deduct a fraction of the costs, which can increase net income (Wykoff, 1970).

At the end of its service life, the machinery may also be scrapped for $10,000, making its salvage value $10,000. The accountant uses these factors to determine depreciation expense, which is equal to the asset's cost less its salvage value, split by its usable life. In this case, the ratio is ($50,000 – $10,000) / 10—depreciation costs, resulting in $4,000 yearly.

As a result, even if the business paid out that sum in cash, the accountant is not required to cost the whole $50,000 in one year. Therefore, the company needs to deduct $4,000 from its net income. The business spends an additional $4,000 the following year, $4,000 the following year, and so forth until the property has a salvage value of $10,000 after ten years (Bierman, 1966).

5.16. CAUSES OF DEPRECIATION

Physical obsolescence and deterioration are two reasons why things depreciate. Below is a summary of the primary contributing factors (Baum, 1993).

KEYWORD

Leasehold refers to a property tenure, where one party buys the right to occupy the property for a given length of time (30 to 99 years).

5.16.1. Physical Deterioration

Due to usage, deterioration, and tear and wear, assets lose value. Regardless matter how good the organization's maintenance plan is, all assets get a usable life and ultimately need to be retired.

5.16.2. Obsolescence

A resource may become outdated because of improved designs, fresh discoveries, or even shifting styles. Due to this, even if the item is still usable and in great physical shape, it can end up being dumped (OKOH et al., 2017).

5.16.3. Exhaustion

A resource might get depleted via use. Mineral mines, oilfields, and other comparable assets fall under this category. There comes a time when the mines or wells are fully depleted—nothing is left—due to the ongoing mineral extraction or oil. As a result, the value of the depleted asset would be zero after one given amount of time (Urbanovsky, 2015).

5.16.4. Efflux of Time

As time goes on, the value of some assets decreases. Examples of these assets include copyrights, licenses, and leasehold holdings (Okoh et al., 2017).

5.17. METHODS OF CALCULATING DEPRECIATION

Depreciation can be calculated in three standard methods. Which are:

- Fixed installment method
- Reducing installment method
- Revaluation method (Nechaev & Rasputina, 2020).

KEYWORD

Fixed asset is property with a useful life greater than one reporting period, and which exceeds an entity's minimum capitalization limit.

5.17.1. Fixed Installment Method

Each year's depreciation amount is equal and constant under the fixed installments approach to depreciation, even as the name suggests. At the year's close, a preset sum is deducted from the asset's book value and credited to the financial statements or accounts for profit and loss (Cross, 1988).

The earliest and most used depreciation technique is this one. Depreciation is levied annually for the duration of the asset at a defined rate. The worth of the asset would be 0 when it has reached the end of its useful life (for example, when a machine stops working). It is often called the initial cost technique or the straight-line foundation for computing depreciation. Some specific assets provide the same services for their whole helpful life and have no value to their owners beyond that. A leasehold home is an excellent illustration. If anybody purchases assets on a 100-year lease, the property will hold no worth to them at the expiration of the lease since it will be returned to the original purchaser. The price of this type of fixed asset is divided by the anticipated amount of time it will be used to get the degradation per year (Sanders, 1953).

5.17.1.1. Advantages of the Fixed Installment Method

- **Simplicity:** The fixed installment strategy is straightforward to comprehend and utilize.
- **Zero Value:** The asset will have no value throughout its actual operating life if this strategy is used (Emory, 1967).
- **Suitable for Assets with an Expiry Period:** This approach is appropriate for items that lose value more quickly over time (e.g., leasehold properties and patents) (Kaden & LaFrance, 1989).

5.17.1.2. Disadvantages of the Fixed Installment Method

- **Concept of Zero Value:** This approach results in an asset's value being zero after its useful life, which is erroneous (i.e., because no assets have zero value).
- **Equal Amount of Depreciation:** This strategy is nonsensical since the depreciation rate stays the same during a machine's operating life. In the early years, depreciation must be higher; in the latter years, it must be smaller (Emory, 1967).
- **No Thought to Interest:** An asset is depreciated by its initial cost; the idea that a similar investment could have earned interest inside a different location is not considered.
- **Difficulty in Additional Purchase of Fixed Asset:** The technique presents challenges regarding depreciation on modifications to assets with an irregular life period (Shen, 2010).

Formula:

$$\text{Depreciation per year} = \frac{\text{Cost of asset}}{\text{Useful life of asset}}$$

KEYWORD

Book value is the value of an asset according to its balance sheet account balance.

5.17.2. Reducing Balance Method

Estimate depreciation; the declining balance approach involves yearly adding a preset percent to an asset's book value. It decreases the amount of depreciation every year compared to what was anticipated the year prior. The book value used to calculate the depreciation charge decreases yearly (Cicală et al., 2008).

To determine depreciation using the diminishing balance approach, use the following formula:

Depreciation = Asset book value x Depreciation rate

Where: Depreciation is the monetary amount of value that is lost. The value of an asset on an accrual basis is its book value. The percent fall in an asset's value is a depreciation rate (Fan, 2000).

Example: Depreciation Calculation Using the Reducing Balance Method

On January 1, 2016, XYZ Limited paid $75,000 for a vehicle. The projected rate is 20% annual depreciation upon that book's value. Required: Determine how much the vehicle will depreciate in 2016, 2017, and 2018.

Solution:

2016

It started in 2016; the book value was $75,000. For 2016, depreciation will be $75,000 x 0.2, or $15,000.

2017

The book value at the start of 2017 is $75,000 – $15,000 = $60,000. Depreciation for 2017 is $60,000 × 0.2 = $12,000.

2018

The book value at the start of 2018 is $60,000 – $12,000 = $48,000. Depreciation for 2018 is $48,000 × 0.2 = $9,600 (Im et al., 2015).

KEYWORD

Revaluation is an upward adjustment to the value of assets, goods or especially the currency from a chosen baseline.

5.17.3. Revaluation Method

The depreciation is determined by subtracting the year's value for the assets at the time of the calendar year using the revaluation technique. A qualified person values the assets owned by the company after every financial year. In contrast, modifications are performed if some assets are added to or sold throughout the year (Goodhaet, 1940). These following assets lend themselves very well to the revaluation approach for computing depreciation:

- Assets that are small in value
- Assets prone to breakage

Typically, one fixed-cost account is used to combine all these assets. These assets include, for instance, books, small office equipment, small tools, flatware, and even loose tools (Missonier, 2007).

Formula:

Depreciation = Beginning value + Addition - Sale - Ending value

Example 1:

For $1,500, a hotel bought dishes on January 1, 2015. A chef gave it $1,250 worth on December 31, 2016. For $2,000 in 2016, a hotel added extra dinnerware to its inventory. This China stock was worth $2,850 at the year's conclusion. Measure the depreciation that will be charged for 2015 and 2016 (Dayan & Berridge, 2014).

Solution:

Depreciation for 2015 is as follows: $1,500 – $1,250 ($Book value on January 1, 2015 – Value put on December 31, 2015) = $250. Depreciation for 2016 is calculated as follows: $1,250 + $2,000 – $2,850 = $400 Book value on January 1, 2016, plus purchases made throughout the year minus value put on December 31, 2016 (Davey, 1989).

Example 2:

Let's assume that such a hotel from Example 1 continued to buy more China in 2017 for $2,400 but sold some ancient pottery for $400. The entire value of the dinnerware stock before the year's end was $4,050. Required: Calculate the 2017 accumulated depreciation. Crockery was acquired throughout the year; less crockery traded during the period equals the depreciation for 2017 divided by the value as of December 31, 2017. = ($2,850 + $2,400 – $400) – $4,050 = $800 (Faisal, 2021).

ACTIVITY 5.1.

Suppose a small business owner purchases a new delivery truck for their company. The truck costs $50,000 and has an estimated useful life of 5 years. The owner plans to use the truck for their business operations and then sell it at the end of its useful life.

What is the yearly depreciation expense for the delivery truck using the straight-line method?

If the owner decides to sell the truck after 3 years of use, what is the book value of the truck at that time?

If the owner decides to sell the truck after 5 years of use, what is the book value of the truck at that time?

These questions can help the business owner understand the concept of depreciation and how it affects the value of their assets over time.

What transactions would you record in the store's general ledger, and how would you classify them?

There should be contents about depreciation and tax implications in the chapter

5.18. SUMMARY

- This chapter covers accounting fundamentals related to assets, liabilities, and depreciation. The first part of the chapter explains the different types of assets, including tangible and intangible. Tangible assets are physical assets such as buildings, equipment, and inventory, while intangible assets are assets that do not have a physical form, such as patents, trademarks, and copyrights. The chapter also covers financial and derivative assets used in investment and trading activities.
- Next, the chapter covers liabilities and obligations a company owes to others. These can be current liabilities, for example, interest payable, unearned revenues, or noncurrent liabilities, like deferred credits or warranty liability.
- The final part of the chapter covers depreciation, which is the gradual reduction in the value of a tangible asset over time. The chapter explains the different types of depreciation methods, including straight-line depreciation, declining balance depreciation, and units of production depreciation. It also covers how to calculate depreciation for tax purposes and how to account for the disposal of assets.
- The chapter provides a comprehensive overview of the critical accounting concepts related to assets, liabilities, and depreciation, which are crucial for effective financial management and reporting.

REVIEW QUESTIONS

1. What is the difference between a tangible and an intangible asset, and how are they accounted for in financial statements?
2. What is a financial asset, and how is it different from a derivative asset?
3. What are the properties of an asset, and how do they affect its classification as current or noncurrent?
4. What is the difference between current and noncurrent liability, and how are they accounted for in financial statements?
5. What is depreciation, and why is it important in accounting?
6. What are the different types of depreciation, and when is each used?
7. How does the choice of depreciation method affect a company's financial statements?
8. What is the difference between book value and market value, and why is it important to consider both in asset valuation?
9. How can intangible assets like patents and trademarks be valued for accounting purposes?
10. What is the impact of an impairment loss on an asset's book value and a company's financial statements?

MULTIPLE CHOICE QUESTIONS

1. **Which of the following is an example of a tangible asset?**
   a. Patent
   b. Building
   c. Trademark
   d. Goodwill
2. **What is a financial asset?**
   a. An asset that has physical substance
   b. An asset that is not easily converted to cash
   c. An asset that represents ownership of a financial claim
   d. An asset that is used in the production of goods and services
3. **Which of the following is an example of a derivative asset?**
   a. Stock
   b. Bond
   c. Futures contract
   d. Real estate
4. **What is the difference between current and noncurrent liabilities?**
   a. Current liabilities are debts that are due within one year, while noncurrent liabilities are debts due after one year
   b. Current liabilities are debts that are due after one year, while noncurrent liabilities are debts due within one year
   c. Current liabilities are debts that are due immediately, while noncurrent liabilities are debts due after one year
   d. There is no difference between current and noncurrent liabilities
5. **What is the purpose of depreciation?**
   a. To reduce the value of an asset to zero
   b. To allocate the cost of an asset over its useful life
   c. To increase the value of an asset over time
   d. To record changes in the market value of an asset
6. **What is the difference between straight-line and accelerated depreciation methods?**
   a. Straight-line depreciation is more commonly used than accelerated depreciation
   b. Straight-line depreciation results in a higher depreciation expense in the early years of an asset's life, while accelerated depreciation results in a higher depreciation expense in the later years

c. Accelerated depreciation results in a higher depreciation expense in the early years of an asset's life, while straight-line depreciation results in a higher depreciation expense in the later years
d. There is no difference between straight-line and accelerated depreciation methods

7. Which of the following is an example of an intangible asset?
a. Land
b. Machinery
c. Copyright
d. Inventory

8. What is goodwill?
a. The value of a company's brand name
b. The difference between the cost of an acquisition and the fair market value of the assets acquired
c. The value of a company's tangible assets
d. The value of a company's intellectual property

9. Which of the following is an example of a property, plant, and equipment (PP&E) asset?
a. Inventory
b. Patents
c. Buildings
d. Accounts receivable

10. What is the difference between a liability and an expense?
a. A liability is a debt that a company owes, while an expense is a cost incurred in the process of generating revenue
b. A liability is a cost incurred in the process of generating revenue, while an expense is a debt that a company owes
c. There is no difference between a liability and an expense
d. A liability

Answers to Multiple Choice Questions

1.	(b)	2.	(c)	3.	(c)	4.	(a)	5.	(b)
6.	(c)	7.	(c)	8.	(b)	9.	(c)	10.	(a)

REFERENCE

1. Ahn, D. H., Conrad, J., & Dittmar, R. F., (2009). Basis assets. *The Review of Financial Studies, 22*(12), 5133–5174.
2. Aleskerova, Y., Fedoryshyna, L., & Koval, N., (2018). Features of loan security for the reproduction of fixed assets for agricultural purposes. *Baltic Journal of Economic Studies, 4*(4), 1–5.
3. Allison, J. R., Lemley, M. A., Moore, K. A., & Trunkey, R. D., (2003). Valuable patents. *Geo. LJ, 92*, 435.
4. An, Y. H., Zagelmeyer, S., & Rygh, A., (2022). Between liability and asset: A critical review of 25 years of foreignness research in international business. *Critical Perspectives on International Business, 18*(5), 666–698.
5. Ang, A., Bekaert, G., & Liu, J., (2005). Why stocks may disappoint. *Journal of Financial Economics, 76*(3), 471–508.
6. Arend, R. J., (2004). The definition of strategic liabilities, and their impact on firm performance. *Journal of Management Studies, 41*(6), 1003–1027.
7. Bakar, M. A., (2018). Concept of revenue, expenses and liabilities in accounting for zakat, waqf and Baitulmal in Malaysia: An analysis from shariah perspective. *International Journal of Zakat, 3*(4), 1–16.
8. Barth, M. E., Kasznik, R., & McNichols, M. F., (2001). Analyst coverage and intangible assets. *Journal of Accounting Research, 39*(1), 1–34.
9. Bartlett, M. S., (1949). Fitting a straight line when both variables are subject to error. *Biometrics, 5*(3), 207–212.
10. Baum, A., (1993). Quality, depreciation, and property performance. *Journal of Real Estate Research, 8*(4), 541–565.
11. Beatty, R. P., & Welch, I., (1996). Issuer expenses and legal liability in initial public offerings. *The Journal of Law and Economics, 39*(2), 545–602.
12. Bedard, J. C., & Graham, L. E., (2002). The effects of decision aid orientation on risk factor identification and audit test planning. *Auditing: A Journal of Practice & Theory, 21*(2), 39–56.
13. Berkens, M. H., (1984). Installment method treatment of a sale of real property with mortgage in excess of basis: Will the correct view please stand up. *U. Miami L. Rev., 39*, 697.
14. Bierman, H., (1966). A further study of depreciation. *The Accounting Review, 41*(2), 271–274.
15. Biryukov, A. N., Dobryshkin, E., Kravchenko, I. N., & Glinsky, M. A., (2019). Optimization of management decisions for choosing strategy of enterprises fixed assets reproduction. *Engineering for Rural Development, 18*, 1726–1735.
16. Brown, C., Dark, J., & Davis, K., (2010). Exchange traded contracts for difference: Design, pricing, and effects. *Journal of Futures Markets, 30*(12), 1108–1149.

17. Byrd, D. T., & Mizruchi, M. S., (2005). Bankers on the board and the debt ratio of firms. *Journal of Corporate Finance, 11*(1–2), 129–173.
18. Campbell, J. Y., & Viceira, L. M., (2001). Who should buy long-term bonds? *American Economic Review, 91*(1), 99–127.
19. Censi, A., Slutsky, K., Wongpiromsarn, T., Yershov, D., Pendleton, S., Fu, J., & Frazzoli, E., (2019). Liability, ethics, and culture-aware behavior specification using rulebooks. In: *2019 International Conference on Robotics and Automation (ICRA)* (pp. 8536–8542). IEEE.
20. Cheatham, C. C., (1989). Economizing on cash investment in current assets. *Managerial Finance, 15*(6), 20–25.
21. Chen, Y. L., Shen, S. L., & Zhou, A., (2022). Assessment of red tide risk by integrating CRITIC weight method, TOPSIS-ASSETS method, and Monte Carlo simulation. *Environmental Pollution, 314*, 120254.
22. Chukwu, G. J., & Egbuhuzor, C. A., (2017). Tangible assets and corporate performance: Evidence from the manufacturing industry in Nigeria. *Research Journal of Financial Sustainability Reporting, 2*(1), 271–277.
23. Cicală, E., Soveja, A., Sallamand, P., Grevey, D., & Jouvard, J. M., (2008). The application of the random balance method in laser machining of metals. *Journal of Materials Processing Technology, 196*(1–3), 393–401.
24. Clemens, J., & Strain, M. R., (2022). Does measurement error explain the increase in subminimum wage payment following minimum wage increases? *Economics Letters, 217*, 110638.
25. Conrad, C. R., & DeMeritt, J. H., (2013). Constrained by the bank and the ballot: Unearned revenue, democracy, and state incentives to repress. *Journal of Peace Research, 50*(1), 105–119.
26. Corbet, S., Lucey, B., Urquhart, A., & Yarovaya, L., (2019). Cryptocurrencies as a financial asset: A systematic analysis. *International Review of Financial Analysis, 62*, 182–199.
27. Cross, III. J. J., (1988). The continuing evolution of the installment method of tax accounting. *Taxes, 66*, 421.
28. D'Mello, R., Gruskin, M., & Kulchania, M., (2018). Shareholders valuation of long-term debt and decline in firms' leverage ratio. *Journal of Corporate Finance, 48*, 352–374.
29. Davey, G. C., (1989). UCS revaluation and conditioning models of acquired fears. *Behavior Research and Therapy, 27*(5), 521–528.
30. Dayan, P., & Berridge, K. C., (2014). Model-based and model-free Pavlovian reward learning: Revaluation, revision, and revelation. *Cognitive, Affective, & Behavioral Neuroscience, 14*, 473–492.
31. Denk, N., Kaufmann, L., & Roesch, J. F., (2012). Liabilities of foreignness revisited: A review of contemporary studies and recommendations for future research. *Journal of International Management, 18*(4), 322–334.

32. Drake, L., (1992). The non-market value of the Swedish agricultural landscape. *European Review of* Agricultural Economics, 19(3), 351–364.
33. Driver, C., Temple, P., & Urga, G. (2006). Contrasts between types of assets in fixed investment equations as a way of testing real options theory. Journal of Business & Economic Statistics, 24(4), 432-443.
34. Emory, M., (1967). Installment method of reporting income its election use and effect. *Cornell L. Rev., 53*, 181.
35. Erik, S. K. A. R. L., (1997). The intangible assets monitor. *Journal of Human Resource Costing & Accounting, 2*(1), 73–97.
36. Faisal, D., (2021). Tax planning analysis through the depreciation and revaluation methods of fixed assets to minimum tax load at pt. Taspen (persero) Tasikmalaya branch. *Jurnal Ilmiah Mahasiswa Ekonomi Akuntansi (JIMEKA), 6*(2), 508–517.
37. Falk, M., & Steiger, R., (2018). An exploration of the debt ratio of ski lift operators. *Sustainability, 10*(9), 2985.
38. Fan, E., (2000). Two new applications of the homogeneous balance method. *Physics Letters A, 265*(5, 6), 353–357.
39. Farbey, B., Land, F., & Targett, D., (1992). Evaluating investments in IT. *Journal of Information Technology, 7*(2), 109–122.
40. Feinschreiber, R., (1968). *Depreciation Method Selection--IMPACT of 1968 Federal Income tax Surcharge* (Vol. 38, No. 000011, p. 789). New York Certified Public Accountant (pre-1986).
41. Francl, M., (2013). Tangible assets. *Nature Chemistry, 5*(3), 147–148.
42. Gastineau, G. L., (2001). Exchange-traded funds: An introduction. *The Journal of Portfolio Management, 27*(3), 88–96.
43. Glode, V., (2011). Why mutual funds "underperform." *Journal of Financial Economics, 99*(3), 546–559.
44. Golovetsky, N. Y., Ivanova, E. V., Galiy, E. A., Vypryazhkina, I. B., & Lebedeva, O. Y., (2019). Improvement of methodological approaches to financial analysis of fixed assets of the enterprise. *Revista ESPACIOS, 40*(34).
45. Goodhaet, R., (1940). A revaluation of the method described by Goodhart and Sinclair for the determination of blood cocarboxylase values. *Journal of Biological Chemistry, 135*, 77–84.
46. Gornik-Tomaszewski, S., & Shoaf, V., (2004). Accounting for noncurrent assets held for sale and discontinued operations converges. *Bank Accounting & Finance, 18*(1), 43–46.
47. Gramlich, J. D., McAnally, M. L., & Thomas, J., (2001). Balance sheet management: The case of short-term obligations reclassified as long-term debt. *Journal of Accounting Research, 39*(2), 283–295.

48. Greco, M., Cricelli, L., & Grimaldi, M., (2013). A strategic management framework of tangible and intangible assets. *European Management Journal, 31*(1), 55–66.
49. Greene, E. D., (1963). Changing from declining balance to straight-line depreciation. *The Accounting Review, 38*(2), 355.
50. Gu, F., & Lev, B., (2011). Intangible assets: Measurement, drivers, and usefulness. In: *Managing Knowledge Assets and Business Value Creation in Organizations: Measures and Dynamics* (pp. 110–124). IGI Global.
51. Guenther, D. A., & Sansing, R. C., (2000). Valuation of the firm in the presence of temporary book-tax differences: The role of deferred tax assets and liabilities. *The Accounting Review, 75*(1), 1–12.
52. Gupta, S., & Lehmann, D. R., (2003). Customers as assets. *Journal of INTERACTIVE MARKETING, 17*(1), 9–24.
53. Harc, M., (2015). The relationship between tangible assets and capital structure of small and medium-sized companies in Croatia. *Ekonomski Vjesnik/Econviews: Review of Contemporary Business, Entrepreneurship and Economic Issues, 28*(1), 213–224.
54. Haslam, C., Tsitsianis, N., Andersson, T., & Gleadle, P., (2015). Real estate investment trusts (REITS): A new business model in the FTSE100. In: *Accounting Forum* (Vol. 39, No. 4, pp. 239–248). Taylor & Francis.
55. Hatfield, H. R., (1936). What they say about depreciation. *The Accounting Review, 11*(1), 18–26.
56. Hein, E., (2006). Interest, debt and capital accumulation—A Kaleckian approach. *International Review of Applied Economics, 20*(3), 337–352.
57. Herring, III. H. C., & Jacobs, F. A., (1977). A controversy over the expected behavior of deferred tax credits. *Journal of Accountancy (pre-1986), 143*(000004), 53.
58. Hlaing, K. P., & Pourjalali, H., (2012). Economic reasons for reporting property, plant, and equipment at fair market value by foreign cross-listed firms in the United States. *Journal of Accounting, Auditing & Finance, 27*(4), 557–576.
59. Honoré, A. M., (2013). Ownership. In: *Readings in the Philosophy of Law* (pp. 563–564). Routledge.
60. Ibbotson, R. G., (2010). The importance of asset allocation. *Financial Analysts Journal, 66*(2), 18–20.
61. Im, D. K., Choi, S., & Kwon, J. H., (2015). Unsteady rotor flow analysis using a diagonally implicit harmonic balance method and an overset mesh topology. *International Journal of Computational Fluid Dynamics, 29*(1), 82–99.
62. Jacobs, M. R., Koornhof, H. J., Robins-Browne, R. M., Stevenson, C. M., Vermaak, Z. A., Freiman, I., & Austrian, R., (1978). Emergence of multiply resistant pneumococci. *New England Journal of Medicine, 299*(14), 735–740.
63. Jorgenson, D. W., (1996). Empirical studies of depreciation. *Economic Inquiry, 34*(1), 24–42.

64. Kaden, A. S., & LaFrance, M. E., (1989). Installment method asset sales by s corporations. *Am. UL Rev., 39*, 915.
65. Kaka, A. P., & Price, A. D. F., (1993). Modelling standard cost commitment curves for contractors' cash flow forecasting. *Construction Management and Economics, 11*(4), 271–283.
66. Kaplan, R. S., & Norton, D. P., (2004). Measuring the strategic readiness of intangible assets. *Harvard Business Review, 82*(2), 52–63.
67. Kim, S. H., & Kim, J. J., (2018). Analysis of defect risk by work types based on warranty liability period in apartments. *Korean Journal of Construction Engineering and Management, 19*(4), 34–42.
68. Klančar, U., Baumgartner, S., Legen, I., Smrdel, P., Kampuš, N. J., Krajcar, D., & Kočevar, K., (2015). Determining the polymer threshold amount for achieving robust drug release from HPMC and HPC matrix tablets containing a high-dose BCS class I model drug: *In vitro* and *in vivo* studies. *AAPS PharmSciTech, 16*, 398–406.
69. Kopriva, R., (2000). *Ensuring Accuracy in Testing for English Language Learners*. Council of Chief State School Officers, One Massachusetts Avenue, NW, Suite 700, Washington, DC 20001-1431.
70. Lewontin, R. C., (1970). The units of selection. *Annual Review of Ecology and Systematics, 1*(1), 1–18.
71. Li, W. C., & Hall, B. H., (2020). Depreciation of business R&D capital. *Review of Income and Wealth, 66*(1), 161–180.
72. Liao, D., (2016). Impact of accelerated depreciation of fixed assets policy on corporate financing behavior—Based on DID, the empirical analysis of the model. *Modern Economy, 7*(09), 1025.
73. Lonvaud-Funel, A., (1999). Lactic acid bacteria in the quality improvement and depreciation of wine. In: *Lactic Acid Bacteria: Genetics, Metabolism and Applications: Proceedings of the Sixth Symposium on Lactic Acid Bacteria: Genetics, Metabolism and Applications* (pp. 317–331). Veldhoven, The Netherlands. Springer Netherlands.
74. Mahoney, J. T., (1995). The management of resources and the resource of management. *Journal of Business Research, 33*(2), 91–101.
75. Matsumoto, K., (1982). The present value of cash flow generated under the double-declining-balance method with switching to the straight-line method—A padagogic note. *The Engineering Economist, 28*(2), 148–157.
76. McCroskey, J. C., & Teven, J. J., (1999). Goodwill: A reexamination of the construct and its measurement. *Communications Monographs, 66*(1), 90–103.
77. Mendonça, S., Pereira, T. S., & Godinho, M. M., (2004). Trademarks as an indicator of innovation and industrial change. *Research Policy, 33*(9), 1385–1404.
78. Mian, S. L., & Smith, Jr. C. W., (1992). Accounts receivable management policy: Theory and evidence. *The Journal of Finance, 47*(1), 169–200.

79. Michalisin, M. D., Smith, R. D., & Kline, D. M., (1997). In search of strategic assets. *The International Journal of Organizational Analysis, 5*(4), 360–387.
80. Mikkelson, W. H., & Partch, M. M., (2003). Do persistent large cash reserves hinder performance? *Journal of Financial and Quantitative Analysis, 38*(2), 275–294.
81. Missonier-Piera, F., (2007). Motives for fixed-asset revaluation: An empirical analysis with Swiss data. *The International Journal of Accounting, 42*(2), 186–205.
82. Nechaev, A., & Rasputina, A., (2020). Integrated depreciation management system. In: *IOP Conference Series: Earth and Environmental Science* (Vol. 421, No. 3, p. 032011). IOP Publishing.
83. Noja, G. G., & Caran, M., (2015). Post-employment benefits in Romania and Serbia: A comparative impact analysis. *Annals of Faculty of Economics* (Vol. 1, No. 2, pp. 237–246). University of Oradea.
84. Okoh, V. P. O., Ebi, U., & Orelaja, A., (2017). Comparative study on the causes of depreciation of process plants in Lagos and Ogun states industrial axes of Nigeria. *International Journal of Latest Engineering and Management Research (IJLEMR), 2*(8), *13, 19.*
85. Okoh, V. P., Ebi, U., & Dada, A. O., (2017). Causes of depreciation in process plants in paper industry: Analysis of the perception of practicing estate surveyors and valuers in Lagos and Ogun States. *International Journal of Research in Business Management (Impact: IJRBM) ISSN (E)*, 2347–4572.
86. Olson, C. A., (1985). Statutes prohibiting cost recovery for cancelled nuclear power plants: Constitutional, pro-consumer. *Wash. UJ Urb & Contemp. L., 28*, 345.
87. Pavlo, A., Paulson, E., Rasin, A., Abadi, D. J., DeWitt, D. J., Madden, S., & Stonebraker, M., (2009). A comparison of approaches to large-scale data analysis. In: *Proceedings of the 2009 ACM SIGMOD International Conference on Management of Data* (pp. 165–178).
88. Pearce, D. W., (2001). The economic value of forest ecosystems. *Ecosystem Health, 7*(4), 284–296.
89. Peloubet, M. E., (1950). Disclosure of current value of LIFO inventories is not normally useful; the figure must be an estimate based on an unreal situation. *Journal of Accountancy (pre-1986), 89*(000006).
90. Preinreich, G. A., (1938). Annual survey of economic theory: The theory of depreciation. *Econometrica: Journal of the Econometric Society*, 219–241.
91. Ramachandran, J., & Pant, A., (2010). The liabilities of origin: An emerging economy perspective on the costs of doing business abroad. In: *The Past, Present and Future of International Business & Management* (Vol. 23, pp. 231–265). Emerald Group Publishing Limited.
92. Raximova, G. M., (2020). Problems of accounting and audit of fixed assets. *Theoretical & Applied Science*, (5), 726–729.

93. Reeds, J., & Shepp, L., (1990). Optimal paths for a car that goes both forwards and backwards. *Pacific Journal of Mathematics, 145*(2), 367–393.

94. Ritchie, T. J., & Macdonald, S. J., (2009). The impact of aromatic ring count on compound developability–are too many aromatic rings a liability in drug design? *Drug Discovery Today, 14*(21–22), 1011–1020.

95. Ross, S. A., (1976). Options and efficiency. *The Quarterly Journal of Economics, 90*(1), 75–89.

96. Rubinstein, M., (1987). Derivative assets analysis. *Journal of Economic Perspectives, 1*(2), 73–93.

97. Sahminan, S., (2007). Effects of exchange rate depreciation on commercial bank failures in Indonesia. *Journal of Financial Stability, 3*(2), 175–193.

98. Sakhno, A., Salkova, I., Polishchuk, N., Kucher, L., & Stashko, I., (2020). Efficiency of managing liabilities of enterprises of different types of economic activities. *European Journal of Sustainable Development, 9*(1), 423–423.

99. Sanders, D. H., (1953). The installment method of accounting as applied to retail credit jewelry stores. *Journal of Accountancy (pre-1986), 96*(1), 89.

100. Seigworth, G. J., & Gregg, M., (2010). An inventory of shimmers. *The Affect Theory Reader, 1*, 25.

101. Sharpe, W. F., & Tint, L. G., (1990). Liabilities-a new approach. *Journal of Portfolio Management, 16*(2), 5–10.

102. Sheehan, K. J., Greene, B. R., Cunningham, C., Crosby, L., & Kenny, R. A., (2014). Early identification of declining balance in higher functioning older adults, an inertial sensor based method. *Gait & Posture, 39*(4), 1034–1039.

103. Shen, H., (2010). Advantages and disadvantages of student loans repayment patterns. *International Education Studies, 3*(1), 45–49.

104. Sigidov, Y. I., Rybyantseva, M. S., Adamenko, A. A., & Yarushkina, E. A., (2016). Methodological aspects of depreciation as an economic category. *International Journal of Economics and Financial Issues, 6*(1), 88–95.

105. Simon, S. I., (1959). The right side of accumulated depreciation. *The Accounting Review, 34*(1), 97–105.

106. Sitorus, C. M., Sianipar, Y. C., & Muda, I., (2021). How noncurrent liabilities ARE reported and analyzed at PT Garuda Indonesia Tbk? *Turkish Online Journal of Qualitative Inquiry, 12*(9).

107. Smyth, D. J., & Hsing, Y., (1995). In search of an optimal debt ratio for economic growth. *Contemporary Economic Policy, 13*(4), 51–59.

108. Sohn, J. H., (2009). Consideration to the depreciation method using accumulated depreciation rate function. *The Journal of the Korea Contents Association, 9*(1), 304–311.

109. Spodniak, P., Chernenko, N., & Nilsson, M., (2014). *Efficiency of Contracts for Differences (CfDs) in the Nordic Electricity Market*. Available at SSRN 2496889.

110. Stulz, R. M., (2010). Credit default swaps and the credit crisis. *Journal of Economic Perspectives, 24*(1), 73–92.

111. Teece, D. J., (1998). Capturing value from knowledge assets: The new economy, markets for know-how, and intangible assets. *California Management Review. 40(3),* 55-79.

112. Teng, J. T., Chang, C. T., & Goyal, S. K., (2005). Optimal pricing and ordering policy under permissible delay in payments. *International Journal of Production Economics, 97*(2), 121–129.

113. Thompson, S. T., Peterson, D., Ho, D., & Papageorgopoulos, D., (2020). Perspective—The next decade of AEMFCs: Near-term targets to accelerate applied R&D. *Journal of The Electrochemical Society, 167*(8), 084514.

114. Thum-Thysen, A., Voigt, P., Bilbao-Osorio, B., Maier, C., & Ognyanova, D., (2019). Investment dynamics in Europe: Distinct drivers and barriers for investing in intangible versus tangible assets? *Structural Change and Economic Dynamics, 51*, 77–88.

115. Urbanovsky, T., (2015). Factors behind the Russian ruble depreciation. *Procedia Economics and Finance, 26*, 242–248.

116. Vanderwalde, A., Spetzler, D., Xiao, N., Gatalica, Z., & Marshall, J., (2018). Microsatellite instability status determined by next-generation sequencing and compared with PD-L1 and tumor mutational burden in 11,348 patients. *Cancer Medicine, 7*(3), 746–756.

117. Waggle, D., & Englis, B., (2000). Asset allocation decisions in retirement accounts: An all-or-nothing proposition? *Financial Services Review, 9*(1), 79–92.

118. Wykoff, F. C., (1970). Capital depreciation in the postwar period: Automobiles. *The Review of Economics and Statistics,* 168–172.

119. Yang, Y., Liu, Y., Cao, S., & Cheng, Y., (2017). A method of evaluating water resource assets and liabilities: A case study of Jinan City, Shandong Province. *Water, 9*(8), 575.

120. York, D., (1966). Least-squares fitting of a straight line. *Canadian Journal of Physics, 44*(5), 1079–1086.

CHAPTER 6

STAKEHOLDER'S EQUITY

UNIT INTRODUCTION

In today's rapidly changing business environment, the traditional concept of shareholder primacy is challenged by a more inclusive approach that recognizes the importance of all stakeholders in a company's success. The idea of stakeholder equity has gained significant momentum in recent years as companies and investors increasingly prioritize environmental, social, and governance (ESG) factors in their decision-making (Sarkki et al., 2021).

Stakeholder equity refers to the value a company creates for all its stakeholders, including customers, employees, suppliers, creditors, and the wider community. This value is not limited to financial returns for shareholders but also includes intangible benefits, such as customer satisfaction, employee engagement, and social and environmental impact. As the world becomes more connected, companies prioritizing stakeholder equity are better positioned to create sustainable, long-term value and maintain a competitive edge. One of the critical challenges in implementing a stakeholder-oriented approach is balancing the competing demands of different stakeholder groups. For example, while shareholders may prioritize short-term financial gains, employees may prioritize long-term job security, and customers may prioritize ethical and sustainable business practices. Companies that effectively manage these competing demands are more likely to create value for all stakeholders and achieve sustainable growth (Torres et al., 2012).

The concept of stakeholder equity is not without its challenges, however. Some critics argue that prioritizing stakeholder interests over shareholder interests may lead to a loss of focus and accountability or that it may be challenging to measure and report on the intangible benefits of stakeholder value (Jimenez & Okhremtchouk, 2021) (Figure 6.1).

Figure 6.1. Illustration of stakeholder equity.

Source: Catherine S, Creative Commons License.

Learning Objectives

At the end of the chapter, the reader will be able to understand

1. The importance of stakeholder equity in the business
2. The purpose of stakeholder's equity
3. The difference between stakeholder's equity and shareholder's equity
4. A different method to calculate stakeholder equity
5. The critical indicators to evaluate the performance of stakeholder equity

Key Terms

1. Community Equity
2. Retained Earnings
3. Shareholder's Equity
4. Stakeholder Equity
5. Supplier Equity
6. Treasury Stock
7. Triple Bottom Line Reporting

6.1. PURPOSE OF STAKEHOLDER EQUITY

The purpose of stakeholder equity is to provide a framework for managing and measuring the value that a company creates for all of its stakeholders. This value goes beyond the financial returns generated for shareholders and considers the impact a company has on its employees, customers, suppliers, communities, and the environment. By viewing the interests and needs of all parties that have a stake in a company's success, stakeholder equity can help companies make decisions aligned with the values and goals of all stakeholders (Brandon, 1998).

Remember

As the world becomes increasingly interconnected and stakeholders become more aware of their power to influence business decisions, companies that prioritize stakeholder equity are likely to be better positioned to create sustainable, long-term value and maintain a competitive edge.

6.1.1. Help Companies

Balance the interests of different stakeholders. By considering the needs and perspectives of all parties involved, companies can balance the interests of different stakeholders and make decisions that are in the best interest of all parties (Bridges et al., 2003).

6.1.2. Enhance Reputation and Brand Image

By considering the impact of its actions on its stakeholders, a company can enhance its reputation and brand image as a responsible and sustainable business. This can help attract and retain customers and employees and improve relationships with suppliers and communities (Gray & Balmer, 1998).

6.1.3. Promote Sustainability and Long-Term Success

By considering the impact of its actions on the environment and communities, a company can promote sustainability and long-term success. This can help reduce the risk of negative environmental and social impacts and ensure the company's continued success over time (Winit & Kantabutra, 2022).

6.1.4. Improve Employee Morale and Engagement

By considering the interests and well-being of employees, companies can improve employee morale and engagement, which can help increase productivity and reduce turnover (Walsh & Sulkowski, 2010).

6.1.5. Attract and Retain Customers

By considering the needs and preferences of customers, companies can create products and services that better meet customer needs, which can help attract and retain customers.

By focusing on stakeholder equity, companies can create value that is sustainable, mutually beneficial, and aligned with the values and goals of all stakeholders. This can help companies positively impact the world and ensure the continued success of their business (Wallace et al., 2014).

KEYWORD

Equity is an ownership interest in property that may be offset by debts or other liabilities.

6.2. STAKEHOLDER VS. SHAREHOLDER EQUITY

Stakeholder equity and shareholder equity are related but distinct concepts in corporate finance. Shareholder equity refers to the ownership interest of shareholders in a company. It is represented on the company's balance sheet as the residual interest in its assets after deducting its liabilities. On the other hand, stakeholder equity considers the interests and values of all parties that have a stake in a company's success, including shareholders, employees, customers, suppliers, and the community (Barsky et al., 1999).

One key difference between the two is that shareholder equity is focused on maximizing returns for shareholders, while stakeholder equity considers the interests and needs of all parties involved. This means that decisions made in the context of stakeholder equity may prioritize the needs of employees, customers, and the community, even if they result in lower profits for shareholders (Jones, 2005).

Another difference is that shareholder equity is a financial measure, while stakeholder equity is a broader, more holistic concept encompassing the relationship between a company and its stakeholders. Shareholder equity can be quantified by financial metrics such as the company's stock price. In contrast, stakeholder equity is more challenging to measure and quantify as it considers stakeholders' values, beliefs, and perceptions. While shareholder and stakeholder equity are related, they have different focuses and implications for corporate decision-making. Shareholder equity is focused on maximizing returns for shareholders, while stakeholder equity considers the interests of all parties involved in a company's success (Carlon & Downs, 2014) (Figure 6.2).

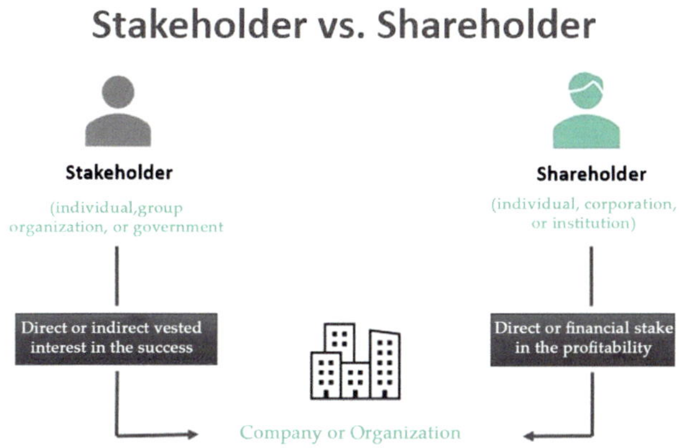

Figure 6.2. Image of difference between Stakeholder and Shareholder equity.

Source: Wallstreetmojo Team, Creative Commons License.

6.3. ADVANTAGES AND DISADVANTAGES

6.3.1. Advantages of Stakeholder Equity

Stakeholder equity refers to the portion of a company's assets attributable to its stakeholders, including shareholders, employees, customers, suppliers, and the community at large. Some potential advantages of stakeholder equity include (Turnbull, 2002) (Figure 6.3):

Figure 6.3. Users of stakeholder equity.

Source: CFI Team, Creative Commons License.

6.3.1.1. Shared Risk and Reward

Stakeholder equity means everyone with a stake in the company shares its risks and rewards. This can help to align everyone's interests and motivate them to work together to achieve the company's goals (Admati et al., 1994) (Figure 6.4).

Figure 6.4. Picture of shared risk and reward.

Source: Lean Construction blog, Creative Commons License.

6.3.1.2. Increased Stakeholder Buy-in

When stakeholders have a direct financial stake in the company's success, they may be more invested in its long-term growth and success. This can increase loyalty and commitment from employees, customers, and suppliers (Fitzpatrick & Mowers, 1997) (Figure 6.5).

Figure 6.5. Illustration of tips for securing stakeholder buy-in.

Source: Lucid chart, Creative Commons License.

6.3.1.3. Improved Financial Stability

Companies with a broad base of stakeholders with equity in the company may be more financially stable and less susceptible to external shocks. This can help to ensure the company's long-term viability (Sulimany et al., 2021).

6.3.1.4. Enhanced Reputation and Social Responsibility

By treating all stakeholders fairly and ensuring they have a stake in the company's success, a company can enhance its reputation as a socially responsible business that values its relationships with all stakeholders (Agyemang & Ansong, 2017).

KEYWORD

Reputation is a ubiquitous, spontaneous, and highly efficient mechanism of social control.

6.3.1.5. Potential for Innovation

When stakeholders are engaged and invested in the company's success, they may be more likely to contribute ideas and innovations to help the company grow and succeed (Sun & Xia, 2022).

6.3.2. Disadvantages of Stakeholder Equity

6.3.2.1. Potential for Conflicting Interests

As stakeholder equity considers the interests of all parties involved, it may be challenging to balance the interests of all stakeholders and make decisions that satisfy everyone. This can lead to conflicts and disagreements between stakeholders, which can be time-consuming and difficult to resolve (Sundaramurthy & Lyon, 1998).

6.3.2.2. Increased Complexity

Stakeholder equity is more complex than shareholder equity and can be more challenging to implement and measure. Companies may need to invest more resources and effort into considering the interests of all stakeholders, which can be complex and resource-intensive (Walker et al., 2018).

6.3.2.3. Potential for Reduced Profitability

By prioritizing the interests of all stakeholders, companies may make decisions that result in lower profits for shareholders. For example, a company may invest in environmental sustainability initiatives that benefit the environment and communities but lower shareholders' profits (Hatherly et al., 2020).

6.4. METHOD TO STAKEHOLDERS' EQUITY

Stakeholder equity cannot be calculated using a specific formula as it is a more general term that refers to the overall value a company creates for its stakeholders. The value a company creates for its stakeholders is a combination of many factors, including its financial performance, reputation, relationships with customers, suppliers, and employees, and its impact on the community and the environment.

However, companies use a few methods to measure and improve their stakeholder equity. These methods include:

KEYWORD

Environmental performance refers to how a country's economic development style relates to its ecological institutions, policies, and the generation of ecological impacts.

6.4.1. Stakeholder Analysis

Companies conduct a stakeholder analysis to identify and understand their stakeholders' needs, expectations, and concerns. This analysis can help companies identify areas where they can improve their stakeholder relationships and create more value for their stakeholders.

6.4.2. Social and Environmental Accounting

Companies use social and environmental accounting to measure and report their social and ecological impacts. This helps companies identify areas where they can reduce their negative impacts and create more positive ones for their stakeholders.

6.4.3. Triple Bottom Line Reporting

Companies use triple bottom line reporting to measure and report their financial, social, and environmental performance. This helps companies to balance their financial performance with their social and environmental performance and create more value for their stakeholders.

Stakeholder equity cannot be calculated using a specific formula, but companies can use various methods to measure and improve their stakeholder relationships and create more value for their stakeholders.

6.5. IMPORTANCE OF STAKEHOLDER EQUITY IN BUSINESS

Stakeholder equity is becoming increasingly important in business as companies recognize the need to consider the interests and expectations of various stakeholders in their operations and decision-making processes. There are several reasons why stakeholder equity is becoming increasingly important (Orts & Strudler, 2002):

Did you Know?

The Global Reporting Initiative (GRI) found that 92% of companies that report on sustainability and stakeholder engagement include at least one indicator related to stakeholder engagement.

6.5.1. Increased Awareness of Social Responsibility

Companies are increasingly aware of their social responsibility to all stakeholders and are looking for ways to create value for everyone impacted by their operations. This includes customers, employees, suppliers, communities, and the environment (Flammer, 2013).

6.5.2. Changing Business Environment

The business environment is changing, and companies are facing increasing pressure from stakeholders to act in sustainable and responsible ways. This includes pressure from investors and customers to reduce their environmental impact and ensure their operations are ethically and socially accountable (Scherrer, 2003).

6.5.3. Long-Term Sustainability

Companies committed to creating value for all stakeholders are more likely to be sustainable in the long term. They can better navigate challenges and opportunities and build lasting relationships with customers, employees, suppliers, and communities (Fulton et al., 2012).

6.5.4. Improved Business Performance

Companies committed to stakeholder equity are more likely to experience improved business performance. For example, companies that invest in their employees are more likely to have engaged and motivated workers, which can lead to increased productivity and innovation (Lau & May 1998).

6.5.5. Better Reputation

Companies committed to stakeholder equity are more likely to be perceived as responsible and trustworthy by their stakeholders. This can lead to improved relationships, increased customer loyalty, and a stronger brand.

Overall, the importance of stakeholder equity in a business is evident. Companies committed to creating value for all stakeholders are more likely to be successful in the long term and enjoy improved business performance and a better reputation (Wang et al., 2021).

6.6. COMPONENTS OF STAKEHOLDER EQUITY

The components of stakeholder equity can vary depending on the company, industry, and country. However, some key elements are commonly considered part of stakeholder equity. These components include (Munilla & Miles, 2005):

6.6.1. Outstanding Shares

The outstanding share count is a fundamental component of stakeholders' equity. It is the quantity of corporate stock sold to clients not repurchased by the corporate. It indicates the total number of shares issued to the public, corporate officers, and company insiders comprising restricted shares (Mietzner & Schweizer, 2014).

This amount comprises the par value of common shares and the par value of any preference shares sold by the corporation. Outstanding shares are also integral to other computations, such as market capitalization and earnings per share calculations (EPS) (Butler et al., 2006) (Figure 6.6).

Figure 6.6. Schematic of the formula of earnings per share (EPS).

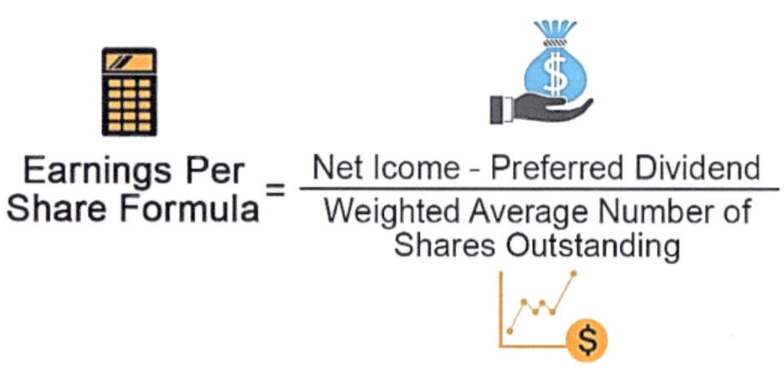

Source: Sayantan Mukhopadhyay, Creative Commons License.

6.6.2. Retained Earnings

A positive balance is generated in the retained profits account when a corporation holds income rather than distributing it as a dividend. Often, retained earnings are used to pay off debt or reinvest in the company (Yemi & Seriki, 2018).

This number comprises stakeholder's equity and is the greatest line item in this computation. Retained earnings can be found on a company's balance sheet below stakeholders' equity or in a brief statement of retained earnings. A company's retained earnings may also be referred to as its "retention ratio" or its "retained surplus" Borisovna, 2020).

TIPS

On the balance sheet of a company, the total shareholders' equity can be reduced by the amount of treasury stock held.

6.6.3. Employee Equity

Employee equity refers to the value a company's employees bring to the organization, which is a critical component of stakeholder equity. Employee equity can encompass a wide range of factors, including (Boukis & Christodoulides, 2020):

6.6.3.1. Skills and Expertise

A company's employees' knowledge, experience, and abilities are critical to its success. Companies with a highly skilled and knowledgeable workforce are better positioned to deliver high-quality products and services and are more likely to have a competitive advantage (Read & Sarasvathy, 2005).

6.6.3.2. Employee Engagement

Engaged employees are more productive, provide better customer service, and are likelier to remain with the company. This can contribute to a positive reputation, improved customer satisfaction, and higher stakeholder equity (Mirvis, 2012).

6.6.3.3. Employee Retention

Employee retention refers to the ability of a company to retain its employees over time. High employee turnover can be costly for a company, as it requires significant recruitment, training, and onboarding investments. Companies that can retain their employees are more likely to have a stable and experienced workforce, which can contribute to higher stakeholder equity (Alshathry et al., 2017).

6.6.3.4. Employee Satisfaction

Employee satisfaction refers to the level of happiness and contentment among a company's employees. Satisfied employees are more likely to be productive, engaged, and committed to the company, which can contribute to higher stakeholder equity (Edmans, 2011).

6.6.3.5. Employee Development

Employee development refers to the opportunities and resources a company provides its employees to help them grow and advance in their careers. Companies that invest in employee development are more likely to have a highly skilled and knowledgeable workforce, which can contribute to higher stakeholder equity (King et al., 2012).

KEYWORD

Employee equity is a form of noncash compensation that provides a share of the company's ownership.

6.6.3.6. Employee Benefits

Employee benefits, such as health insurance, retirement plans, and paid time off, can also contribute to employment equity. These benefits can help attract and retain employees and improve overall employee satisfaction and engagement.

Investing in its employees can build a strong and valued workforce that contributes to its overall stakeholder equity. Employee equity can help to improve customer satisfaction, brand recognition, community relations, and financial performance (Palladino, 2022).

6.6.4. Treasury Stock

It refers to the number of shares bought back by the corporation from individual stakeholders. A treasury is where a firm stores its shares of stock for safekeeping and potential future usage. The shares may be sold later to raise funds, or they may be used to avoid an unfriendly takeover.

This number is deducted from the overall equity of a corporation because, once it has been repurchased, it will reflect a lower number of shares that are available to be purchased by investors (Cho, 2017).

In the area of its balance sheet devoted to equity, a company will document its treasury stock holdings with a negative number. There are a few different names that can be used to refer to treasury stock, including "treasury shares" and "reacquired stock" (Teng & Hachiya, 2010) (Figure 6.7).

Figure 6.7. Image of treasury stock.

Source: Niti Gupta, Creative Commons License.

6.6.5. Customer Equity

Customer equity refers to the value a company's customers bring to the organization, a critical component of stakeholder equity. Customer equity encompasses a wide range of factors, including (Persson & Ryals, 2010):

6.6.5.1. Customer Loyalty

Customer loyalty refers to the degree to which a customer is committed to a company over time. Companies with high customer loyalty are more likely to have a stable and predictable revenue stream, which can contribute to higher stakeholder equity (Rachbini et al., 2019).

6.6.5.2. Customer Satisfaction

Customer satisfaction refers to the level of happiness and contentment among a company's customers. Satisfied customers are more likely to be loyal, recommend the company to others, and make repeat purchases, which can contribute to higher stakeholder equity (Luo et al., 2012).

6.6.5.3. Customer Lifetime Value

Customer lifetime value refers to the total value a customer is expected to bring to a company throughout their relationship. Companies that maximize customer lifetime value are more likely to have a stable and predictable revenue stream, contributing to higher stakeholder equity (Stahl et al., 2003).

6.6.5.4. Customer Advocacy

Customer advocacy refers to the degree to which a customer is willing to speak positively about a company to others. Companies with a high degree of customer advocacy are more likely to have a positive reputation, which can contribute to higher stakeholder equity (Lawer & Knox, 2006).

KEYWORD

Turnover is a concept in accounting that shows how quickly a company runs its business.

6.6.5.5. Customer Retention

Customer retention refers to the ability of a company to retain its customers over time. High customer turnover can be costly for a company, as it requires significant investments in marketing and sales to attract new customers. Companies that can retain their customers are more likely to have a stable and predictable revenue stream, which can contribute to higher stakeholder equity (Srivastava & Singh, 2021).

Investing in its customers can build strong and valuable relationships that contribute to its overall stakeholder equity. Customer equity can help improve brand recognition, community relations, and financial performance, which are critical components of stakeholder equity. Companies prioritizing customer equity are more likely to have a competitive advantage in the marketplace and are better positioned for long-term success (Mokhtaruddin et al., 2018).

6.6.6. Supplier Equity

Supplier equity refers to the value a company's suppliers bring to the organization, a critical component of stakeholder equity. Supplier equity encompasses a wide range of factors, including (Kannan, 2018):

6.6.6.1. Supplier Loyalty

Supplier loyalty refers to the degree to which a supplier is committed to a company over time. Companies with a high degree of supplier loyalty are more likely to have a stable and predictable supply chain, which can contribute to higher stakeholder equity (Zhang et al., 2014).

6.6.6.2. Supplier Satisfaction

Supplier satisfaction refers to happiness and contentment among a company's suppliers. Satisfied suppliers are more likely to provide high-quality products and services, be flexible with delivery times, and offer competitive pricing, contributing to higher stakeholder equity (Lindwall et al., 2010).

KEYWORD

Competitive pricing is the process of selecting strategic price points to best take advantage of a product or service based market relative to competition.

6.6.6.3. Supplier Reputation

Supplier reputation refers to the perceived quality of a company's suppliers. Companies that work with high-quality suppliers are more likely to have a positive reputation, which can contribute to higher stakeholder equity (Suh & Houston, 2010).

6.6.6.4. Supplier Relationship

Supplier relationship refers to the level of trust and collaboration between a company and its suppliers. Companies with strong and positive relationships with their suppliers are more likely to have a stable and predictable supply chain, contributing to higher stakeholder equity (Banerjee et al., 2008).

6.6.6.5. Supplier Reliability

Supplier reliability refers to the degree to which a supplier can deliver products and services as promised. Companies that work with reliable suppliers are more likely to have a stable and predictable supply chain, which can contribute to higher stakeholder equity (Walton & Marucheck, 1997). Investing in its suppliers can build strong and valuable relationships that contribute to its overall stakeholder equity. Supplier equity can help improve product quality, delivery times, and financial performance, which are critical components of stakeholder equity. Companies prioritizing supplier equity are more likely to have a competitive advantage in the marketplace and are better positioned for long-term success (Selnes & Gønhaug, 2000).

6.6.7. Community Equity

Community equity refers to the value that a company brings to the communities in which it operates. It encompasses a wide range of factors, including (Mirkovski et al., 2019):

6.6.7.1. Community Involvement

Community involvement refers to the degree to which a company is involved in local activities and initiatives. Companies highly involved in their communities are more likely to be seen as good corporate citizens, which can contribute to higher stakeholder equity (Simpson, 2001).

6.6.7.2. Community Engagement

Community engagement refers to the level of communication and interaction between a company and the communities in which it operates. Companies that engage actively with their communities are more likely to build strong and positive relationships, which can contribute to higher stakeholder equity (Scull & Cuthill, 2010).

KEYWORD

Corporate means relating to large companies, or to a particular large company.

6.6.7.3. Community Impact

Community impact refers to a company's positive or negative impact on the communities in which it operates. Companies that positively impact their communities are more likely to be seen as good corporate citizens, which can contribute to higher stakeholder equity (Cornforth & Brown, 2013).

6.6.7.4. Community Reputation

Community reputation refers to the perceived quality of a company in the communities in which it operates. Companies with a positive reputation are more likely to have strong and positive relationships with the communities in which they serve, which can contribute to higher stakeholder equity (Waddock, 2000).

6.6.7.5. Community Contributions

Community contributions refer to a company's financial or in-kind donations to local initiatives or organizations. Companies that make significant contributions to their communities are more likely to be seen as good corporate citizens, which can contribute to higher stakeholder equity (Wallerstein & Duran, 2010).

Investing in the communities in which it operates can build strong and positive relationships that contribute to its overall stakeholder equity. Community equity can help to improve the company's reputation, financial performance, and overall sustainability, all of which are critical components of stakeholder equity. Companies prioritizing community equity are more likely to have a competitive advantage in the marketplace and are better positioned for long-term success (Rendon et al., 2021).

6.7. STAKEHOLDER EQUITY PERFORMANCE INDICATORS

Measuring stakeholder equity can be challenging, as it encompasses a variety of intangible and tangible elements that contribute to a company's overall value and reputation. However, there are several metrics that organizations can use to track and evaluate their stakeholder equity over time. Some of these metrics include (Sawhney & Zabin, 2002):

6.7.1. Customer Satisfaction

This measures the level of satisfaction among a company's customers, which is an essential factor in determining stakeholder equity. A high level of customer satisfaction indicates that the company is delivering on its promises and providing value to its customers, which can contribute to a positive reputation and higher stakeholder equity (Churchill & Surprenant, 1982) (Figure 6.8).

Figure 6.8. Illustration of customer satisfaction.

Source: Unsplash, Creative Commons License.

6.7.2. Employee Engagement

Employee engagement refers to the level of involvement, commitment, and satisfaction among a company's employees. Engaged employees are more productive, provide better customer service, and are more likely to remain with the company, which can contribute to a positive reputation and higher stakeholder equity (Mittal et al., 2018).

6.7.3. Brand Recognition

The recognition and reputation of a company's brand are essential to its stakeholder equity. Brands well known and highly regarded by customers, employees, and other stakeholders can command a premium price and have higher stakeholder equity (Naidoo & Abratt, 2018).

KEYWORD

Economic Development is programs, policies or activities that seek to improve the economic well-being and quality of life for a community.

6.7.4. Community Relations

Companies with a positive relationship with the communities in which they operate can also benefit from higher stakeholder equity. This includes initiatives contributing to local economic development, supporting education and training, and promoting sustainability and environmental responsibility (Kemp & Owen, 2013).

6.7.5. Corporate Social Responsibility

Corporate social responsibility (CSR) initiatives are another critical component of stakeholder equity. CSR initiatives demonstrate a company's commitment to ethical and responsible business practices and can help to build trust and credibility with stakeholders (Deng et al., 2013).

6.7.6. Financial Performance

Finally, a company's financial performance is a critical component of stakeholder equity. This includes measures such as revenue growth, profitability, and return on investment, as well as the stability and sustainability of the company's financial position over time.

By regularly measuring and tracking these metrics, companies can better understand the value they are providing to their stakeholders and make informed decisions about improving and maintaining their stakeholder equity over time (Jo & Kim, 2008).

6.8. LIMITATIONS OF MEASURING STAKEHOLDER EQUITY

Despite the importance of measuring stakeholder equity, several limitations must be considered:

6.8.1. Data Availability

Measuring stakeholder equity requires a wide range of data, including customer satisfaction, employee engagement, community involvement, and supplier relationships. The availability of this data can be limited, making it difficult to obtain an accurate and comprehensive view of stakeholder equity (Federer et al., 2018).

KEYWORD

Stakeholder value is a business concept that companies use to create the best possible levels of return for their stakeholders.

6.8.2. Subjectivity

Measuring stakeholder equity can be subjective, requiring companies to judge the value of their relationships with different stakeholders. This can lead to inconsistencies in measuring stakeholder equity across companies and over time (Allenby et al., 1998).

6.8.3. Cost

Measuring stakeholder equity can be expensive, requiring companies to invest in data collection and analysis. This can be a barrier to companies with limited resources, minimal, and medium-sized enterprises (Richardson & Welker, 2001).

6.8.4. Complexity

Measuring stakeholder equity can be complex, as it requires companies to consider the impact of a wide range of factors on stakeholder value, including social, environmental, and economic factors (Chatzipanagiotou et al., 2016).

6.8.5. Lack of Standardization

There is currently a lack of standardization in measuring stakeholder equity, which can make it difficult for companies to compare their performance with others and benchmark their stakeholder equity over time.

Despite these limitations, the importance of measuring stakeholder equity cannot be overstated. By measuring stakeholder equity, companies can better understand the impact of their business practices on all of their stakeholders and make informed decisions that promote long-term success and sustainability (Suchy, 2010).

ACTIVITY 6.1.

In a real scenario, a company is facing pressure from both its shareholders and environmental activists. The company is considering investing in a new manufacturing facility that will increase production and revenue, but it will also increase its environmental impact. At the same time, the company's customers are becoming more environmentally conscious and are pushing for the company to prioritize sustainable business practices. As a stakeholder-oriented company, how can the company balance these competing demands and make a decision that creates value for all stakeholders? What methods and tools can the company use to measure and improve its stakeholder equity? How can the company effectively communicate its decision and actions to its stakeholders?

6.9. SUMMARY

- Stakeholder equity is a concept that emphasizes the importance of creating value for all stakeholders in a business. This includes customers, employees, suppliers, creditors, and the community. Unlike shareholder equity, which focuses solely on the value created for shareholders, stakeholder equity takes a more holistic approach. It recognizes that a business's success depends on the value it creates for all its stakeholders.
- Companies can use various methods to calculate stakeholder equity, such as surveys and feedback, social, and environmental impact assessments, financial analysis, stakeholder mapping, and case studies. However, stakeholder equity is a more qualitative concept requiring a comprehensive measurement and evaluation approach. Companies should focus on creating value for all stakeholders to achieve long-term success and sustainable growth. Indicators such as customer satisfaction, employee engagement, community relations, and financial performance impact can be used to evaluate the performance of stakeholder equity. By prioritizing stakeholder equity, companies can build a positive reputation, foster trust and loyalty among their stakeholders, and achieve long-term success.

REVIEW QUESTIONS

1. What is stakeholder equity, and why is it important in business?
2. What is the purpose of stakeholder equity, and how does it differ from shareholder equity?
3. What are some of the methods that can be used to calculate stakeholder equity in a company?
4. What are some critical indicators that can be used to evaluate the performance of stakeholder equity in a company?
5. Why is it essential for companies to consider the needs and interests of all stakeholders when making business decisions?
6. How can companies improve their stakeholder equity and create more value for their stakeholders?

MULTIPLE CHOICE QUESTIONS

1. Which of the following is a stakeholder in a company?

a. Shareholder

b. Customer

c. Employee

d. All of the above

2. **What is the purpose of stakeholder equity?**
   a. To measure the financial value of a company's stakeholders
   b. To evaluate the impact of a company's business decisions on its stakeholders
   c. To calculate the dividends paid to shareholders
   d. To determine the market value of a company's stock
3. **What is the difference between stakeholder equity and shareholder equity?**
   a. Stakeholder equity refers to the value created for all stakeholders, while shareholder equity refers only to the value created for shareholders.
   b. Stakeholder equity is a financial measure, while shareholder equity is qualitative.
   c. Stakeholder equity is based on the number of shares owned by shareholders, while stakeholder equity is based on the number of stakeholders.
   d. There is no difference between stakeholder equity and shareholder equity.
4. **Which of the following is not a method to calculate stakeholder equity?**
   a. Surveys and feedback
   b. Social and environmental impact assessments
   c. Financial ratio analysis
   d. Stakeholder mapping
5. **Which of the following is an important indicator to evaluate the performance of stakeholder equity?**
   a. Revenue growth
   b. Profit margin
   c. Employee turnover rate
   d. All of the above
6. **Which of the following is an example of a non-financial measure of stakeholder equity?**
   a. Return on investment
   b. Customer satisfaction
   c. Earnings per share
   d. Market share
7. **Which of the following is an example of a stakeholder other than a shareholder?**
   a. Supplier
   b. CEO
   c. Board of Directors
   d. None of the above

Answers to Multiple Choice Questions

1. (d) 2. (b) 3. (a) 4. (c) 5. (c)
6. (b) 7. (a)

REFERENCES

1. Admati, A. R., Pfleiderer, P., & Zechner, J., (1994). Large shareholder activism, risk sharing, and financial market equilibrium. *Journal of Political Economy, 102*(6), 1097–1130.
2. Agyemang, O. S., & Ansong, A., (2017). Corporate social responsibility and firm performance of Ghanaian SMEs: Mediating role of access to capital and firm reputation. *Journal of Global Responsibility, 8*(1), 47–62.
3. Allenby, B., Yasui, I., Lehni, M., Züst, R., & Hunkeler, D., (1998). Ecometrics' stakeholder subjectivity: Values, issues, and effects. *Environmental Quality Management, 8*(1), 11–18.
4. Alshathry, S., Clarke, M., & Goodman, S., (2017). The role of employer brand equity in employee attraction and retention: A unified framework. *International Journal of Organizational Analysis, 25*(3), 413–431.
5. Banerjee, S., Dasgupta, S., & Kim, Y., (2008). Buyer–supplier relationships and the stakeholder theory of capital structure. *The Journal of Finance, 63*(5), 2507–2552.
6. Barsky, N. P., Hussein, M. E., & Jablonsky, S. F., (1999). Shareholder and stakeholder value in corporate downsizing–the case of United technologies corporation. *Accounting, Auditing & Accountability Journal, 1*, 1–05.
7. Bergevin, P. M., (1993). The stockholders' equity section of a Japanese company: The Minolta camera company case. *Journal of Accounting Education, 11*(2), 301–311.
8. Borisovna, I. T., (2020). Shareholders' equity consists of share capital and retained earnings. The share capital is the value of funds that shareholders have invested in the company. When a company is first formed, shareholders will typically put in cash. *Balkan Scientific Review*, 81.
9. Boukis, A., & Christodoulides, G., (2020). Investigating key antecedents and outcomes of employee-based brand equity. *European Management Review, 17*(1), 41–55.
10. Brandon, P. R., (1998). Stakeholder participation for the purpose of helping ensure evaluation validity: Bridging the gap between collaborative and non-collaborative evaluations. *American Journal of Evaluation, 19*(3), 325–337.
11. Bridges, S., Marcum, W., & Harrison, J. K., (2003). The relation between employee perceptions of stakeholder balance and corporate financial performance. *SAM Advanced Management Journal, 68*(2), 50.
12. Butler, P., Pinkerton, K., & Reinstein, D., (2006). The guideline publicly traded company method and the market value of "invested" capital: Should market value

of "stakeholder" capital be the appropriate reference? *Business Valuation Review, 25*(2), 78–82.

13. Carlon, D. M., & Downs, A., (2014). Stakeholder valuing: A process for identifying the interrelationships between firm and stakeholder attributes. *Administrative Sciences, 4*(2), 137–154.
14. Chandra, V., (2023). *The Effect of Income Statement on Retained Earnings and Statement of Stockholders' Equity.* Available at SSRN 4339250.
15. Chatzipanagiotou, K., Veloutsou, C., & Christodoulides, G., (2016). Decoding the complexity of the consumer-based brand equity process. *Journal of Business Research, 69*(11), 5479–5486.
16. Cho, S. I., (2017). Treasury stock sales and management rights protection: Conflicts of interest between an owner-manager and small shareholders. *KDI Journal of Economic Policy, 39*(3), 63–98.
17. Churchill, Jr. G. A., & Surprenant, C., (1982). An investigation into the determinants of customer satisfaction. *Journal of Marketing Research, 19*(4), 491–504.
18. Cornforth, C., & Brown, W. A., (2013). Community-engagement Governance™: Engaging stakeholders for community impact Judy Freiwirth. In: *Nonprofit Governance* (pp. 199–225). Routledge.
19. Deng, X., Kang, J. K., & Low, B. S., (2013). Corporate social responsibility and stakeholder value maximization: Evidence from mergers. *Journal of Financial Economics, 110*(1), 87–109.
20. Edmans, A., (2011). Does the stock market fully value intangibles? Employee satisfaction and equity prices. *Journal of Financial Economics, 101*(3), 621–640.
21. Federer, L. M., Belter, C. W., Joubert, D. J., Livinski, A., Lu, Y. L., Snyders, L. N., & Thompson, H., (2018). Data sharing in PloS one: An analysis of data availability statements. *PloS One, 13*(5), e0194768.
22. Fitzpatrick, J. E., & Mowers, M., (1997). Success and the four block schedule: Stakeholders buy in! *NASSP Bulletin, 81*(588), 51–56.
23. Flammer, C., (2013). Corporate social responsibility and shareholder reaction: The environmental awareness of investors. *Academy of Management Journal, 56*(3), 758–781.
24. Fulton, M., Kahn, B., & Sharples, C., (2012). *Sustainable Investing: Establishing Long-Term Value and Performance.* Available at SSRN 2222740.
25. Fung, B., (2014). The demand and need for transparency and disclosure in corporate governance. *Universal Journal of Management, 2*(2), 72–80.
26. Gray, E. R., & Balmer, J. M., (1998). Managing corporate image and corporate reputation. *Long Range Planning, 31*(5), 695–702.
27. Hatherly, D., Mitchell, R. K., Mitchell, J. R., & Lee, J. H., (2020). Reimagining profits and stakeholder capital to address tensions among stakeholders. *Business & Society, 59*(2), 322–350.

28. Jimenez, R. M., & Okhremtchouk, I. S., (2021). Introduction: Education stakeholders striving for equity and culturally relevant approaches. *Taboo, 20*(2), 4–8.

29. Jo, H., & Kim, Y., (2008). Ethics and disclosure: A study of the financial performance of firms in the seasoned equity offerings market. *Journal of Business Ethics, 80*, 855–878.

30. Jones, R., (2005). Finding sources of brand value: Developing a stakeholder model of brand equity. *Journal of Brand Management, 13*, 10–32.

31. Kannan, D., (2018). Role of multiple stakeholders and the critical success factor theory for the sustainable supplier selection process. *International Journal of Production Economics, 195*, 391–418.

32. Karpoff, J. M., Malatesta, P. H., & Walkling, R. A., (1996). Corporate governance and shareholder initiatives: Empirical evidence. *Journal of Financial Economics, 42*(3), 365–395.

33. Kemp, D., & Owen, J. R., (2013). Community relations and mining: Core to business but not "core business." *Resources Policy, 38*(4), 523–531.

34. King, C., Grace, D., & Funk, D. C., (2012). Employee brand equity: Scale development and validation. *Journal of Brand Management, 19*, 268–288.

35. Lau, R. S. M., & May, B. E., (1998). A win-win paradigm for quality of work life and business performance. *Human Resource Development Quarterly, 9*(3), 211–226.

36. Lawer, C., & Knox, S., (2006). Customer advocacy and brand development. *Journal of Product & Brand Management, 15*(2), 121–129.

37. Lindwall, C., Ellmo, A., Rehme, J., & Kowalkowski, C., (2010). Increasing customer attractiveness through upstream brand equity. In: *The International IPSERA Workshop on CUSTOMER Attractiveness, Supplier Satisfaction and Customer Value* (pp. 1–20). IPSERA.

38. Lionis, C., Papadakaki, M., Saridaki, A., Dowrick, C., O'Donnell, C. A., Mair, F. S., & MacFarlane, A., (2016). Engaging migrants and other stakeholders to improve communication in cross-cultural consultation in primary care: A theoretically informed participatory study. *BMJ Open, 6*(7), e010822.

39. Luo, X., Wieseke, J., & Homburg, C., (2012). Incentivizing CEOs to build customer- and employee-firm relations for higher customer satisfaction and firm value. *Journal of the Academy of Marketing Science, 40*, 745–758.

40. McCandless, S., (2018). Improving community relations: How police strategies to improve accountability for social equity affect citizen perceptions. *Public Integrity, 20*(4), 370–385.

41. Mietzner, M., & Schweizer, D., (2014). Hedge funds versus private equity funds as shareholder activists in Germany—Differences in value creation. *Journal of Economics and Finance, 38*, 181–208.

42. Mirkovski, K., Yin, C., Liu, L., & Yang, J., (2019). Exploring the contingent effect of community equity on users' intention to share information. *Information Systems Frontiers, 21*, 845–860.
43. Mirvis, P., (2012). Employee engagement and CSR: Transactional, relational, and developmental approaches. *California Management Review, 54*(4), 93–117.
44. Mittal, V., Han, K., & Westbrook, R. A., (2018). Customer engagement and employee engagement: A research review and agenda. *Customer Engagement Marketing,* 173–201.
45. Mokhtaruddin, S. A., Che, W. C. A., Alam, S. S., & Khalid, N. R., (2018). The influence of relationship marketing orientation (RMO) on customer retention in travel agency services. *International Journal of Academic Research in Business and Social Sciences, 8*(2), 713–724.
46. Munilla, L., & Miles, M., (2005). The corporate social responsibility continuum as a component of stakeholder theory. *Business and Society Review, 110*(4), 371–387.
47. Naidoo, C., & Abratt, R., (2018). Brands that do good: Insight into social brand equity. *Journal of Brand Management, 25*, 3–13.
48. Ogden, S., & Watson, R., (1999). Corporate performance and stakeholder management: Balancing shareholder and customer interests in the UK privatized water industry. *Academy of Management Journal, 42*(5), 526–538.
49. Orts, E. W., & Strudler, A., (2002). The ethical and environmental limits of stakeholder theory. *Business Ethics Quarterly,* 215–233.
50. Palladino, L., (2022). The potential benefits of employee equity funds in the United States. *Journal of Participation and Employee Ownership, 5*(1), 56–78.
51. Park, Y. W., Voss, G. B., & Voss, Z. G., (2022). Advancing customer diversity, equity, and inclusion: Measurement, stakeholder influence, and the role of marketing. *Journal of the Academy of Marketing Science*, 1–24.
52. Persson, A., & Ryals, L., (2010). Customer assets and customer equity: Management and measurement issues. *Marketing Theory, 10*(4), 417–436.
53. Rachbini, W., Hatta, I. H., & Evi, T., (2019). Determinants of trust and customer loyalty on C2C e-marketplace in Indonesia. *International Journal of Civil Engineering and Technology, 10*(3).
54. Read, S., & Sarasvathy, S. D., (2005). Knowing what to do and doing what you know: Effectuation as a form of entrepreneurial expertise. *The Journal of Private Equity, 9*(1), 45–62.
55. Rendon, C., Osman, K. K., & Faust, K. M., (2021). Path towards community resilience: Examining stakeholders' coordination at the intersection of the built, natural, and social systems. *Sustainable Cities and Society, 68*, 102774.
56. Richardson, A. J., & Welker, M., (2001). Social disclosure, financial disclosure and the cost of equity capital. *Accounting, Organizations and Society, 26*(7, 8), 597–616.

57. Sarkki, S., Heikkinen, H. I., & Löf, A., (2021). Reindeer herders as stakeholders or rights-holders? Introducing a social equity-based conceptualization relevant for indigenous and local communities. *Nordic Perspectives on the Responsible Development of the Arctic: Pathways to Action*, 271–292.
58. Sawhney, M., & Zabin, J., (2002). Managing and measuring relational equity in the network economy. *Journal of the Academy of Marketing Science, 30*(4), 313–332.
59. Scherrer, P. S., (2003). Management turnarounds: Diagnosing business ailments. *Corporate Governance: The International Journal of Business in Society, 1*, 1–25.
60. Scull, S., & Cuthill, M., (2010). Engaged outreach: Using community engagement to facilitate access to higher education for people from low socio-economic backgrounds. *Higher Education Research & Development, 29*(1), 59–74.
61. Selnes, F., & Gønhaug, K., (2000). Effects of supplier reliability and benevolence in business marketing. *Journal of Business Research, 49*(3), 259–271.
62. Simpson, K., (2001). Strategic planning and community involvement as contributors to sustainable tourism development. *Current Issues in Tourism, 4*(1), 3–41.
63. Srivastava, S., & Singh, N., (2021). Do corporate social responsibility (CSR) initiatives boost customer retention in the hotel industry? A moderation-mediation approach. *Journal of Hospitality Marketing & Management, 30*(4), 459–485.
64. Stahl, H. K., Matzler, K., & Hinterhuber, H. H., (2003). Linking customer lifetime value with shareholder value. *Industrial Marketing Management, 32*(4), 267–279.
65. Suchy, K., (2010). A lack of standardization: The basis for the ethical issues surrounding quality and performance reports. *Journal of Healthcare Management, 55*(4), 241–251.
66. Suh, T., & Houston, M. B., (2010). Distinguishing supplier reputation from trust in buyer–supplier relationships. *Industrial Marketing Management, 39*(5), 744–751.
67. Sulimany, H. G., Ramakrishnan, S., Chaudhry, A., & Bazhair, A. H., (2021). Impact of corporate governance and financial sustainability on shareholder value. *Studies of Applied Economics, 39*(4).
68. Sun, Y., & Xia, J., (2022). Stakeholder interest to mitigate the agency problem in enterprise innovation and the moderating effect of ownership concentration and financial constraints. *Creativity and Innovation Management, 31*(4), 599–613.
69. Sundaramurthy, C., & Lyon, D. W., (1998). Shareholder governance proposals and conflict of interests between inside and outside shareholders. *Journal of Managerial Issues,* 30–44.
70. Teng, M., & Hachiya, T., (2010). *The Pump-Priming Effect of Regulatory Reform on Stock Repurchases: Evidence from Lifting the Ban on Treasury Stocks in Japan* (Vol. 1, pp. 1–20). Graduate School of Commerce and Management Center for Japanese Business Studies, Hitotsubashi University.
71. Torres, A., Bijmolt, T. H., Tribó, J. A., & Verhoef, P., (2012). Generating global brand equity through corporate social responsibility to key stakeholders. *International Journal of Research in Marketing, 29*(1), 13–24.

72. Turlington, J., Fafatas, S., & Oliver, E. G., (2019). Is it US GAAP or IFRS? Understanding how R&D costs affect ratio analysis. *Business Horizons, 62*(4), 427–436.
73. Turnbull, S., (1997). Stakeholder cooperation. *Journal of Cooperative Studies, 29*(3), 18–52.
74. Turnbull, S., (2002). The competitive advantages of stakeholder mutuals. In: *The New Mutualism in Public Policy* (pp. 171–201). Routledge.
75. Waddock, S., (2000). The multiple bottom lines of corporate citizenship: Social investing, reputation, and responsibility audits. *Business and Society Review, 105*(3), 323–345.
76. Walker, R. M., Lee, M. J., James, O., & Ho, S. M., (2018). Analyzing the complexity of performance information use: Experiments with stakeholders to disaggregate dimensions of performance, data sources, and data types. *Public Administration Review, 78*(6), 852–863.
77. Wallace, M., Lings, I., Cameron, R., & Sheldon, N., (2014). Attracting and retaining staff: The role of branding and industry image. *Workforce Development: Perspectives and Issues*, 19–36.
78. Wallerstein, N., & Duran, B., (2010). Community-based participatory research contributions to intervention research: The intersection of science and practice to improve health equity. *American Journal of Public Health, 100*(S1), S40–S46.
79. Walsh, C., & Sulkowski, A. J., (2010). A greener company makes for happier employees more so than does a more valuable one: A regression analysis of employee satisfaction, perceived environmental performance and firm financial value. *Interdisciplinary Environmental Review, 11*(4), 274–282.
80. Walton, S. V., & Marucheck, A. S., (1997). The relationship between EDI and supplier reliability. *International Journal of Purchasing and Materials Management, 33*(2), 30–35.
81. Wang, H. M., Yu, T. H. K., & Hsiao, C. Y., (2021). The causal effect of corporate social responsibility and corporate reputation on brand equity: A fuzzy-set qualitative comparative analysis. *Journal of Promotion Management, 27*(5), 630–641.
82. Winit, W., & Kantabutra, S., (2022). Enhancing the prospect of corporate sustainability via brand equity: A stakeholder model. *Sustainability, 14*(9), 4998.
83. Yemi, A. E., & Seriki, A. I., (2018). Retained earnings and firms' market value: Nigeria experience. *The Business & Management Review, 9*(3), 482–496.
84. Zhang, M., Ma, L., Su, J., & Zhang, W., (2014). Do suppliers applaud corporate social performance? *Journal of Business Ethics, 121*, 543–557.

CHAPTER 7

FINANCIAL RATIO ANALYSIS AND PERFORMANCE EVALUATION

UNIT INTRODUCTION

Ratio Analysis is a quantitative technique that provides valuable insights into a company's financial health, including its operational efficiency, profitability, and liquidity. This is achieved by analyzing its accounting reports. It is a crucial element of fundamental equity analysis (Halkos & Tzeremes, 2012).

A company can employ comparative data to track its performance over time and guess future performance. Moreover, this data compares a company's financial footing with the market's averages and other companies within the same sector (Anthony et al., 2019).

Ratio analysis is easy to use as all figures required to compute the ratios are available on a firm's accounting statements. Ratios are used as comparison points between firms to analyze market commodities (Schönbohm, 2013). Additionally, they provide insight into how a company performs compared to its historical figures. Management can modify its policy to make its stock more tempting. Therefore, a sound knowledge of the variables that operate the ratios is necessary. Ratios are generally used with other ratios rather than in isolation (Islam, 2014).

Although evaluating a company's financial staging is crucial to assessing its operations' effectiveness, performance evaluation involves analyzing and measuring various business areas, including departments, employees, products, and services. Performance evaluation enables businesses to identify areas that need improvement, recognize achievements, and make informed decisions based on data and analysis. This chapter examines various performance evaluation methods and their importance in helping businesses achieve their goals and objectives (Shaverdi et al., 2014).

Learning Objectives

At the end of this chapter, the reader will be able to understand the following:

1. The concept of ratio analysis
2. The importance of performance evaluation in the company
3. The classifications of ratio analysis
4. The methods to implement ratio analysis
5. The essential uses and users of financial ratio
6. The important types of performance evaluation
7. Advantages of performance evaluation

Key Terms

1. 360-Degree Evaluation
2. Coverage Ratio
3. Efficiency Ratio
4. Liquidity Ratios
5. Profitability Ratio
6. Ration Analysis
7. Solvency Ratio

7.1. PURPOSE AND SIGNIFICANCE OF FINANCIAL RATIO ANALYSIS

Financial ratio analysis is a crucial technique to assess a company's financial performance and condition, including investors, creditors, and management. Financial ratio analysis is used to understand a company's strengths and weaknesses and make decisions regarding the company's prospects for the future (Edmister, 1972).

Financial ratio analysis is critical because it lets people comprehend the connections between various financial measures, including a firm's income, expenses, assets, liabilities, and equity. By evaluating these measurements, anyone can better comprehend a company's financial health, including its liquidity, solvency, profitability, and efficiency (Salmi & Martikainen, 1994).

For instance, a company's ability to pay its short-term debts is determined by its liquidity ratios. In contrast, its capacity to fulfill its long-term obligations is determined by its solvency ratios. Efficiency ratios assess how well a company manages its resources and controls its costs, whereas profitability ratios assess its capacity to make a profit. Financial ratio analysis is useful for determining whether to invest in a company, lend it money, or manage it in general. It enables people to objectively evaluate a company's position and financial performance and compare other businesses and industries (Altman, 1968).

Remember

Stakeholders use ratio analysis to determine a company's economic performance by examining both past and present accounting reports.

7.2. TYPES OF RATIO ANALYSIS

The financial ratios can be categorized into the given five divisions (Figure 7.1):

Figure 7.1. Image of types of financial ratio.

Source: Shraddha Sureka, Creative Commons License.

7.2.1. Liquidity Ratios

Liquidity ratios evaluate a firm's ability to meet its short-term goals using its quick or current assets. Examples of liquidity ratios include quick and working capital (Madushanka & Jathurika, 2018).

7.2.1.1. Current Ratio

Before putting money into a firm, it is vital to measure its liquidity. Liquidity is the proficiency with which a company can transform commodities into cash to meet urgent needs. (Cote & Latham, 1999).

KEYWORD

Working capital ratio is calculated simply by dividing total current assets by total current liabilities

The working capital/current ratio is the proportion of a company's assets exceeding its current liabilities. This measure stipulates a business's potential to utilize its assets to satisfy its current financial obligations. The working capital ratio compares a company's existing assets to its current liabilities to determine liquidity. The working capital ratio can be computed by dividing current assets by liabilities (Nazir & Afza, 2009).

Current Ratio = Current Assets / Current Liabilities

Let's say an Enterprise has $8 million in current assets and $4 million in current liabilities. $8 million/$ 4 million equals a working capital ratio of 2. A high working capital ratio is a sign of good short-term liquidity. For example, if two indistinguishable businesses have a ratio of 2, but one has a larger amount of cash among its current assets, it will be able to meet its obligations more swiftly than the other business (Afza & Nazir, 2007). Conversely, a ratio of one suggests that a business may be experiencing liquidity challenges and could struggle to meet its short-term obligations. However, this situation may be temporary and could improve shortly (Fazzari & Petersen, 1993). Overall, a working capital ratio of two or higher suggests that a business has sound liquidity and should be able to cover its short-term debts. It may signify a business with excess short-term assets, some of which would be better allocated to business expansion (Pass & Pike, 1984).

Determining a firm's potential to meet its short-term obligations can be challenging to categorize the broad array of liabilities and assets on a balance sheet (Sagan, 1955).

7.2.1.2. Quick Ratio

The quick ratio (acid test) is another metric for liquidity. It shows a firm's potential to pay short-term obligations with assets that can be conveniently transformed into cash (Warrad, 2014).

After subtracting inventories and installments, the quick ratio is computed by dividing current liabilities by current assets. The algorithm eliminates it as it could take time to sell goods and transform them into liquid assets (Kumoro et al., 2020).

The XYZ Company has $4 million in current obligations, $2 million in inventory, and $8 million in current assets. It also has $2 million in prepaid expenses. With $8 million minus $2 million divided by $4 million, the quick ratio is 1.5. It shows that the firm has sufficient cash to manage its expenses and continue operating (Tumanggor, 2020).

If the quick ratio is less than 1, there may be insufficient liquid assets to cover current liabilities. The business might need to raise money or take other measures (Wijaya & Sedana, 2020) (Figure 7.2).

Liquidity Ratios

$$\text{Current Ratio} = \frac{\text{Current assets}}{\text{Current liabilities}}$$

$$\text{Quick Ratio} = \frac{\text{Current assets} - \text{Inventory}}{\text{Current liabilities}}$$

Figure 7.2. Picture of the formula of current ratio and quick ratio.

Source: Michael Brown, Creative Commons License.

7.2.2. Leverage Ratio

Leverage ratios, also called financial solvency ratios, determine a business's ability to remain financially stable over the long run by evaluating its debt levels about its assets, earnings, and equity. These ratios assess the probability of a business being able to settle its long-term debt and the interest on that debt. Examples of solvency ratios are debt-assets, interest coverage, and debt-equity ratios (Ibendahl, 2016) (Figure 7.3).

Figure 7.3. Illustration of types of leverage ratio.

Source: Milan Jha, Creative Commons License.

7.2.2.1. Debt-to-Equity Ratio

What if the primary recipient of investment has uncontrolled debt? This could lead to higher fixed costs, lower earnings for dividends, and risk for shareholders (Sari et al., 2021).

The D/E ratio is a monetary metric determining the proportion of borrowed funds a firm uses to finance its operations. It can also show whether the shareholder equity is enough to cover all the company's debts. Investors rely on this ratio to compare the level of leverage used by different companies within the same market. This analysis can assist them in identifying potentially lower-risk investments. (Nuryani & Sunarsi, 2020).

Debt-Equity Ratio = Total Liabilities / Total Shareholders' Equity

Divide the total liabilities by the shareholders' equity to get the debt-to-equity ratio. Suppose Company XYZ has $13.3 million in shareholders' equity and loans totaling $3.1 million. That results in a sensible ratio of 0.23, which is appropriate in most circumstances.

Nonetheless, the ratio must be analyzed in light of market standards and the company's unique criteria (Heikal et al., 2014) (Figure 7.4).

Figure 7.4. Pictorial representation of debt to equity ratio.

Source: investor one, Creative Commons License.

7.2.2.2. Debt-Assets Ratio

A debt-to-asset ratio calculates what portion of a company's assets are funded by debt. This ratio is computed by subtracting the total debt from the business's assets (Feder, 1980).

Total debt / total assets = debt-assets ratios.

A higher debt-to-assets ratio means that a significant percentage of a company's assets are funded by debt, which can be problematic if it struggles to pay its long-term obligations. A lower debt-to-assets ratio indicates that a lesser percentage of a firm's assets are funded by debt, meaning financial stability (Fosberg, 2008).

7.2.2.3. Interest Coverage Ratio

The interest coverage ratio is a financial statistic gauges a firm's capacity to pay interest on its debt. Divided by interest expense, a firm's earnings determine this ratio before interest and taxes (EBIT).

EBIT / Interest expenditure = interest coverage ratio

A firm's ability to cover its interest costs increases with a better interest coverage ratio, which signifies financial health. Yet, a lower interest coverage ratio shows that a business may struggle to meet its interest costs, which can indicate financial danger (Setiany, 2021).

Did you Know?

A working capital ratio of 2:1 is considered healthy, indicating that a company has twice the amount of current assets compared to its current liabilities.

7.2.3. Profitability Ratios

These statistics show how successfully a business can profit from its operations.

ROE: Return on Equity Return on equity (ROE) determines the coherence with which a business generates profits from its shareholders. For calculating ROE for common stockholders, net income is determined before paying ordinary share dividends and after paying preferred share dividends. The resulting value is divided by total shareholders' equity (Lesakova, 2007).

Let's imagine the net income for XYZ corporation is $1.3 million. Equity held by shareholders totals $8 million. The ROE is then 16.25%. The better a corporation makes money from shareholder equity, the greater its ROE will be (Husain & Sunardi, 2020) (Figure 7.5).

Figure 7.5. Description of return on equity formula.

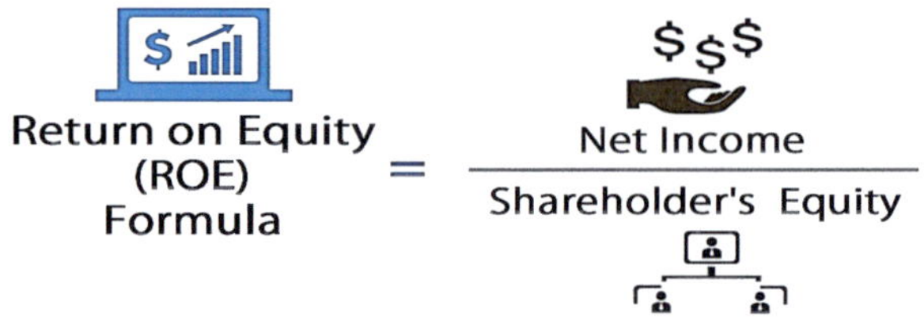

Souce: ENVzag, Creative Commons License.

7.2.4. Efficiency Ratios

Efficiency ratios (activity ratios) evaluate how efficiently a business employs its assets and liabilities to drive sales and optimize profits. Among the crucial efficiency ratios are turnover, inventory, accounts receivable (AR), and total asset turnover (Khumawala et al., 2005).

7.2.4.1. Inventory Turnover Ratio

Inventory turnover explains how effectively a business sells things at a lower cost. The cost of goods sold divided by inventory is the inventory turnover ratio.

A greater ratio suggests that the business can abruptly convert inventory to sales. Low inventory turnover rates indicate the business stocking outmoded products (Sunjoko & Arilyn, 2016) (Figure 7.6).

Figure 7.6. The schematic of formula of inventory turnover formula.

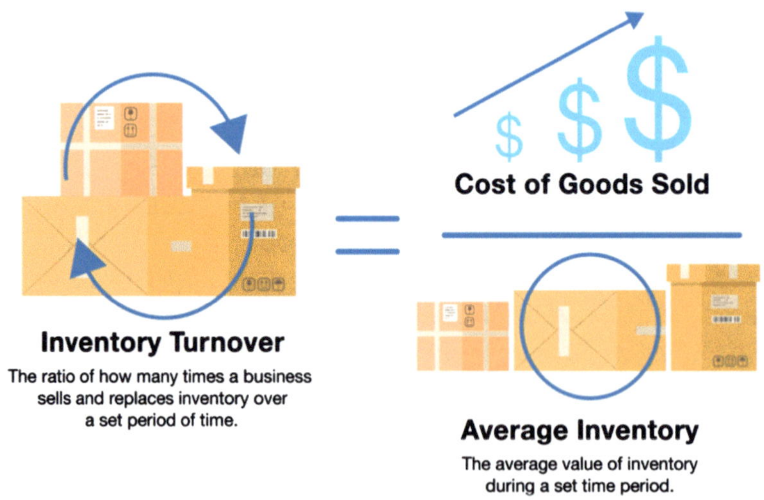

Source: Scott Schulfer, Creative Commons License.

7.2.4.2. Accounts Receivable Turnover Ratio

The potency of a business to recover cash from credit sales made throughout the year is determined by the AR turnover.

Credit Sales / Accounts Receivable = Accounts Receivable Turnover Ratio

When the ratio is higher, collections are higher, and when the balance is lower, cash collections are lower (Manullang et al., 2020).

7.2.4.3. Total Assets Turnover Ratio

This financial ratio shows how rapidly a company's total assets can produce revenue.

Total Assets / Net Sales is the asset turnover ratio.

For instance, a higher asset turnover ratio suggests the equipment is adequate. A lower ratio implies that the equipment is outdated and unable to produce sales rapidly (Irman & Purwati, 2020).

> **KEYWORD**
>
> **Asset turnover** is considered to be a Profitability Ratio, which is a group of financial ratios that measure how efficiently a company uses assets.

7.2.5. Market Prospect Ratios

These ratios are frequently utilized in fundamental analysis. Investors use these measures to forecast earnings and future performance, including the dividend yield ratio, P/E ratio, and earnings per share (EPS) (Mack, 1956).

For example, a stock with a P/E ratio of seven would be undervalued if the average P/E ratio of all the businesses in the S&P 500 index is 20, and the bulk of the companies have a P/E between 15 and 25. One with a P/E ratio of 50 would be regarded as being overvalued. (Sargent, 1998).

7.2.5.1. Dividend Yield Ratio

When financed at the market price, the dividend yield ratio displays the return on investment.

Dividend Yield Ratio (Black & Scholes, 1974) is defined *as Dividend Per Share (DPS) / Share Price.*

7.2.5.2. Price-Earnings Ratio (P/E)

Investors use this ratio to find out the developmental potential of a stock. It shows how much people would spend to get $1 in compensation. It is widely used to assess the potential value of several stocks (Beaver & Morse, 1978).

Current Share price / EPS = Price-Earnings Ratio

If a company's stock price at the close of trade was $46.51 and its EPS for the prior year was an average of $4.90, the P/E ratio would be 9.49 ($46.51/$4.90). Investment costs would amount to $9.49 per dollar of annual returns. Investors had paid over 20 times the EPS for several commodities when they anticipated the company's future earnings expansion would provide a reasonable return on investment (Goodman & Peavy, 1983).

If a corporation never makes or loses money, then the P/E ratio is worthless. The not-appropriate symbol, N/A, will be displayed. When interpreted correctly and used, ratios can enhance your investments' performance (Breen, 1968).

7.2.5.3. Earnings per Share (EPS)

The company's earnings or losses are shared when the goods are bought. A company's profitability is assessed by EPS. Investors employ it to determine a firm's worth (Almeida, 2019) (Figure 7.7).

EPS is calculated as Earnings for the Period (Net Income) / Outstanding Shares.

Figure 7.7. Image of earning per share formula.

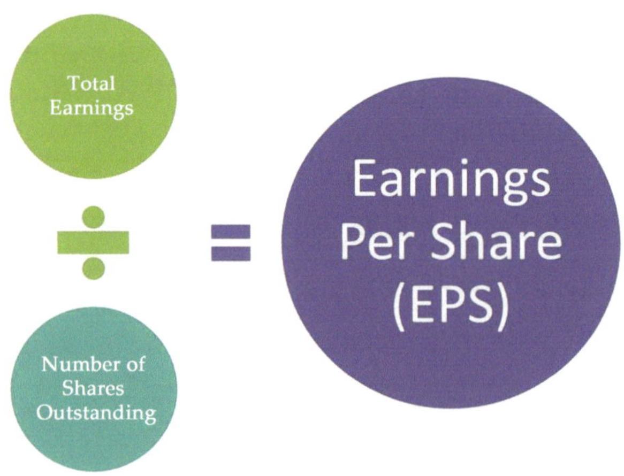

Source: AMarendra Agrwal, Creative Commons License.

7.3. BENEFITS OF FINANCIAL RATIO

There are a few different names for financial ratios, but two common ones are accounting and finance ratios. These ratios are essential for assessing the efficiency with which a company converts its assets and operating expenses into revenue and profits over a given time frame. (Arkan, 2016) (Figure 7.8).

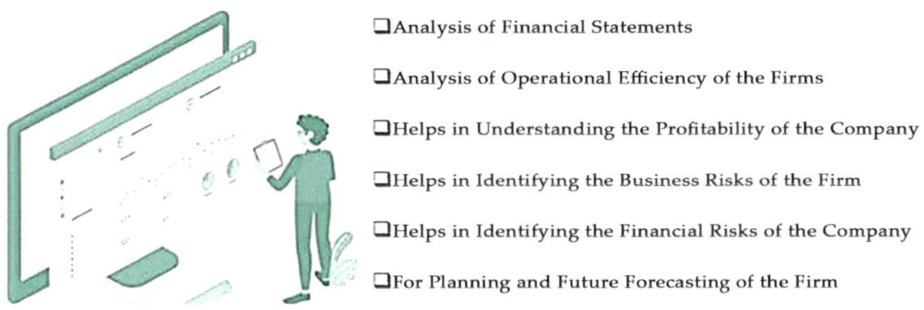

Figure 7.8. Picture of benefits of financial ratio.

Source: Pritha Banerjee, Creative Commons License.

7.3.1. Analyzing Financial Statements

A thorough analysis of the financial statements and data is essential for the stakeholders of a firm. When it pertains to financial outcomes, each stakeholder has specific interests. Long-term dividend payments growth and the firm's ability to generate earnings are of more interest to equity investors. Creditors want the guarantee that they receive prompt payment of their debts (Mahotra & Malhotra, 2008).

7.3.2. Understanding Company Profitability

Profitability ratios also assess a business' profitability. Understanding the company's ability to generate profits is convenient by looking at return on assets and equity. Total net income divided by total assets equals a return on assets. It is the amount of profit a business makes on every dollar spent. Net income divided by shareholder equity is the return on equity. This ratio explains how effectively a business manages investment capital: gross profit and net profit margin. Margins assist in analyzing a company's capacity to transform sales into profits (Howell & Soucy, 1990).

7.3.3. Analyzing Operational Efficiency of Firms

The level of firm efficiency can be analyzed with the help of specific ratios, such as the inventory turnover ratio, fixed asset turnover, and account receivables turnover ratio. These ratios can be contrasted to those of other companies in the same industry to determine which ones are better managed (Chuang et al., 2019).

7.3.4. Evaluating the Liquidity of the Firms

A company's ability to meet its short-term obligations hinges on its liquidity. Here, the obligations that can be fulfilled within a year, loans with a one-year maturity, and the business cycle are being referred—the unpaid wages, creditors, taxes, bills, etc., The quick and current ratios are used to analyze a company's liquidity (Richards & Laughlin, 1980).

KEYWORD

Business risk is the exposure a company or organization has to factor(s) that will lower its profits or lead it to fail.

7.3.5. Identifying the Business Threats

The most significant benefit of ratio analysis is the ability to understand the company's business better. Assessing the leverages enables the company to comprehend the business risk, specifically how its profitability is affected by the deployment of fixed costs and the amount of existing debt (Scott, 2004).

7.3.6. Identifying Company's Financial Risks

The potential to identify financial hazards is another advantage of ratio analysis. For instance, measurements such as the leverage ratio, interest coverage ratio, DSCR ratio, etc., aid the company in inspecting how dependent it is on outside capital and whether it can pay off the debt with its existing assets (Lewent & Kearney, 1990).

7.3.7. Planning and Future Forecasting of the Firm

Managers and analysts can aid external stakeholders, such as investors, make future decisions by spotting trends. They can choose whether to put money into a project (Herbig et al., 1993).

7.4. APPLICATIONS OF RATIO ANALYSIS

The foundation of ratio analysis is the examination of many numbers to find a conclusion. Its intrinsic worth may not warrant much consideration. Ratio analysis compares one set of financial data to another to decide whether a company's financial condition is healthy, poor, improving, or collapsing (Karande & Chakraborty, 2012).

7.4.1. Ratio Analysis over Time

A company's growth over time can be adequately comprehended using ratio analysis. The company is less concerned with its current state and more inclined toward learning about its past performance, the effectiveness of recent changes, and the persistence of potential risks. Ratio analysis is a substantial part of large-scale planning and decision-making processes. (Patrone, 1981).

Consider seasonality and the impact of short-term variations in account balances on month-over-month ratio calculations. Following that, a business inspects how the ratio has modified over time, including if it is improving, how quickly it is changing, and whether it wants the ratio to evolve (Horrigan, 1968).

KEYWORD

Gross profit margin is calculated by subtracting direct expenses or cost of goods sold (COGS) from net sales (gross revenues minus returns, allowances and discounts).

7.4.2. Ratio Analysis across Companies

Suppose that a business has a gross profit margin of 10%. This ratio may become profitable until it finds out that every rival is receiving a gross profit margin of 25%. Using ratio analysis, a company can better understand how its performance compares to similar companies (Borde et al., 1994).

To get the most out of a ratio study, compare companies in the same industry. Likewise, consider how different company sizes and finance arrangements could impact a business's efficiency. Consider the inner workings of enterprises that sell many items (some tech firms sell both products and services, which might have varying impacts on ratio analysis) (Tan et al., 1997).

Simply put, different industries have different expectations for ratios. A technological business that relies more heavily on private investor finance may view a debt-to-equity ratio considered standard for a utility company that can access affordable debt as unsustainable. (Rashid, 2018).

7.4.3. Ratio Analysis Against Benchmarks

TIPS

A corporation should select a particular financial ratio to examine over time and then calculates that ratio at a defined interval.

Businesses may create internal standards for the precision of their ratio analysis calculations. These judgments might aim for operational growth or keep present levels (Joiner & Wormsley, 2005). Lenders and other third parties often impose their standards as well. Financial health is often a requirement of lending institutions. If these conditions are not implemented, the entire loan may be called, or the company may be compelled to pay a higher interest rate to make up for the added loss. Lenders frequently use metrics like the DSCR to evaluate their investments in a company. (Schmidgall & DeFranco, 2004).

7.5. USES OF FINANCIAL RATIO ANALYSIS

There are two primary goals for analyzing financial ratios:

7.5.1. Track Company Performance

For example, if a company's debt-to-asset ratio keeps going up, that could indicate that it has a lot of debt and is at risk of default.

7.5.2. Compare Company Performance

Financial ratios are compared to those of the company's significant competitors to determine whether or not a firm is doing better than the average in its industry. An analyst, for instance, can tell which company is making the best use of its resources by comparing the return on assets of different businesses (Myková & Hájek, 2017).

7.6. USERS OF FINANCIAL RATIO ANALYSIS

Multiple stakeholders, both inside and outside the organization, can benefit from financial ratios:

7.6.1. External Users

7.6.1.1. Investors

Investors use financial ratios to determine if a company's stock or securities are a good investment. Investors measure a company's profitability and growth potential with the help of financial measurements, including return on investment, EPS, and price-to-earnings ratio (Asiri, 2015).

7.6.1.2. Creditors

Creditors use financial ratios like banks and bondholders to gauge a company's solvency. They measure the firm's liquidity and solvency with the help of ratios like debt-to-equity and interest coverage ratios and cash flow-to-debt ratios (Ingram, 1983).

KEYWORD

Price-to-earnings (P/E) ratio is the ratio for valuing a company that measures its current share price relative to its per-share earnings.

7.6.2. Internal Users

7.6.2.1. Management

Financial ratios are used by management to keep tabs on the business's health, pinpoint problem areas, and make educated choices about where to put the firm's limited resources. To determine the company's efficacy and profitability, they calculate metrics including return on assets, inventory turnover, and gross profit margin (Babalola & Abiola, 2013).

7.6.2.2. Employees

Financial ratios are used by staff members to assess the stability and capacity of their employer's business and to assess their financial health. To evaluate the effectiveness of the company's management and determine the possibility of career advancement within the organization, they may also employ ratios like EPS and return on investment (Bae et al., 2005).

7.7. METHOD TO INTERPRET FINANCIAL RATIOS

Analyzing the numbers of various ratios and determining what they signify about a company's financial performance constitutes financial ratio interpretation. Comparing a company's ratios to industry norms or benchmarks and its historical data is typically part of this interpretation process (Delen et al., 2013).

The following are some standard procedures for interpreting financial ratios:

- Determine the ratios that will be examined: Choose the most pertinent to the company and sector being assessed. Liquidity, profitability, efficiency, and solvency are the four primary categories of ratios.
- Gather data: Get the financial information required to construct the ratios.
- Determine the ratios: Use the financial information to determine the pertinent firm ratios.
- Compare to industry benchmarks: To gauge how the company is doing compared to its competitors, compare the ratios to industry benchmarks or guidelines (Blocker et al., 2003).
- Search for trends: To find any recurring patterns in performance over time, compare the company's ratios to its historical statistics. This might indicate whether the organization is growing or losing ground in certain regions.
- Review the ratios: Go over the ratios and note any areas where the employee management might be stronger or weaker. For instance, a low liquidity ratio would suggest a business is in danger of running out of funds. Still, a high profitability ratio might indicate that a company is doing well in making profits.
- Think about restrictions: Recognize the drawbacks of financial ratios because they don't give a complete view of a firm's financial footing. When analyzing financial ratios, other aspects like the state of the market or the company's strategic orientation should also be considered (Ak et al., 2013).

Understanding the ratios' meaning and the circumstances in which they are applied is necessary for adequately comprehending financial ratios. Investors and financial analysts can acquire essential insights into a company's financial performance by carefully examining financial ratios and comparing them to industry benchmarks and historical data (Taffler, 1982).

KEYWORD

Liquidity refers to the efficiency or ease with which an asset or security can be converted into ready cash without affecting its market price.

7.8. LIMITATIONS OF FINANCIAL RATION ANALYSIS

7.8.1. Does Not Consider the Size of the Company

Ratio analysis ignores the company's size, the resulting negotiating leverage, and a large company's economies of scale over a micro-enterprise, which pulls the user's attention away from the company's numbers. Such factors that have an impact on the company's operations are not taken into consideration (Nerviana, 2016).

7.8.2. Does Not Consider Contingent Liability

Ratio analysis also has the disadvantage of not considering any unexpected liabilities. A contingent liability is determined by unforeseen outside factors, such as litigation issues.

Such occurrences will majorly impact the business's finances if they have an unwanted effect. (Bova et al., 2019) (Figure 7.9).

Figure 7.9. Image of contingent liability.

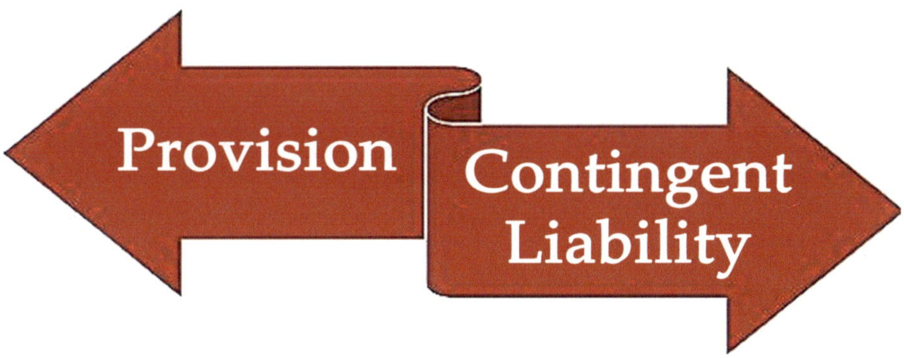

Source: key Differences, Creative Commons License.

7.8.3. Does Not Compliant with Unified Accounting Principles

Ratio analysis does not consider how the company's accounting practices are used to recognize income and expenses. Ratio analysis will bring an unfair comparison of the companies that does not represent an accurate comparison of the businesses (Astami & Tower, 2006).

For example, businesses that report deflation using the Straight Line Method and those that use the Falling Balance Method will have different net profits. Ratio analysis will not represent this in financial statements, much like how businesses not exposed to currency swings will be affected differently (Gietzmann & Trombetta, 2003).

7.8.4. Susceptible to Creative Accounting

Businesses that use novel accounting techniques run the risk of misinterpreting their financial statements. Accounting policies implemented by organizations have a significant impact on ratio analysis. Extraordinary Income may be included in a company's revenue. It may relabel a business cost as a one-time expense, substantially impacting its accounting statements and the resulting ratio analysis. Businesses purposefully exploit the uncertainty inherent in accounting by implementing accounting policies that skew data in the direction chosen by the management (Vasile, 2013). If the rules and laws of a company are changed, it will become impossible to compare the ratios. For instance, switching from the LIFO Inventory technique to the FIFO method may cause a significant variation in the company's profitability and liquidity ratios during inflationary periods, exhibiting the trend analysis exercise useless (Sabau et al., 2020) (Figure 7.10).

Figure 7.10. Illustration of first in first out (FIFO).

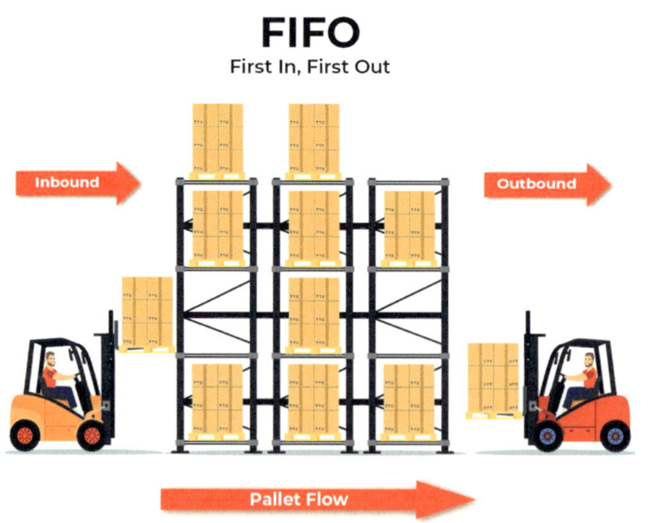

Source: Jake Rheude, Creative Commons License.

7.8.5. Does Not Contrast Distinct industries

The absence of industry-specific standardization is another pitfall. Inspecting businesses that run in several industries using the basic ratio analysis is difficult. Firms in the real estate industry will have a very low return on capital employed (ROCE) since their assets are modified offense, increasing the capital employed; however, there are some industries where assets are not required to be revalued at such a frequency, making it very hard to compare statements based on ratio analysis (Gupta & Huefner, 1972). Ratio Analysis doesn't take into account the particular dynamics of the industry and other linked industries, so a company in the trading business with a current ratio of 3:1 may look excellent in comparison to a company in real estate with a current ratio of 1:1 (Bordeianu & Radu, 2020).

7.8.6. Only Based on Historical

Another disadvantage is that it considers the past will repeat itself based on historical data issued by the company, which may or may not be accurate (Piotroski, 2000).

KEYWORD

Outstanding debt is the overall amount businesses owe their lenders or creditors, including accrued interest.

7.8.7. Does Not Consider the Impact of Inflation

Ratio analysis does not take inflation into account. If a rise in sales is only due to inflation, the company's revenues appear to have climbed over the prior year, but in reality, they would have remained constant (Rousseau & Wachtel, 2001).

7.8.8. Does Not Take Market Circumstances Into Account

Ratio analysis does not consider how market conditions affect a company's efficiency. For example, compared to a recessionary era, a rise in the Company's Outstanding Debt Receivables during an economic expansion cycle when sales increase will be seen negatively (Restianti & Agustina, 2018).

7.8.9. Failure in Capturing the Impact of Seasonality

Seasonality not being considered is another drawback of financial ratio analysis. Seasonality factors influence many organizations, but ratio analysis fails to account for this, causing an incorrect explanation of ratio analysis.

For example, a company that manufactures woolen clothing may experience unexpected inventory levels before the winter due to large-scale manufacturing done ahead of time to meet peak season demand for woolen clothing. If seasonal effects are not considered, which Ratio Analysis does not do, such Inventory levels will exhibit an unlikely rise in Inventory levels compared to other months (Nagar & Rajan, 2001).

7.8.10. Assesses the Company on a Certain Date

Ratio analysis uses the balance sheet figures to represent the company's position on a specific date. Most of these values are depicted on the income statement and historical cost, respectively, which indicate the results for the entire year at the current price. The intended consumers may be quite disparately affected by the analysis of such ratios (Holt et al., 1994).

7.9. EXAMPLE OF RATIO ANALYSIS

Ratio analysis, for better or worse, can predict how a business will do in the future. Companies that consistently turn a profit tend to have solid ratios across the board, and a sudden decrease in any of these metrics could trigger a widespread stock selloff. Here are some simple cases to consider (Thanassoulis et al., 1996).

Investors use the net profit margin, the bottom line, to compare the financial health of organizations in the same sector. You can calculate the company's net profit to its total sales. Instead of poring over financials, this ratio can tell an investor how profitable certain businesses are. Suppose, for instance, ABC, and DEF operate in the same industry and have 50% and 10% profit margins, respectively. Investors can analyze the two businesses and determine that while DEF only turned 10% of its revenues into profits, ABC converted 50% into earnings (Liesz & Maranville, 2008).

Assuming the businesses in the above scenario have P/E ratios of 100 for ABC and 10 for DEF. The average investor comes to the deduction that investors are willing to pay $100 for every $1 that ABC earns in earnings but only $10 for every $1 that DEF generates (Choi et al., 1983).

7.10. PERFORMANCE EVALUATION

The process of gauging and evaluating the effectiveness of a business's activities is referred to as performance evaluation. The company's financial performance is objectively assessed, including its profitability, liquidity, solvency, and effectiveness (Lin et al., 2005) (Figure 7.11).

Figure 7.11. Image of performance evaluation.

Source: Evaluation Forms, Creative Commons License.

7.11. IMPORTANCE OF PERFORMANCE EVALUATION IN BUSINESS

Measuring, assessing, and reporting an organization's performance is part of the crucial business process known as performance evaluation. Organizations can use it to determine their weaknesses and strengths and adjust to achieve their objectives. The following examples show the value of performance review in business:

7.11.1. Aids in Setting Goals

Businesses can use performance evaluation as a platform to define goals that are precise, measurable, doable, realistic, and time-bound (SMART). This aids in coordinating personal and group aims with the company's strategic goals (Lee et al., 1995) (Figure 7.12).

Figure 7.12. Schematic of SMART model.

Source: Toolshero, Creative Commons License.

7.11.2. Improves Communication

Communication between managers and employees is facilitated by performance evaluation, which enhances communication. It allows managers to comment on an employee's performance, strengths, and development opportunities. Also, it will enable staff members to let management know how they find their jobs and any difficulties they may have.

7.11.3. Identify Training and Development Needs

Finding knowledge, skill, and ability gaps in employees is more accessible with performance evaluation. Using this data, training, and development programs are created to assist staff in acquiring the skills required to carry out their tasks more successfully (Indjejikian & Matjka, 2012).

7.11.4. Facilitates Performance Improvement

Employee performance improvement areas are found through performance reviews. This information is then used to offer feedback, training, and mentorship to assist employees in performing better.

7.11.5. Rewards and Recognition

Employee rewards for good performance are based on performance evaluation. This encourages workers to give their best effort (Bassioni et al., 2005).

7.11.6. Enables Performance-Based Decisions

Data from performance reviews can be used to inform choices about hiring, firing, promotions, and other personnel actions. Additionally, it offers information that can be used to make decisions on the budget, strategic planning, and allocation of resources (Tseng et al., 2009).

KEYWORD

Financial health is a term used to describe the state of one's personal monetary affairs.

7.12. USES OF FINANCIAL RATION IN PERFORMANCE EVALUATION

Financial ratios are a crucial instrument for assessing performance. They offer a quantitative method of evaluating an organization's performance and financial health. The following examples illustrate how financial ratios evaluate performance: (Barnes, 1987).

7.12.1. Comparison With Industry Standards

Financial ratios assess how well a firm performs compared to industry norms. This aids in determining areas where the organization is succeeding and those that want development. An organization may not be employing its assets effectively if, for instance, its return on assets ratio is lower than the industry average (Drury, 1981).

7.12.2. Financial Position Assessment

Financial ratios are used to assess a company's financial standing. The debt-to-equity ratio, for instance, is used to determine the company's leverage. If the company has a larger debt-to-equity ratio, it is more indebted and perhaps more financially risky (Pal, 2015).

7.12.3. Financial Trends Recognition

Financial ratios are used to track long-term financial developments. For instance, if a business's return on investment has been steadily dropping over the previous several years, that may be a sign that it is not making enough money to pay for the investment (Hosaka, 2019).

7.12.4. Assessment of Liquidity

Financial ratios are used to evaluate an organization's liquidity. For instance, the current ratio assesses the organization's capacity to settle its current liabilities. A current ratio of less than one shows that the business would struggle to settle its short-term obligations (Emery & Cogger, 1982).

7.12.5. Measurement of Profitability

KEYWORD

Profit margin is a financial ratio that measures the percentage of profit earned by a company in relation to its revenue.

Financial ratios are used to assess an organization's profitability. For instance, the gross profit margin is utilized to determine the profitability of an entire business. A higher gross profit margin shows that the company makes more money from its sales (Finishtya, 2019).

7.12.6. Support Decision-Making

In an organization, financial ratios are employed to support decision-making. Financial ratios, for instance, can be used to gauge the financial impact of a prospective purchase or investment (Kung & Wen, 2007).

7.13. TYPES OF PERFORMANCE EVALUATION

7.13.1. Self-Evaluation

Self-evaluations are a form of performance review in which workers rate their work. A survey, a questionnaire, or a written report can be used for this. Employees are encouraged to evaluate their performance and pinpoint development areas through self-evaluation. Also, it helps workers assume accountability for their growth and gives them a feeling of ownership over their performance.

Employees may overestimate their skills or deficiencies since self-evaluation is subject to subjectivity. Employees may not deliver an appropriate appraisal if they do not fully comprehend their function or responsibilities (Chen et al., 2016).

7.13.2. 360-Degrees Evaluation

A 360-degree review is a thorough evaluation that gathers feedback from numerous sources, such as peers, managers, and employees. The appraisal is based on comments from the employee's coworkers, clients, and suppliers. Compared to other evaluations, this type gives a full view of the employee's performance and aids in identifying strengths and flaws.

Yet, conducting 360-degree reviews can take a lot of time and resources. They may not be completely objective and can also be influenced by interpersonal ties (Brutus et al., 1998) (Figure 7.13).

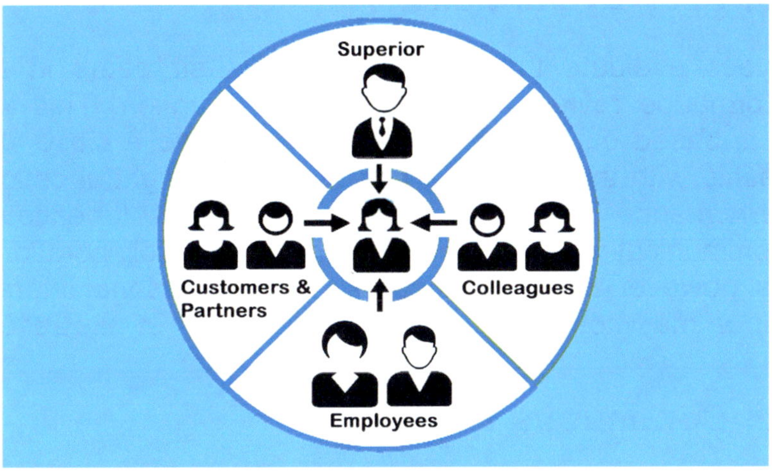

Figure 7.13. Image of 360-degree Evaluation.

Source: T2 Informatik, Creative Commons License.

7.13.3. Manager Assessment

The most typical form of performance evaluation is a management evaluation. It is a supervisor's firsthand evaluation of a worker's performance. Employee performance is reviewed by managers, who also assist in setting performance objectives. This evaluation targets specific tasks and goals and depends on the supervisor's expertise and the employee's experiences.

However, management assessments can be tainted by the boss's biases and may not give a complete picture of the worker's performance (Kangari et al., 1992).

7.13.4. Objective-Based Evaluation

Performance reviews based on pre-established goals and objectives are called objective-based evaluations. Rather than more generic performance metrics, this review style concentrates on the employee's capacity to accomplish specific goals and targets. Objective-based evaluations can help track development and inspire workers to reach their objectives. Nevertheless, objective-based evaluations may not give a whole picture of the employee's performance because they are concentrated on achieving particular goals rather than more general performance indicators (Chen, 2008).

7.13.5. Peer Evaluation

Employees evaluate the performance of their peers in a type of performance review known as peer evaluation. This kind of review is based on input from people who have a close working relationship with the employee and can offer insightful criticism of their performance. Peer reviews are an effective tool for encouraging open communication and fostering teamwork and collaboration. Peer reviews, however, might be influenced by interpersonal interactions and hence may not be entirely unbiased (Ding et al., 2019).

KEYWORD

Staff development is a process of practices and procedures that helps develop the knowledge, competencies, and skills of the people in the organization.

7.13.6. Continuous Evaluation

Instead of being a one-time event, continuous assessment is a constant procedure that evaluates employee performance. This kind of assessment offers more regular feedback and can support the early problem-solving of difficulties. The identification of training needs and the promotion of staff development can both be accomplished through ongoing evaluations.

Continuous reviews, however, can be demanding and costly regarding resources and technology (Sim et al., 2010).

7.14. INTERPRETATION OF PERFORMANCE METRICS

7.14.1. Revenue

A crucial performance metric for any firm is revenue. Generally, a successful company has high revenue, but it's necessary to consider revenue in light of other elements. For instance, if sales are rising but expenses are rising more quickly, this can mean that the company is not profitable. Similarly, if revenue is falling, but costs are coming down more rapidly, the company may be getting more efficient. Analyzing revenue by product line or region can be useful in finding areas for development or expansion (Bader et al., 2007).

7.14.2. Profit Margin

The portion of income left over after all costs have been paid is the profit margin. A large profit margin shows that a company is operating effectively and is in a solid position to compete. On the contrary, a low-profit margin means ineffective cost control, poor pricing tactics, or a challenge differentiating the company from rivals. To find development opportunities, it is crucial to monitor profit margins over time and compared to industry benchmarks (Reddy, 2013).

KEYWORD

Cost control is the process of identifying, eliminating or reducing unnecessary business expenses in order to increase profits.

7.14.3. Customer Contentment

Customers' levels of fulfillment with a good or service are measured by customer satisfaction. For customer retention and word-of-mouth marketing, increased customer happiness is crucial. Businesses can find improvement areas and gauge changes' effects by tracking customer satisfaction via surveys, social media, or other feedback channels. Also, measuring customer satisfaction by clientele segment might assist in locating possibilities to enhance services for particular clientele (Lee & Hwan, 2005).

7.14.4. Employee Turnover

The frequency of employee departures from a company is measured by staff turnover. Businesses may incur hiring, training, and lost productivity costs due to high turnover. Conversely, a low turnover rate shows that staff members are motivated and dedicated to the company. Identifying problem areas and directing initiatives for increasing employee retention can be done by analyzing turnover by department or job function (Awwad & Heyari, 2022).

7.14.5. Website Traffic

A website's traffic is a gauge of how many people visit it. High website traffic is typically a sign of a successful company, but comparing traffic to other variables like conversion rates is vital. For instance, if a website receives a lot of traffic but few conversions, this may mean that the website has to be enhanced for improved user experience (Culotta et al., 2015).

7.14.6. Sales Growth

The pace of growth or decline in sales is measured by sales growth. Strong sales growth might indicate a thriving business, but it's necessary to consider other elements like profit margins, client retention, and competition. A corporation may compromise profitability for expansion, for instance, if sales growth is rapid but profit margins are poor. In contrast, if profit margins are strong but sales growth is slow, the company may prioritize sustaining profitability over growth (Deitiana, 2015).

KEYWORD

Sales growth is a metric that measures the ability of your sales team to increase revenue over a fixed period of time.

7.15. PERFORMANCE EVALUATION STEPS TO IMPROVE BUSINESS

7.15.1. Establish Specific, Measurable Objectives

This is a crucial initial step as it lays the groundwork for the whole performance review process. Set clear and quantifiable goals to guarantee that everyone knows what they are aiming for and can track their progress. The objectives must be clear, pertinent, and doable within a predetermined time frame. These objectives should be defined at all organizational levels and in line with the organization's overarching mission and vision (Galar et al., 2012).

7.15.2. Collect Relevant Data

It's crucial to get pertinent data while assessing performance. A range of sources, including financial records, customer reviews, staff surveys, and website analytics, can be used to collect data. Ensuring the data gathered is trustworthy, correct, and pertinent to the assessed objectives is critical. Collecting data from many sources is crucial since diverse data can help provide a holistic view of the organization's performance (Hashemian et al., 2012).

7.15.3. Analyze the Data

After the data has been gathered, it is crucial to examine it thoroughly. Discovering areas of weakness and strengths and chances for progress; entails recognizing patterns in the data. To collect a variety of viewpoints and insights, it is crucial to involve all stakeholders in the analysis process. This enhances the evaluation's thoroughness and paints a more accurate image of the company's performance (Halkos & Salamouris, 2004).

KEYWORD

Data analysis is the process of inspecting, cleansing, transforming, and modeling data with the goal of discovering useful information, informing conclusions, and supporting decision-making.

7.15.4. Develop an Action Plan

After data analysis, it is vital to create an action plan to target areas for improvement. The action plan must have precise deadlines and be explicit, attainable, and measurable. All parties involved should be included, with each person having a specific function and duty. The data analysis should serve as the foundation for the action plan, which should focus on the areas that need improvement. Given the resources available to the company, it's critical to make sure the program is feasible and realistic (Kim & Im, 2017).

7.15.5. Implement the Action Plan

Once the action plan has been created, it must be implemented. It should be closely watched to ensure successful implementation produces the anticipated objectives. As the implementation process moves forward, changes to the plan can be required. All parties involved in the execution should know their roles and responsibilities in attaining the action plan's objectives (Grozdanovska et al., 2017).

7.15.6. Evaluate the Results

To measure the action plan's effectiveness, assessing the outcomes is crucial. This assessment should concentrate on the degree to which the strategy produced the anticipated results and point out any areas that could use improvement. The evaluation's findings can be used for future performance assessments and enhancements. To ensure the company is moving closer to its objectives, it is crucial to continuously assess the action plan and make adjustments as necessary (Jeovita, 2015).

7.16. ADVANTAGES OF PERFORMANCE EVALUATION

Organizations can gain from performance reviews in several ways, including:

7.16.1. Improving Employee Performance

Employees can better grasp their performance objectives and work to enhance their abilities and performance by understanding their strengths and areas for improvement due to performance reviews (McAfee & Champagne, 1993).

7.16.2. Aligning Employee and Organizational Goals

Performance reviews can help guarantee that workers pursue the same objectives as the business, ensuring that their efforts align with its vision and goals (Paarlberg & Perry, 2007).

7.16.3. Facilitating Communication and Feedback

Managers and employees have an organized forum to evaluate performance, offer criticism, and pinpoint areas for improvement during performance assessments (Roter et al., 2004).

7.16.4. Identifying Training and Development Needs

Performance reviews can assist in uncovering employees' skill and knowledge gaps, which training and development programs can fill (Tannenbaum & Yukl, 1992).

7.16.5. Supporting Decision Making

Performance reviews can offer insightful information to help with decisions regarding pay, promotions, and terminations (Cinelli, 2017).

7.16.6. Driving Organizational Change

Setting targets and objectives for the future can be done using performance evaluations, which can also be used to focus on areas where the organization needs to alter or improve.

In general, performance evaluation is a crucial tool for firms to use to guarantee that their staff members meet performance standards and contribute to the company's goals and objectives.

ACTIVITY 7.1.

A company has been in business for several years, and the management team is considering expanding into a new market. They have done some initial research and believe that the new market has significant growth potential. However, they are concerned about whether the company's financial health is strong enough to support the expansion.

What financial ratios should the management team analyze to assess the company's financial health? How should they use this information to make an informed decision about whether to move forward with the expansion plan? Additionally, how can they use performance evaluation methods to ensure that the company is prepared to succeed in the new market?

7.17. SUMMARY

The chapter discusses using ratio analysis as a quantitative technique to gain insights into a company's financial health, operational efficiency, profitability, and liquidity. Stakeholders can use ratio analysis to determine a company's economic performance by examining its past and present accounting reports. The chapter highlights that ratios are useful as comparison points between firms to analyze market commodities and provide insights into how a company performs compared to its historical figures. The chapter also emphasizes the importance of performance evaluation in helping businesses identify areas that need improvement, recognize achievements, and make informed decisions based on data and analysis. It further explains various performance evaluation methods and how they can help businesses achieve their goals and objectives. Overall, the chapter provides a comprehensive overview of how ratio analysis and performance evaluation are essential in assessing a company's financial health and making informed business decisions.

REVIEW QUESTIONS

1. What is financial ratio analysis, and how is it used to assess a company's financial performance?
2. What are the different types of financial ratios, and what information do they provide?
3. How do stakeholders use financial ratio analysis to make informed investment decisions?
4. What are the limitations of financial ratio analysis, and how can they be addressed?
5. How can a company improve its working capital ratio?
6. What is performance evaluation, and why is it essential for businesses?
7. What are some standard performance evaluation methods, and how are they used?
8. How can businesses use performance evaluation to improve their operations and achieve their goals?

MULTIPLE CHOICE QUESTIONS

1. What is the purpose of financial ratio analysis?

a. To determine employee performance
b. To evaluate market trends
c. To assess a company's financial health
d. To identify areas for expansion

2. **What does the working capital ratio measure?**
   a. A company's ability to meet short-term financial obligations
   b. The effectiveness of a company's inventory management
   c. The level of risk associated with a company's investments
   d. The level of profit generated by a company's sales
3. **Which of the following is an example of a liquidity ratio?**
   a. Debt-to-Equity Ratio
   b. Gross Margin Ratio
   c. Current Ratio
   d. Return on Investment Ratio
4. **What does the quick ratio measure?**
   a. A company's ability to pay off its long-term debts
   b. The level of risk associated with a company's investments
   c. A company's ability to meet short-term financial obligations without relying on inventory
   d. The level of profit generated by a company's sales
5. **Which ratio measures the percentage of net income generated from each sales dollar?**
   a. Current Ratio
   b. Gross Margin Ratio
   c. Return on Equity Ratio
   d. Inventory Turnover Ratio
6. **How is the debt-to-equity ratio calculated?**
   a. Total Liabilities / Total Assets
   b. Total Liabilities / Shareholders' Equity
   c. Total Debt / Total Assets
   d. Total Debt / Shareholders' Equity
7. **Which ratio measures a company's ability to generate profit from its assets?**
   a. Return on Investment Ratio
   b. Working Capital Ratio
   c. Gross Margin Ratio
   d. Debt-to-Equity Ratio

Answers to Multiple Choice Questions

1.	(c)	2.	(a)	3.	(c)	4.	(c)	5.	(b)
6.	(b)	7.	(a)	8.	(c)	9.	(d)	10.	(c)

REFERENCES

1. Afza, T., & Nazir, M. S., (2007). Is it better to be aggressive or conservative in managing working capital. *Journal of Quality and Technology Management, 3*(2), 11–21.
2. Ak, B. K., Dechow, P. M., Sun, Y., & Wang, A. Y., (2013). The use of financial ratio models to help investors predict and interpret significant corporate events. *Australian Journal of Management, 38*(3), 553–598.
3. Almeida, H., (2019). Is it time to get rid of earnings-per-share (EPS)? *Review of Corporate Finance Studies, 8*(1), 174–206.
4. Altman, E. I., (1968). Financial ratios, discriminant analysis and the prediction of corporate bankruptcy. *The Journal of Finance, 23*(4), 589–609.
5. Anthony, P., Behnoee, B., Hassanpour, M., & Pamucar, D., (2019). Financial performance evaluation of seven Indian chemical companies. *Decision Making: Applications in Management and Engineering, 2*(2), 81–99.
6. Arkan, T., (2016). The importance of financial ratios in predicting stock price trends: A case study in emerging markets. *Finanse, Rynki Finansowe, Ubezpieczenia*, (79), 13–26.
7. Asiri, B. K., (2015). How investors perceive financial ratios at different growth opportunities and financial leverages. *Journal of Business Studies Quarterly, 6*(3), 1.
8. Astami, E. W., & Tower, G., (2006). Accounting-policy choice and firm characteristics in the Asia Pacific region: An international empirical test of costly contracting theory. *The International Journal of Accounting, 41*(1), 1–21.
9. Awwad, M. S., & Heyari, H. I., (2022). Predicting employee turnover using financial indicators in the pharmaceutical industry. *Industrial and Commercial Training, (ahead-of-print), 1*, 1–15.
10. Babalola, Y. A., & Abiola, F. R., (2013). Financial ratio analysis of firms: A tool for decision making. *International Journal of Management Sciences, 1*(4), 132–137.
11. Bader, M. K. I., Mohamad, S., Ariff, M., & Hassan, T., (2007). Cost revenue, and profit efficiency of conventional versus Islamic banks: Financial ratios approach. *Review of Islamic Economics, 11*(1), 89–106.
12. Bae, M. K., Hanna, S., & Baek, E., (2005). Before and after the economic crisis: Changes in financial ratios of the self-employed households. *Consumer Interests Annual, 51*, 290–295.

13. Barnes, P., (1987). The analysis and use of financial ratios. *Journal of Business Finance dan Accounting, 14*(4), 449.
14. Bassioni, H. A., Price, A. D. F., & Hassan, T. M., (2005). Building a conceptual framework for measuring business performance in construction: An empirical evaluation. *Construction Management and Economics, 23*(5), 495–507.
15. Beaver, W., & Morse, D., (1978). What determines price-earnings ratios? *Financial Analysts Journal, 34*(4), 65–76.
16. Bititci, U. S., Firat, S. U. O., & Garengo, P., (2013). How to compare performances of firms operating in different sectors? *Production Planning & Control, 24*(12), 1032–1049.
17. Black, F., & Scholes, M., (1974). The effects of dividend yield and dividend policy on common stock prices and returns. *Journal of Financial Economics, 1*(1), 1–22.
18. Blocker, A., Ibendahl, G., & Anderson, J., (2003). *Interpreting Farm Financial Ratios, 1*, 1–10.
19. Borde, S. F., Chambliss, K., & Madura, J., (1994). Explaining variation in risk across insurance companies. *Journal of Financial Services Research, 8*, 177–191.
20. Bordeianu, G. D., & Radu, F., (2020). Basic types of financial ratios used to measure a company's performance. *Economy Transdisciplinarity Cognition, 23*(2).
21. Bova, E., Ruiz-Arranz, M., Toscani, F. G., & Ture, H. E., (2019). The impact of contingent liability realizations on public finances. *International Tax and Public Finance, 26*, 381–417.
22. Breen, W., (1968). Low price-earnings ratios and industry relatives. *Financial Analysts Journal, 24*(4), 125–127.
23. Brutus, S., Fleenor, J. W., & London, M., (1998). Does 360-degree feedback work in different industries? A between-industry comparison of the reliability and validity of multi-source performance ratings. *Journal of Management Development, 17*(3), 177–190.
24. Chen, C. C., (2008). A model for customer-focused objective-based performance evaluation of logistics service providers. *Asia Pacific Journal of Marketing and Logistics, 20*(3), 309–322.
25. Chen, C. H. V., Yuan, M. L., Cheng, J. W., & Seifert, R., (2016). Linking transformational leadership and core self-evaluation to job performance: The mediating role of felt accountability. *The North American Journal of Economics and Finance, 35*, 234–246.
26. Choi, F. D., Hino, H., Min, S. K., Nam, S. O., Ujiie, J., & Stonehill, A. I., (1983). Analyzing foreign financial statements: The use and misuse of international ratio analysis. *Journal of International Business Studies*, 113–131.
27. Chuang, H. H. C., Oliva, R., & Heim, G. R., (2019). Examining the link between retailer inventory leanness and operational efficiency: Moderating roles of firm size and demand uncertainty. *Production and Operations Management, 28*(9), 2338–2364.

28. Cinelli, M., (2017). The art of supporting decision-making. *Exchanges: The Interdisciplinary Research Journal, 4*(2), 298–308.
29. Cote, J. M., & Latham, C. K., (1999). The merchandising ratio: A comprehensive measure of working capital strategy. *Issues in Accounting Education, 14*(2), 255–267.
30. Culotta, A., Kumar, N., & Cutler, J., (2015, February). Predicting the demographics of twitter users from website traffic data. In: *Proceedings of the AAAI Conference on Artificial Intelligence* (Vol. 29, No. 1).
31. Deitiana, T., (2015). *Influence Of Financial Ratio and Sales Growth on Dividend and Implication of Stock Price on Manufactured Companies Listed on Indonesian Stock Exchange* (Vol. 1, pp. 1–20). Doctoral dissertation, Faculty of Economics & Business, Padjadjaran University.
32. Delen, D., Kuzey, C., & Uyar, A., (2013). Measuring firm performance using financial ratios: A decision tree approach. *Expert Systems with Applications, 40*(10), 3970–3983.
33. Ding, K., Peng, X., & Wang, Y., (2019). A machine learning-based peer selection method with financial ratios. *Accounting Horizons, 33*(3), 75–87.
34. Dothan, M., (2006). Costs of financial distress and interest coverage ratios. *Journal of Financial Research, 29*(2), 147–162.
35. Drury, J. C., (1981). A study of industry financial ratios. *Management Decision, 19*(1), 24–35.
36. Edmister, R. O., (1972). An empirical test of financial ratio analysis for small business failure prediction. *Journal of Financial and Quantitative Analysis, 7*(2), 1477–1493.
37. Emery, G. W., & Cogger, K. O., (1982). The measurement of liquidity. *Journal of Accounting Research*, 290–303.
38. Fazzari, S. M., & Petersen, B. C., (1993). Working capital and fixed investment: New evidence on financing constraints. *The RAND Journal of Economics,* 328–342.
39. Feder, G., (1980). A note on debt, assets and lending under default risk. *Journal of Financial and Quantitative Analysis, 15*(1), 191–200.
40. Finishtya, F. C., (2019). The role of cash flow of operational, profitability, and financial leverage in predicting financial distress on manufacturing company in Indonesia. *Jurnal Aplikasi Manajemen, 17*(1), 110–117.
41. Fosberg, R. H., (2008). Debt capacity and debt financing. *Journal of Business & Economics Research (JBER)*, *6*(8).
42. Galar, D., Parida, A., Kumar, U., Baglee, D., & Morant, A., (2012, May). The measurement of maintenance function efficiency through financial KPIs. In: *Journal of Physics: Conference Series* (Vol. 364, No. 1, p. 012112). IOP Publishing.
43. Gietzmann, M. B., & Trombetta, M., (2003). Disclosure interactions: Accounting policy choice and voluntary disclosure effects on the cost of raising outside capital. *Accounting and Business Research, 33*(3), 187–205.
44. Goodman, D. A., & Peavy, III. J. W., (1983). Industry relative price-earnings ratios as indicators of investment returns. *Financial Analysts Journal, 39*(4), 60–66.

45. Grozdanovska, V., Bojkovska, K., & Jankulovski, N., (2017). Financial management and financial planning in the organizations. *European Journal of Business and Management, 9*(02).
46. Gupta, M. C., & Huefner, R. J., (1972). A cluster analysis study of financial ratios and industry characteristics. *Journal of Accounting Research*, 77–95.
47. Halkos, G. E., & Salamouris, D. S., (2004). Efficiency measurement of the Greek commercial banks with the use of financial ratios: A data envelopment analysis approach. *Management Accounting Research, 15*(2), 201–224.
48. Halkos, G. E., & Tzeremes, N. G., (2012). Industry performance evaluation with the use of financial ratios: An application of bootstrapped DEA. *Expert Systems with Applications, 39*(5), 5872–5880.
49. Hashemian, M., Knowles, D., Calver, J., Qian, W., Bullock, M. C., Bell, S., & Stanley, K. G., (2012). iEpi: An end to end solution for collecting, conditioning and utilizing epidemiologically relevant data. In: *Proceedings of the 2nd ACM International Workshop on Pervasive Wireless Healthcare* (pp. 3–8).
50. Heikal, M., Khaddafi, M., & Ummah, A., (2014). Influence analysis of return on assets (ROA), return on equity (ROE), net profit margin (NPM), debt to equity ratio (DER), and current ratio (CR), against corporate profit growth in automotive in Indonesia stock exchange. *International Journal of Academic Research in Business and Social Sciences, 4*(12), 101.
51. Herbig, P., Milewicz, J., & Golden, J. E., (1993). Forecasting: Who, what, when and how. *The Journal of Business Forecasting, 12*(2), 16.
52. Holt, G. D., Olomolaiye, P. O., & Harris, F. C., (1994). Evaluating prequalification criteria in contractor selection. *Building and Environment, 29*(4), 437–448.
53. Horrigan, J. O., (1968). A short history of financial ratio analysis. *The Accounting Review, 43*(2), 284–294.
54. Hosaka, T., (2019). Bankruptcy prediction using imaged financial ratios and convolutional neural networks. *Expert Systems with Applications, 117*, 287–299.
55. Howell, R. A., & Soucy, S. R., (1990). Customer profitability-As critical as product profitability. *Strategic Finance, 72*(4), 43.
56. Husain, T., & Sunardi, N., (2020). Firm's value prediction based on profitability ratios and dividend policy. *Finance & Economics Review, 2*(2), 13–26.
57. Ibendahl, G., (2016). Using solvency ratios to predict future profitability. *Journal of ASFMRA*, 195–201.
58. Indjejikian, R. J., & Matějka, M., (2012). Accounting decentralization and performance evaluation of business unit managers. *The Accounting Review, 87*(1), 261–290.
59. Ingram, R. W., (1983). The importance of state accounting practices for creditor decisions. *Journal of Accounting and Public Policy, 2*(1), 5–17.
60. Irman, M., & Purwati, A. A., (2020). Analysis on the influence of current ratio, debt to equity ratio and total asset turnover toward return on assets on the otomotive and

component company that has been registered in Indonesia stock exchange within 2011–2017. *International Journal of Economics Development Research (IJEDR), 1*(1), 36–44.

61. Islam, M. A., (2014). An analysis of the financial performance of national bank limited using financial ratio. *Journal of Behavioral Economics, Finance, Entrepreneurship, Accounting and Transport,* 2(5), 121–129.
62. Ježovita, A., (2015). Variations between financial ratios for evaluating financial position related to the size of a company. *Review of Innovation and Competitiveness: A Journal of Economic and Social Research, 1*(1), 115–136.
63. Joiner, K. A., & Wormsley, S., (2005). Strategies for defining financial benchmarks for the research mission in academic health centers. *Academic Medicine, 80*(3), 211–217.
64. Jordan, C. E., Clark, S. J., & Smith, W. R., (2007). Should earnings per share (EPS) be taught as a means of comparing intercompany performance? *Journal of Education for Business, 82*(6), 343–348.
65. Kangari, R., Farid, F., & Elgharib, H. M., (1992). Financial performance analysis for construction industry. *Journal of Construction Engineering and Management, 118*(2), 349–361.
66. Karande, P., & Chakraborty, S., (2012). Application of multi-objective optimization on the basis of ratio analysis (MOORA) method for materials selection. *Materials & Design, 37*, 317–324.
67. Kemelgor, B. H., Johnson, S. D., & Srinivasan, S., (2000). Forces driving organizational change: A business school perspective. *Journal of Education for Business, 75*(3), 133–137.
68. Khumawala, S. B., Parsons, L. M., & Gordon, T. P., (2005). TRACKS: Assessing the quality of not-for-profit efficiency ratios: Do donors use joint cost allocation disclosures? *Journal of Accounting, Auditing & Finance, 20*(3), 287–309.
69. Kim, J., & Im, C., (2017). Study on corporate social responsibility (CSR): Focus on tax avoidance and financial ratio analysis. *Sustainability, 9*(10), 1710.
70. Kung, C. Y., & Wen, K. L., (2007). Applying grey relational analysis and grey decision-making to evaluate the relationship between company attributes and its financial performance—A case study of venture capital enterprises in Taiwan. *Decision Support Systems, 43*(3), 842–852.
71. Lee, H., Kwak, W., & Han, I., (1995). Developing a business performance evaluation system: An analytic hierarchical model. *The Engineering Economist, 40*(4), 343–357.
72. Lee, M. C., & Hwan, S., (2005). Relationships among service quality, customer satisfaction and profitability in the Taiwanese banking industry. *International Journal of Management, 22*(4), 635.
73. Lesakova, L., (2007, June). Uses and limitations of profitability ratio analysis in managerial practice. In: *International Conference on Management, Enterprise and Benchmarking* (Vol. 259).

74. Lewent, J. C., & Kearney, A. J., (1990). Identifying, measuring, and hedging currency risk at Merck. *Journal of Applied Corporate Finance, 2*(4), 19–28.

75. Liesz, T. J., & Maranville, S. J., (2008). Ratio analysis featuring the Dupont method: An overlooked topic in the finance module of small business management and entrepreneurship courses. *Small Business Institute Journal, 1*(1).

76. Lin, W. C., Liu, C. F., & Chu, C. W., (2005). Performance efficiency evaluation of the Taiwan's shipping industry: An application of data envelopment analysis. In: *Proceedings of the Eastern Asia Society for Transportation Studies* (Vol. 5, No. 1, pp. 467–476). CiteSeer.

77. Mack, R. P., (1956). Retailers' buying: The market prospect. In: *Consumption and Business Fluctuations: A Case Study of the Shoe, Leather, Hide Sequence* (pp. 113–127). NBER.

78. Madushanka, K. H. I., & Jathurika, M., (2018). The impact of liquidity ratios on profitability. *International Research Journal of Advanced Engineering and Science, 3*(4), 157–161.

79. Mahotra, D. K., & Malhotra, R., (2008). Analyzing financial statements using data envelopment analysis. *Com. Lending Rev., 23*, 25.

80. Manullang, A. E. A., Togatorop, D., Purba, P. R. D., Manik, E. A. Y., Simorangkir, E. N., & Lase, R. K., (2020). The significance of accounts receivable turnover, debt to equity ratio, current ratio to the probability of manufacturing companies. *International Journal of Social Science and Business, 4*(3), 464–471.

81. McAfee, R. B., & Champagne, P. J., (1993). Performance management: A strategy for improving employee performance and productivity. *Journal of Managerial Psychology, 8*(5), 24–32.

82. Mysková, R., & Hájek, P., (2017). Comprehensive assessment of firm financial performance using financial ratios and linguistic analysis of annual reports. *Journal of International Studies, 10*(4).

83. Nagar, V., & Rajan, M. V., (2001). The revenue implications of financial and operational measures of product quality. *The Accounting Review, 76*(4), 495–513.

84. Nazir, M. S., & Afza, T., (2009). Working capital requirements and the determining factors in Pakistan. *IUP Journal of Applied Finance, 15*(4), 28.

85. Nerviana, R., (2016). The effect of financial ratios and company size on dividend policy. *The Indonesian Accounting Review, 5*(1), 23–32.

86. Nuryani, Y., & Sunarsi, D., (2020). The effect of current ratio and debt to equity ratio on deviding growth. *JASa (Jurnal Akuntansi, Audit dan Sistem Informasi Akuntansi)*, *4*(2), 304–312.

87. Paarlberg, L. E., & Perry, J. L., (2007). Values management: Aligning employee values and organization goals. *The American Review of Public Administration, 37*(4), 387–408.

88. Pal, S., (2015). Evaluation of financial performance in terms of financial ratios-an empirical study on Indian automobile industry. *International Journal of Business Management and Research (IJBMR), 5*(3), 1–8.
89. Pass, C. L., & Pike, R. H., (1984). An overview of working capital management and corporate financing. *Managerial Finance, 10*(3), 1–11.
90. Patrone, F. L., (1981). Financial ratio analysis for the small business. *Journal of Small Business Management (pre-1986), 19*(000001), 35.
91. Piotroski, J. D., (2000). Value investing: The use of historical financial statement information to separate winners from losers. *Journal of Accounting Research*, 1–41.
92. Rashid, C. A., (2018). Efficiency of financial ratios analysis for evaluating companies' liquidity. *International Journal of Social Sciences & Educational Studies, 4*(4), 110.
93. Kumoro, D. F. C., Novitasari, D., Yuwono, T., & Asbari, M. (2020). Analysis of the Effect of Quick Ratio (QR), total assets turn over (TATO), and debt to equity ratio (DER) on return on equity (ROE) at PT. XYZ. *Journal of Industrial Engineering & Management Research, 1*(3), 166–183.
94. Reddy, C. V., (2013). An analysis of profitability ratios of Dr Reddy's Laboratories Ltd. *International Journal of Applied Financial Management Perspectives, 2*(4), 642.
95. Restianti, T., & Agustina, L., (2018). The effect of financial ratios on financial distress conditions in sub industrial sector company. *Accounting Analysis Journal, 7*(1), 25–33.
96. Richards, V. D., & Laughlin, E. J., (1980). A cash conversion cycle approach to liquidity analysis. *Financial Management*, 32–38.
97. Roter, D. L., Larson, S., Shinitzky, H., Chernoff, R., Serwint, J. R., Adamo, G., & Wissow, L., (2004). Use of an innovative video feedback technique to enhance communication skills training. *Medical Education, 38*(2), 145–157.
98. Rousseau, P. L., & Wachtel, P., (2001). Inflation, financial development and growth. *Economic Theory, Dynamics and Markets: Essays in Honor of Ryuzo Sato,* 309–324.
99. Sabau, A. I., Safta, I. L., Miron, G. M., & Achim, M. V., (2020, September). Manipulation of financial information through creative accounting: Case study at companies listed on the Romanian stock exchange. In: *RSEP Conferences* (Vol. 18, pp. 64–80).
100. Sagan, J., (1955). Toward a theory of working capital management. *The Journal of Finance, 10*(2), 121–129.
101. Salmi, T., & Martikainen, T., (1994). *A Review of the Theoretical and Empirical Basis of Financial Ratio Analysis* (1). News Group.
102. Sargent, T. C., (1998). *The BU Ratio: Prospect and Retrospect* (Vol. 1, pp. 1–05). Department of Finance.
103. Sari, D. P., Suryani, W., & Sabrina, H., (2021). Pengaruh debt to asset ratio dan debt to equity ratio terhadap kinerja keuangan pada perusahaan otomotif yang terdaftar di bei periode 2015–2018. *Jurnal Ilmiah Manajemen Dan Bisnis (Jimbi), 2*(1), 72–80.
104. Schmidgall, R. S., & DeFranco, A. L., (2004). Ratio analysis: Financial benchmarks for the club industry. *The Journal of Hospitality Financial Management, 12*(1), 1–14.

105. Schönbohm, A., (2013). *Performance Measurement and Management with Financial Ratios: The BASF SE Case* (No. 72). Working Paper.
106. Scott, J. E., (2004). Measuring dimensions of perceived e-business risks. *Information Systems and e-Business Management, 2*, 31–55.
107. Setiany, E., (2021). The effect of investment, free cash flow, earnings management, and interest coverage ratio on financial distress. *Journal of Social Science, 2*(1), 64–69.
108. Shaverdi, M., Heshmati, M. R., & Ramezani, I., (2014). Application of fuzzy AHP approach for financial performance evaluation of Iranian petrochemical sector. *Procedia Computer Science, 31*, 995–1004.
109. Sim, K., Aung, Z., & Gopalkrishnan, V., (2010). Discovering correlated subspace clusters in 3D continuous-valued data. In: *2010 IEEE International Conference on Data Mining* (pp. 471–480). IEEE.
110. Sunjoko, M. I., & Arilyn, E. J., (2016). Effects of inventory turnover, total asset turnover, fixed asset turnover, current ratio and average collection period on profitability. *Jurnal Bisnis Dan Akuntansi, 18*(1), 79–83.
111. Taffler, R. J., (1982). Forecasting company failure in the UK using discriminant analysis and financial ratio data. *Journal of the Royal Statistical Society: Series A (General), 145*(3), 342–358.
112. Tan, P. M., Chye, K., H., & Chin, L. L., (1997). Stability of financial ratios: A study of listed companies in Singapore. *Asian Review of Accounting, 5*(1), 19–39.
113. Tannenbaum, S. I., & Yukl, G., (1992). Training and development in work organizations. *Annual Review of Psychology, 43*(1), 399–441.
114. Thanassoulis, E., Boussofiane, A., & Dyson, R. G., (1996). A comparison of data envelopment analysis and ratio analysis as tools for performance assessment. *Omega, 24*(3), 229–244.
115. Tseng, F. M., Chiu, Y. J., & Chen, J. S., (2009). Measuring business performance in the high-tech manufacturing industry: A case study of Taiwan's large-sized TFT-LCD panel companies. *Omega, 37*(3), 686–697.
116. Tumanggor, M., (2020). The influence of current ratio, quick ratio and net profit margin on return on assets at PT. hero supermarket Tbk. *PINISI Discretion Review, 3*(2), 137–146.
117. Vasile, P. R., (2013). The impact of creative accounting on financial audit. *Studia Universitatis Vasile Goldiş, Arad-Seria Ştiinţe Economice, 23*(4), 56–62.
118. Warrad, L., (2014). The impact of liquidity through quick ratio on share price: Evidence from Jordanian banks. *European Journal of Accounting Auditing and Finance Research, 2*(8), 9–14.
119. Wijaya, D. P., & Sedana, I. B. P., (2020). Effects of quick ratio, return on assets, and exchange rates on stock returns. *Am. J. Humanities Soc. Sci. Res., 4*, 323–329.

CHAPTER 8

CHALLENGES AND PROSPECTS OF FINANCIAL ACCOUNTING

UNIT INTRODUCTION

Financial accounting is a vital function in any organization, responsible for collecting, analyzing, and communicating financial information to stakeholders. The financial landscape is constantly evolving, and financial accounting faces its own set of challenges in keeping up with these changes. These challenges can hinder the ability to report financial information accurately and make informed decisions based on that information (Haller, 2002).

However, during these challenges, there are also exciting prospects for the future of financial accounting. New technologies are being developed that have the potential to revolutionize financial accounting processes and improve accuracy. Sustainability and corporate social responsibility (CSR) are increasingly becoming essential factors in financial reporting, reflecting the growing need to consider the broader impact of financial decisions on society and the environment (Makarenko, 2017).

In this chapter, we will detail the challenges and prospects of financial accounting. We will examine the current landscape of financial accounting, explore the potential of new technologies to improve financial accounting processes, and discuss the importance of accurate financial reporting. We will also analyze the role of sustainability and CSR in financial accounting and consider the potential impact of emerging trends and technologies on the field (Rezaee & Turner, 2002) (Figure 8.1).

Figure 8.1. Illustration of components of finance.

Source: Ishita Birmani, Creative Commons License.

Learning Objectives

At the end of this chapter, the reader will be able to understand

1. The gravity of challenges in financial accounting
2. The impact of accounting scandals on the finances of the company
3. The potential of new technologies to cater to the challenges
4. The concept of Robotic Process Automation
5. The significance of artificial intelligence (AI) and machine learning (ML)

Key Terms

1. Artificial Intelligence
2. Cloud Computing
3. Enron and WorldCom accounting scandals
4. International Financial Reporting Standards (IFRS)
5. Internet of Things (IoT)
6. Machine Learning
7. Robotic Process Automation (RPA)
8. The Sarbanes-Oxley Act (SOX)

8.1. CHALLENGES OF FINANCIAL ACCOUNTING

Financial accounting is a critical function for organizations of all sizes and sectors, but it is also an increasingly complex and challenging field. One of the primary challenges facing financial accounting today is the increasing complexity of financial reporting requirements (Arnold, 2009). With globalization's rise and the world economy's increasing interconnectedness, financial reporting standards have become more complicated to navigate. This has increased the demand for highly skilled accounting professionals who interpret and apply complex financial reporting standards (Chhabra & Pattanayak, 2014).

Another challenge facing financial accounting is the lack of global accounting standards. While several IFRS are in place, these standards are not universally adopted, and there is significant variation in financial reporting requirements from country to country. This can create challenges for multinational organizations, which must navigate a patchwork of different reporting standards to comply with local regulations (Mohamed & Lashine, 2003). It can also create challenges for investors and other stakeholders, who must interpret financial statements that may be prepared using different accounting methods and standards. This lack of standardization can create confusion and reduce the comparability and reliability of financial information, which can impact investment decisions and business performance (Randall, 1999).

Overall, financial accounting challenges are significant and require ongoing attention and investment to ensure that financial reporting remains accurate, reliable, and useful for stakeholders. Some challenges are as follows (Crookes & Conway, 2018).

The challenges of financial accounting also include;

- Accounting automation
- Lack of skills and professionalism
- Changing client relations for certified public accountants (CPAs)
- Complicated tax laws
- Security of financial data

TIPS

To address the challenge of increasing complexity of financial reporting, organizations, and accounting professionals must invest in ongoing training and professional development to keep up with changes in accounting standards and financial reporting requirements.

8.2. RISE IN COMPLEXITY OF FINANCIAL REPORTING

This challenge arises from several factors, including the increasing complexity of financial transactions and changes in accounting standards (Chychyla et al., 2019). The complexity of financial transactions has increased significantly over the past few decades, driven in part by technological advances and the growing complexity of business structures. This has made it more difficult for accounting professionals to accurately record and report financial transactions. For example, complex financial instruments such as derivatives, which are used to manage risk, can be challenging to value and account for accurately. In addition, many modern business models, such as those used by technology companies, involve complex revenue recognition issues, which can be challenging to navigate and require significant expertise (Bimo et al., 2019). Another factor contributing to the increasing complexity of financial reporting is changes in accounting standards. Over the past few years, accounting standards have undergone significant changes, particularly with the adoption of IFRS and the introduction of new accounting standards, such as the new revenue recognition standard (ASC 606). These changes have required organizations to invest significant resources to comply with new reporting requirements and ensure accurate and reliable financial statements (Bratten et al., 2019). Overall, the increasing complexity of financial reporting is a significant challenge for organizations and accounting professionals. Still, with suitable investments in technology and training, it is possible to navigate this challenge and ensure that financial reporting remains accurate and reliable (Mutiso & Kamau, 2013) (Figure 8.2).

Figure 8.2. The graphical representation of the relationship between the percentage of GAAP concepts and the number of words in standards associated with a GAAP concept.

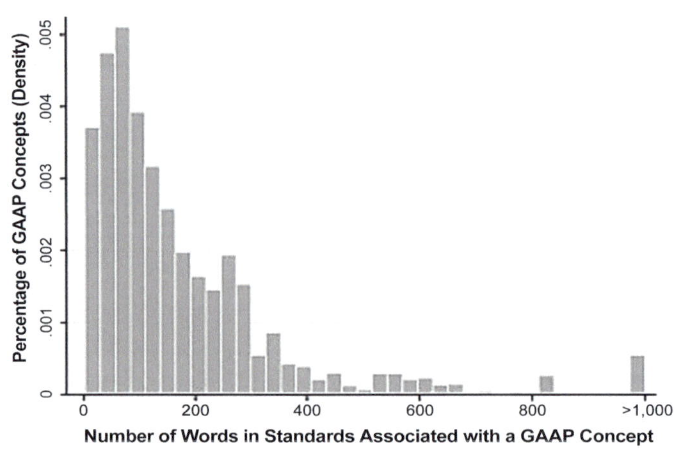

Source: Roman et al. Creative Commons License.

8.3. LACK OF GLOBAL ACCOUNTING STANDARDS

8.3.1. Patchwork of Different Reporting Standards

One of the primary challenges resulting from the lack of global accounting standards is the patchwork of different reporting standards across other countries and regions. This can create significant challenges for multinational organizations, which must navigate a complex web of accounting standards to comply with local regulations. For example, a company operating in Europe, North America, and Asia may be required to use different accounting standards in each region, making it challenging to create accurate and consistent financial reports (Héritier, 1996).

The patchwork of different reporting standards also challenges investors and other stakeholders, who must interpret financial statements that may be prepared using different accounting methods and means (Hijink & Veld, 2019). This can make it difficult to compare the financial performance of other companies and reduce the comparability and reliability of financial information (Figure 8.3).

Figure 8.3. Picture of financial performance.

Source: Geetha Ravichandran, Creative Commons License.

8.3.2. Cost and Complexity of Compliance

Another challenge resulting from the lack of global accounting standards is the cost and complexity of compliance. With different accounting across different regions, companies must invest significant resources. This can include hiring local accounting professionals, investing in training and development, and implementing new accounting systems and processes (Mills, 1996).

The cost and complexity of compliance can create significant challenges for small and medium-sized enterprises (SMEs), which may not have the resources to invest in compliance with multiple accounting standards. This can create a barrier to entry for SMEs, limiting competition and innovation in different markets. In addition, the cost of compliance can impact the overall profitability of organizations, reducing the resources available for investment in other areas of the business (Eichfelder & Vaillancourt, 2014) (Figure 8.4).

Figure 8.4. Image of cost and complexity.

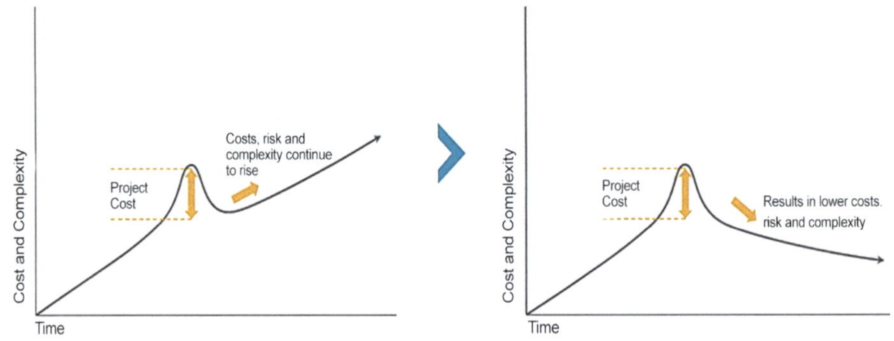

Source: Jayant Raman, Creative Commons License.

8.3.3. Impact on Emerging Markets

The lack of global accounting standards can also significantly impact emerging markets, which may be less developed in accounting standards and financial reporting infrastructure. This can create challenges for companies operating in these markets, which may struggle to produce accurate and reliable financial statements (Hunter & Smith, 2009).

The lack of global accounting standards can also limit the flow of investment into emerging markets, as investors may be wary of the risks associated with investing in markets with weaker accounting standards. This can create a barrier to economic development in these markets, limiting growth and opportunity. To address this challenge, there is a growing need for increased investment in accounting infrastructure and training in emerging markets to build the capacity to produce accurate and reliable financial statements (Mbatha & Ngibe, 2017) (Figure 8.5).

Figure 8.5. Pictorial representation of common characteristics of emerging market.

Source: The Investopedia team, Creative Commons License.

8.4. DIFFICULTY IN VALUING ASSETS AND LIABILITIES

8.4.1. Complex Financial Instruments

The increasing use of complex financial instruments has made it difficult to value assets and liabilities accurately. These instruments have unique characteristics and risks that can be difficult to assess, and the lack of transparency in financial markets can further complicate the valuation process. For example, derivatives such as options and futures are often used to hedge against market risks, but their value is highly dependent on underlying market conditions. This can make it challenging to accurately value these instruments, as market conditions are constantly changing (Cheung & Chung, 1996).

In addition, securitization has become increasingly common, which involves packaging multiple assets into a single security that can be bought and sold. However, the complexity of securitization can make it difficult to assess the value of underlying assets. If the value of these assets is not accurately reported, it can lead to significant misreporting of financial statements, ultimately harming organizations' financial health (Young, 1996).

8.4.2. Changes in Market Conditions

Changes in market conditions can have a significant impact on the valuation of assets and liabilities. For example, interest rates can affect the value of fixed-income securities, such as bonds. If interest rates rise, the value of these securities will decline as investors demand higher yields to compensate for the increased risk. Similarly, changes in exchange rates can impact the value of assets denominated in foreign currencies. If the value of the local currency appreciates, the value of these assets will decline in the local currency (Mullins, 1996). Inflation rates can also impact the value of assets and liabilities. Inflation can erode the purchasing power of assets denominated in a fixed currency, such as cash or bonds, and can also impact the value of liabilities, such as debt. If inflation rates are higher than expected, it can lead to significant misreporting of financial statements, ultimately harming organizations' financial health (Tang & Yan, 2010).

8.4.3. Judgment Calls

Estimating assets and liabilities often require judgment calls from accountants and financial analysts. Various factors can influence these judgment calls, including company culture, incentives, and individual biases. For example, accountants may be incentivized to report higher earnings to meet targets, leading to the overvaluation of assets and liabilities. Inaccurate judgment calls can result in misreporting of financial statements, which can have significant implications for the overall financial health of organizations (Soederberg, 2004).

Remember

The lack of consistency in financial reporting can also impact investment decisions and business performance, as investors may have difficulty assessing the financial health and future prospects of different companies.

Organizations can establish rigorous valuation policies and procedures to address this challenge and ensure that the individuals responsible for valuation are independent and objective. By creating a culture of transparency and accountability, organizations can help to ensure that the valuation of assets and liabilities is accurate and reliable (Lerrick, 2005).

8.4.4. Regulatory Requirements

Regulatory requirements can impact the valuation of assets and liabilities and may require organizations to use specific valuation methods or disclose additional information in financial statements. For example, the IFRS require organizations to use fair value accounting for specific financial instruments (Wagenhofer, 2016). Failure to comply with regulatory requirements can result in penalties and damage organizations' reputations. The complexity of regulatory requirements can also make it difficult to accurately report the value of assets and liabilities on financial statements. Organizations can establish vital compliance programs to address this challenge and ensure they have the resources and expertise to comply with regulatory requirements (Rahman & Rahim, 2003).

8.5. ACCOUNTING SCANDALS

8.5.1. Enron and WorldCom Scandals

In the early 2000s, the Enron and WorldCom accounting scandals shook the financial world and exposed significant flaws in financial accounting practices (Giroux, 2008). Enron used complex accounting methods to manipulate financial statements, while WorldCom used fraudulent accounting practices to inflate revenue and profits. These scandals led to the bankruptcy of both companies and a loss of public trust in corporate accounting practices. The impact of these scandals was felt worldwide and resulted in greater scrutiny and regulation of financial reporting (Brickey, 2003) (Figure 8.6).

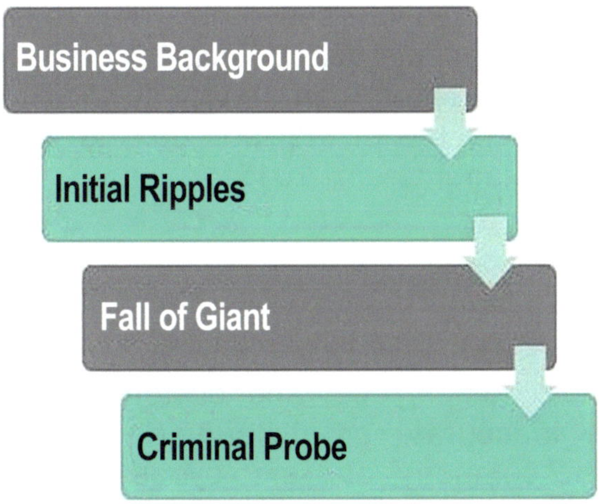

Figure 8.6. Illustration of Enron scandal.

Source: WallstreetMojo, Creative Commons License.

8.5.2. Sarbanes-Oxley Act

In response to the Enron and WorldCom scandals, the U.S. government passed the Sarbanes-Oxley Act (SOX) in 2002. SOX introduced a range of new regulations and requirements designed to improve transparency and accountability in financial reporting (Lobo & Zhou, 2006). These regulations include requirements for increased disclosure, stronger internal controls, and independent audits. SOX also created the Public Company Accounting Oversight Board (PCAOB), which oversees auditors of public companies and ensures that they comply with the requirements set out in the act (Sarbanes, 2002) (Figure 8.7).

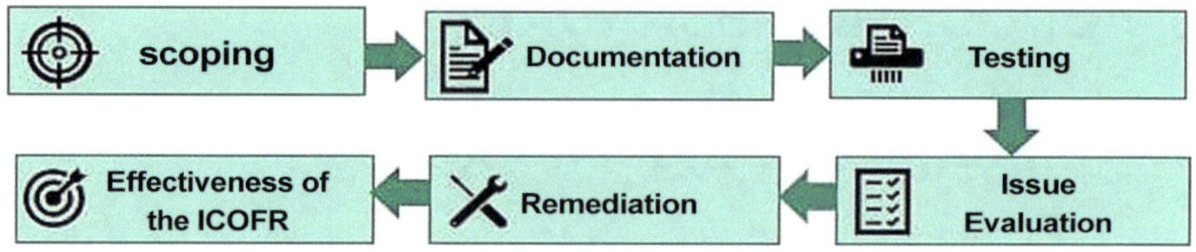

Figure 8.7. Image of Sarbanes-Oxley Act.

Source: Wallstreet Mojo, Creative Commons License.

8.5.3. Auditor Independence

One key area of focus in the aftermath of accounting scandals has been auditor independence. Auditors play a critical role in ensuring the accuracy and transparency of financial statements. Still, conflicts of interest can arise when auditors also provide consulting or other services to the companies they audit (Kinney, 1999). To address this issue, regulators have introduced new requirements designed to strengthen auditor independence. These include restrictions on the types of services auditors can provide to their clients and the need for greater disclosure of the fees paid to auditors for non-audit services (Tepalagul & Lin, 2015).

8.5.4. Impact on Stakeholders

Accounting scandals can significantly impact a range of stakeholders, including investors, employees, and customers. When financial statements are inaccurate or misleading, investors may lose confidence in the company, and employees may lose their jobs. Customers may also be impacted if a company's financial troubles result in a product quality or service decline. As a result, there is a strong need for greater transparency and accuracy in financial reporting to protect the interests of all stakeholders (Akther & Xu, 2020).

8.6. NEED FOR GREATER TRANSPARENCY

Technology advances can improve transparency in financial accounting, as they enable more efficient and accurate processing of financial data. For example, blockchain technology can create a secure and transparent ledger of financial transactions. At the same time, data analytics tools can help to identify potential fraud or errors in financial statements (Taipaleenmäki & Ikäheimo, 2013). However, the use of technology also presents new challenges, such as the need to ensure the security and accuracy of financial data. Regulators and businesses must ensure that they are keeping up with the latest technology and best practices to leverage the potential benefits of technology while minimizing the risks (Hodge et al., 2004).

As well as accounting scandals often have their roots in broader ethical and cultural issues within organizations. In some cases, pressure to meet financial targets or to maintain a particular image can lead to unethical behavior or financial reporting practices (Jaijairam, 2017). To address these issues, organizations must foster a culture of transparency and ethical behavior and ensure employees are trained on the importance of accurate and transparent financial reporting. This requires a top-down commitment to transparency and ethical behavior, including setting clear policies and procedures and taking swift action to address any issues that arise (Satava et al., 2006).

KEYWORD

Unethical behavior is an action that falls outside of what is considered morally right or proper for a person, a profession, or an industry.

Overall, greater transparency in financial accounting is essential to building trust and confidence in financial reporting, both for businesses and the public. Addressing the root causes of accounting scandals and improving transparency and accountability (Sims & Brinkmann, 2003).

8.7. PROSPECTS OF FINANCIAL ACCOUNTING

Financial accounting is an essential component of modern business operations. Its primary purpose is to record, analyze, and report valuable financial information for decision-making, planning, and controlling business operations. Financial accounting has evolved significantly over the years, and it is expected to continue to change to meet the changing needs of businesses (Groot & Budding, 2008).

One of the significant changes in financial accounting is the increasing use of technology. Businesses are adopting new technologies such as cloud computing, big data analytics, and artificial intelligence (AI) to improve the efficiency and accuracy of financial accounting processes (Calmel, 2014). These new technologies are transforming financial accounting by making it easier to collect, analyze, and report financial information in real-time. With the increasing availability of these technologies, businesses can take advantage of the data to make informed decisions and optimize their financial performance (Barik & Sharma, 2019).

The prospects of financial accounting are shaped by ongoing technological advancements and the need for increased transparency and accountability (Murodovich & Ziyadullaevna, 2022). With the increasing complexity of business operations, financial accounting will play a critical role in helping businesses manage their finances and make informed decisions. As companies continue to evolve and adapt to the changing economic landscape, financial accounting will need to change and evolve to meet their needs broadly (Ahmed et al., 2019).

8.8. DEVELOPMENT OF NEW FINANCIAL INSTRUMENTS AND REPORTING STANDARDS

KEYWORD

Transparency is the quality of being easily seen through, while transparency in a business or governance context refers to being open and honest.

The financial industry is constantly evolving, and with new business models and technological advancements, financial instruments and reporting standards must also evolve to address the challenges that arise. The demand for more comprehensive and reliable financial reporting is a growing trend in the financial sector. This demand has led to the development new financial instruments and reporting standards that ensure consistency, transparency, and accuracy in financial reporting (Llewellyn, 2005).

One example of new financial instruments is the emergence of ETFs, which provide investors with more flexibility and risk management tools than traditional mutual funds (Barlaup et al., 2009). Another example is the development of complex financial derivatives, which require specialized knowledge and expertise in financial accounting to ensure accurate reporting. These new instruments can pose challenges for financial accounting as they need the development of new accounting standards and principles (Roychowdhury et al., 2019).

To address these challenges, accounting bodies such as the IFRS have been established (Kapellas & Siougle, 2017). The IFRS provides a common framework for financial reporting that covers areas such as revenue recognition, asset valuation, financial instruments, and liabilities management. The IFRS has become increasingly important as more companies operate globally and require common accounting standards (Abiola & Ojo, 2012).

Developing new financial instruments and reporting standards is critical to ensure that financial reporting remains relevant and valuable in a rapidly changing financial landscape. This requires continuous monitoring of emerging trends and challenges and the development of new financial instruments and standards to address these issues (Ghose, 2007).

8.9. EXPANSION OF FINANCIAL ACCOUNTING SERVICES TO SMBS

In recent years, there has been an increasing demand for financial accounting services from small and medium-sized businesses (SMBs) as they have realized the importance of maintaining accurate financial records and complying with tax regulations (Bentley et al., 2016). Financial accounting services provide SMBs with the necessary tools and expertise to manage their finances effectively, which can help them make informed decisions about their business operations (Scholes et al., 1990).

Expanding financial accounting services to SMBs involves providing them with a range of accounting services such as bookkeeping, tax preparation, financial statement preparation, and audit support. Professional accountants usually offer these services with the expertise and experience to handle the financial accounting needs of SMBs (Francis & Rowell, 1978).

Did you Know?

75% of executives believe that AI will enable their companies to move into new businesses.

One of the main benefits of financial accounting services for SMBs is that it can help them to save time and money. By outsourcing financial accounting services to professionals, SMBs can focus on other aspects of their business, such as marketing, product development, and customer service. This can help them grow their business and increase profitability (Horngren et al., 2002).

Another benefit of financial accounting services for SMBs is that they can help them comply with tax regulations. Tax laws are complex, and they are subject to frequent changes. By using financial accounting services, SMBs can ensure that they comply with tax regulations, which can help them avoid penalties and fines (Capon et al., 1994).

In conclusion, expanding financial accounting services to SMBs is an important trend in the financial industry (Alviniussen & Jankensgard, 2009). It provides SMBs with the necessary tools and expertise to manage their finances effectively, which can help them to make informed decisions about their business operations. It also helps SMBs to save time and money and ensures compliance with tax regulations (Kern & Formoso, 2006).

8.10. EMERGENCE OF NEW TECHNOLOGIES

8.10.1. Artificial Intelligence (AI) and Machine Learning

Artificial Intelligence (AI) and ML are rapidly transforming the landscape of financial accounting, offering significant potential to improve financial reporting processes. With AI and ML, companies can process massive amounts of data in real-time and automate decision-making (Lytras & Visvizi, 2021). One of the primary benefits of AI and ML is that they can analyze complex financial data, identify patterns and trends, and provide valuable insights that can help companies make better business decisions. For instance, AI, and ML can help companies predict future financial trends, identify potential risk areas, and even provide suggestions for potential cost savings (Cangemi & Taylor, 2018).

KEYWORD

Audit is the examination of the financial report of an organisation - as presented in the annual report - by someone independent of that organisation.

Another significant benefit of AI and ML is that they can help to improve the accuracy and reliability of financial reporting. By automating many of the routine accounting tasks, AI, and ML can help reduce the likelihood of errors and ensure that financial reports are produced promptly and consistently (Nagendran et al., 2020). For example, AI, and ML can be used to automate the process of reconciling accounts, detecting fraud, and identifying errors in financial statements. Additionally, these technologies can help to streamline the audit process, enabling auditors to focus on high-risk areas and make more informed decisions (Pothumsetty, 2020).

Despite these benefits, some challenges are associated with using AI and ML in financial accounting. One of the primary challenges is ensuring the accuracy of the data used to train these systems. Without high-quality data, the insights provided by AI and ML can be inaccurate or misleading. Additionally, the use of AI and ML raises some ethical concerns, particularly regarding the potential for these technologies to replace human workers. Therefore, it is essential to implement these technologies responsibly and ethically, considering the potential impact on employees and other stakeholders (Verma et al., 2022) (Figure 8.8).

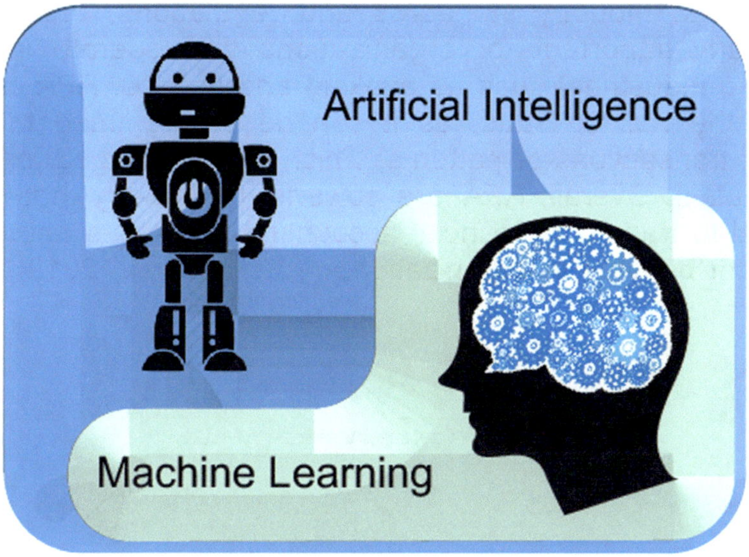

Figure 8.8. Illustration of AI and machine learning.

Source: Javapoint, Creative Commons License.

8.10.2. Robotic Process Automation (RPA)

Robotic Process Automation (RPA) is a technology that has revolutionized the financial accounting industry by automating repetitive and time-consuming tasks. RPA is a software program that uses AI and ML to automate tasks such as data entry, invoice processing, and report generation (Devarajan, 2018). Using RPA in financial accounting has significantly reduced the time and cost of manual tasks and increased the accuracy and efficiency of financial reporting. With RPA, accountants can free up their time to focus on higher-value tasks such as analysis, forecasting, and strategic planning (Kokina & Blanchette, 2019).

One of the primary benefits of RPA is that it can work 24/7, ensuring that financial processes are always up-to-date and accurate. In addition, RPA can reduce the risk of human error, which can be a significant problem in financial accounting. For example, if a human accountant makes a mistake in data entry, it can lead to errors in the financial statements, which can have severe consequences for the organization. By automating these tasks, RPA can ensure that data is accurately entered into the system and is free from human error (Aguirre & Rodriguez, 2017).

Another benefit of RPA is that it can provide consistency and standardization in financial processes. RPA can be programmed to follow specific rules and regulations, ensuring financial processes comply with industry standards and regulations. This can be particularly important for organizations that operate in highly regulated industries, such as banking and finance. RPA can also reduce the risk of fraud, as it can be programmed to detect unusual transactions or patterns, which can be flagged for further investigation. Overall, RPA is a powerful technology that has the potential to transform financial accounting processes and provide significant benefits to organizations (Yatskiv et al., 2019) (Figure 8.9).

Figure 8.9. Schematic of benefits of RPA.

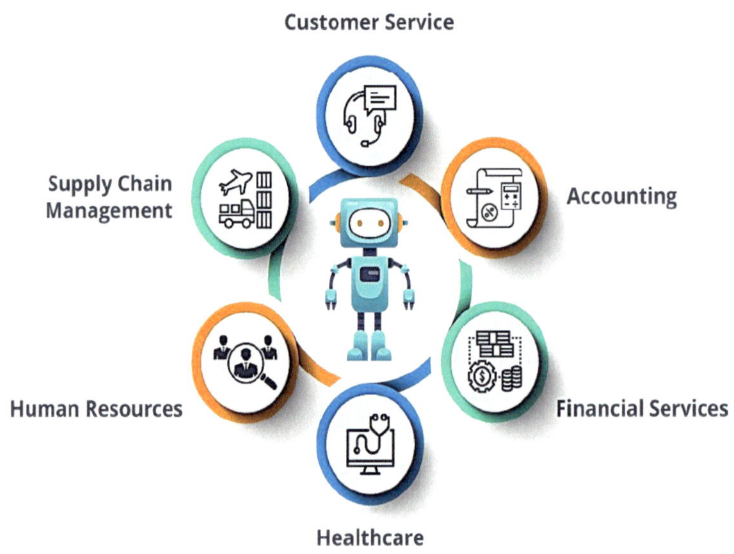

Source: Processmaker, Creative Commons License.

8.10.3. Internet of Things (IoT)

The Internet of Things (IoT) refers to a network of devices, vehicles, appliances, and other objects embedded with sensors, software, and connectivity that enables them to collect and exchange data. In the context of financial accounting, IoT has the potential to revolutionize how financial data is collected, processed, and analyzed (Li, 2022). By embedding sensors and other devices in financial assets such as inventory, companies can track and monitor their assets in real-time, thereby improving their inventory management processes. Additionally, IoT can enable companies to track the performance of their equipment and assets, which can help improve their maintenance processes and avoid breakdowns and other issues (Ghosh et al., 2021).

Moreover, IoT can help improve the accuracy and completeness of financial data by automating data collection processes. For instance, IoT-enabled devices can automatically collect data on sales, production, and other operational metrics, which can be used to generate financial reports and additional critical financial information. This can help reduce errors and inaccuracies often arising from manual data entry and processing. Additionally, IoT can enable companies to collect data on customer behavior, which can help improve marketing and sales strategies (Zaychenko et al., 2021).

However, there are also some challenges and risks associated with the use of IoT in financial accounting. One of the biggest challenges is the security of the IoT network. As IoT devices are often connected to the internet, they are vulnerable to cyber-attacks, compromising the confidentiality and integrity of financial data. Additionally, the sheer volume of data generated by IoT devices can be overwhelming, and it can be challenging to analyze and process the data promptly and effectively. Therefore, companies need to implement robust security measures and invest in data analytics capabilities to fully leverage IoT's potential in financial accounting (Tang et al., 2018) (Figure 8.10).

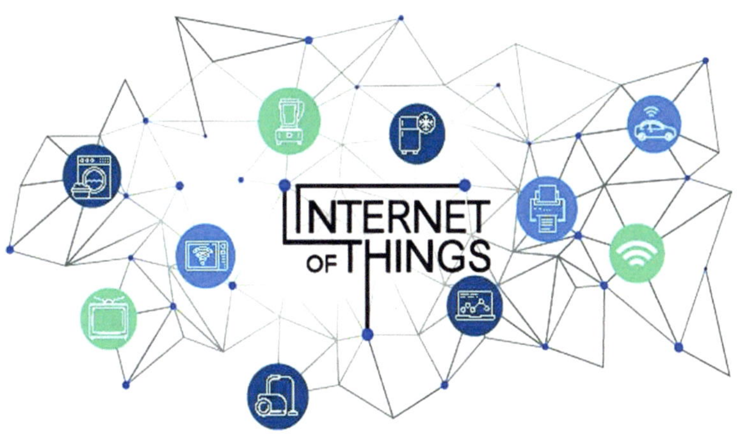

Figure 8.10. Picture of internet of things (IoT).

Source: SimonBr, Creative Commons License.

8.10.4. Cloud Computing

Cloud computing refers to delivering computing services, including storage, software, and processing power, over the internet. The technology offers an innovative and efficient way for financial accounting firms to handle large amounts of data without significantly investing in hardware or software. With cloud computing, companies can store and manage their data in remote data centers, eliminating the need for on-site infrastructure. This approach can lead to significant cost savings while allowing firms to focus on their core competencies. Additionally, cloud computing offers high data security, reliability, and scalability levels, making it an attractive solution for accounting firms (Chen & Metawa, 2020).

The adoption of cloud computing in financial accounting can potentially revolutionize the industry. With the ability to access real-time data from any device, cloud computing can significantly improve efficiency, decision-making, and collaboration. In addition, cloud computing offers advanced tools for data analysis, including AI and ML, which can enhance the accuracy of financial reports and provide valuable insights into financial performance. The scalability of cloud computing also means that firms can quickly scale up or down their operations to meet changing demands without incurring high costs or downtime. Overall, cloud computing has the potential to transform the way financial accounting firms operate, making them more agile, efficient, and competitive (Li, 2021).

KEYWORD

Collaboration is the process of two or more people, entities or organizations working together to complete a task or achieve a goal.

Despite the potential benefits, cloud computing also challenges financial accounting firms. One of the primary concerns is the security of data. As financial data is sensitive and confidential, accounting firms must ensure that their cloud service providers have adequate security measures to protect against cyber threats and data breaches. Additionally, firms must comply with regulations governing data privacy and security, such as the General Data Protection Regulation (GDPR) in the European Union. Another challenge is the risk of service disruptions and downtime, which can impact the availability and reliability of financial data. Accounting firms must work closely with their cloud service providers to ensure high uptime and rapid disaster recovery in case of service disruptions. Despite these challenges, the potential benefits of cloud computing make it a compelling technology for financial accounting firms looking to modernize their operations and improve their competitive position in the marketplace (Taghipour et al., 2020).

8.10.5. Data Visualization and Business Intelligence Tools

Data visualization and business intelligence tools are increasingly important for financial accounting processes. These tools allow businesses to extract meaningful insights from large data sets to make better decisions. Data visualization tools can take complex financial data and present it more visually appealing and easily understandable, helping users quickly identify trends, patterns, and anomalies. This can assist businesses in identifying potential risks and opportunities and developing strategies to address them. Business intelligence tools also help improve financial accounting processes by creating custom reports and dashboards, providing real-time updates on financial performance, and automating repetitive tasks (Shao et al., 2022).

One key benefit of data visualization and business intelligence tools is their ability to provide accurate and timely information. By automating data collection and analysis, these tools can help organizations quickly identify potential issues and take corrective action. This can be especially useful in financial accounting, where errors or discrepancies can have significant consequences. By providing up-to-date and accurate data, these tools can help businesses to make more informed decisions, reduce risks, and improve financial performance (Prevedello et al., 2010).

Another benefit of data visualization and business intelligence tools is their ability to provide a deeper understanding of financial data. By presenting complex data in a visual format, these tools can help users to identify patterns and trends that may not be immediately obvious. This can lead to more informed decision-making and a better understanding of financial performance and potential risks. Additionally, these tools can help businesses to identify and address inefficiencies in their financial accounting processes, leading to cost savings and increased productivity (Xia & Gong, 2014).

ACTIVITY 8.1.

In 2015, a multinational corporation was accused of overstating its revenue by $1.2 billion over the course of several years. The company's stock price plummeted, and investigations revealed that the executives had been involved in fraudulent accounting practices to inflate their financial performance. The scandal eventually led to the resignation of the CEO and other top executives, as well as a significant financial settlement paid to investors.

Based on this scenario, discuss the potential long-term effects of accounting scandals on a company, its stakeholders, and the broader financial system. What measures can be taken to prevent such scandals from occurring in the future, and what role can auditors and regulators play in ensuring transparency and accountability in corporate accounting practices?

8.11. SUMMARY

- This chapter outlines the current and future challenges and prospects of financial accounting. The challenges discussed in the chapter include the increasing complexity of financial reporting, the lack of global accounting standards, and the difficulty valuing assets and liabilities. These challenges can make it challenging for businesses to remain compliant with accounting standards, particularly for international companies.
- On the other hand, the chapter also highlights some financial accounting prospects. These include the development of new financial instruments and reporting standards to address emerging trends and challenges, expanding financial accounting services to SMBs, and increasing the use of technology in financial accounting.
- In conclusion, the chapter provides an insightful overview of the challenges and prospects of financial accounting. It highlights the importance of financial accounting in modern business operations and the need for businesses to keep up with changing trends and developments. The chapter provides a valuable resource for individuals interested in financial accounting and its role in modern business operations.

REVIEW QUESTIONS

1. What are the main challenges facing financial accounting in the current economic landscape?
2. How can the lack of global accounting standards impact financial reporting for businesses operating globally?
3. What are some of the prospects for financial accounting in the future?
4. How is technology expected to impact financial accounting in the future?
5. How can businesses overcome the challenges of financial accounting in the current economic landscape?
6. How can businesses leverage emerging trends and prospects in financial accounting to gain a competitive advantage in their industry?

MULTIPLE CHOICE QUESTIONS

1. Which of the following is a challenge of financial accounting?

a. Development of new financial instruments and reporting standards
b. Increasing demand for skilled accounting professionals
c. Difficulty in valuing assets and liabilities
d. Expansion of financial accounting services to SMBs

2. **Which of the following is a prospect of financial accounting?**
   a. Lack of global accounting standards
   b. Rise in complexity of financial reporting
   c. Adoption of new technologies such as cloud computing and AI
   d. Increased complexity of business operations
3. **What is the primary purpose of financial accounting?**
   a. To record and analyze financial information for tax purposes
   b. To record and analyze financial information for decision-making, planning, and controlling business operations
   c. To record and analyze financial information for marketing purposes
   d. To record and analyze financial information for HR purposes
4. **What is one of the significant changes in financial accounting?**
   a. Decreased use of technology
   b. Decreased demand for transparency and accountability
   c. Increased use of technology such as cloud computing and big data analytics
   d. Decreased demand for accurate and reliable financial reporting
5. **Which of the following is a challenge of financial accounting related to globalization?**
   a. Difficulty in valuing assets and liabilities
   b. Rise in complexity of financial reporting
   c. Lack of global accounting standards
   d. Expansion of financial accounting services to SMBs

Answers to Multiple Choice Questions

1. (c) 2. (c) 3. (b) 4. (c) 5. (c)

REFERENCES

1. Abiola, J. O., & Ojo, S. O., (2012). Compliance with regulatory financial reporting and corporate governance practices in selected primary mortgage institutions in Nigeria. *International Journal of Business and Social Science, 3*(15), 246–254.
2. Aguirre, S., & Rodriguez, A., (2017). Automation of a business process using robotic process automation (RPA): A case study. In: *Applied Computer Sciences in Engineering: 4th Workshop on Engineering Applications, WEA 2017, Cartagena, Colombia, 2017, Proceedings 4* (pp. 65–71). Springer International Publishing.

3. Ahmed, H., Tajul, A. F. A., Karbhari, Y., & Shafii, Z., (2019). Diverse accounting standards on disclosures of Islamic financial transactions: Prospects and challenges of narrowing gaps. *Accounting, Auditing & Accountability Journal, 32*(3), 866–896.
4. Akther, T., & Xu, F., (2020). Existence of the audit expectation gap and its impact on stakeholders' confidence: The moderating role of the financial reporting council. *International Journal of Financial Studies, 8*(1), 4.
5. Alviniussen, A., & Jankensgard, H., (2009). Enterprise risk budgeting: Bringing risk management into the financial planning process. *Journal of Applied Finance (Formerly Financial Practice and Education), 19*(12).
6. Arnold, P. J., (2009). Global financial crisis: The challenge to accounting research. *Accounting, Organizations and Society, 34*(6, 7), 803–809.
7. Barik, R., & Sharma, P., (2019). Analyzing the progress and prospects of financial inclusion in India. *Journal of Public Affairs, 19*(4), e1948.
8. Barlaup, K., Iren, D. H., & Stuart, I., (2009). Restoring trust in auditing: Ethical discernment and the Adelphia scandal. *Managerial Auditing Journal, 24*(2), 183–203.
9. Bentley-Goode, K. A., Newton, N. J., & Thompson, A., (2016). *Business Strategy and Internal Control Over Financial Reporting*. Available at SSRN 2637688.
10. Bimo, I. D., Siregar, S. V., Hermawan, A. A., & Wardhani, R., (2019). Internal control over financial reporting, organizational complexity, and financial reporting quality. *International Journal of Economics & Management, 13*(2).
11. Bratten, B., Causholli, M., & Omer, T. C., (2019). Audit firm tenure, bank complexity, and financial reporting quality. *Contemporary Accounting Research, 36*(1), 295–325.
12. Brickey, K. F., (2003). From Enron to WorldCom and beyond: Life and crime after Sarbanes-Oxley. *Wash. ULQ, 81*, 357.
13. Calmel, M. P., (2014). Harmonization of EPSASs (European public sector accounting standards): Developments and prospects. *Accounting, Economics and Law, 4*(3), 215–236.
14. Cangemi, M. P., & Taylor, P., (2018). Harnessing artificial intelligence to deliver real-time intelligence and business process improvements. *EDPACS, 57*(4), 1–6.
15. Capon, N., Farley, J. U., & Hulbert, J. M., (1994). Strategic planning and financial performance: More evidence. *Journal of Management Studies, 31*(1), 105–110.
16. Chen, X., & Metawa, N., (2020). Enterprise financial management information system based on cloud computing in big data environment. *Journal of Intelligent & Fuzzy Systems, 39*(4), 5223–5232.
17. Cheung, J. K., & Chung, R., (1996). Valuation of complex financial instruments via basic components. *Review of Quantitative Finance and Accounting, 7*, 163–176.
18. Chhabra, K. S., & Pattanayak, J. K., (2014). Financial accounting practices among small enterprises: Issues and challenges. *IUP Journal of Accounting Research & Audit Practices, 13*(3).

19. Chychyla, R., Leone, A. J., & Minutti-Meza, M., (2019). Complexity of financial reporting standards and accounting expertise. *Journal of Accounting and Economics, 67*(1), 226–253.
20. Cordery, C., (2013). Regulating small and medium charities: Does it improve transparency and accountability? *Voluntas: International Journal of Voluntary and Nonprofit Organizations, 24*, 831–851.
21. Crookes, L., & Conway, E., (2018). Technology challenges in accounting and finance. *Contemporary Issues in Accounting: The Current Developments in Accounting Beyond the Numbers*, 61–83.
22. Devarajan, Y., (2018). A study of robotic process automation use cases today for tomorrow's business. *International Journal of Computer Techniques, 5*(6), 12–18.
23. Efimova, O. V., (2018). Integrating sustainability issues into investment decision evaluation. *Journal of Reviews on Global Economics, 7*(495), 668–681.
24. Eichfelder, S., & Vaillancourt, F., (2014). *Tax Compliance Costs: A Review of Cost Burdens and Cost Structures.* Available at SSRN 2535664.
25. Epstein, M. J., (2003). The identification, measurement, and reporting of corporate social impacts: Past, present, and future. In: *Advances in Environmental Accounting & Management* (Vol. 2, pp. 1–29). Emerald Group Publishing Limited.
26. Francis, J. C., & Rowell, D. R., (1978). A simultaneous equation model of the firm for financial analysis and planning. *Financial Management*, 29–44.
27. Ghose, A., (2007). Information disclosure and regulatory compliance: Economic issues. In: *Managing Information Assurance in Financial Services* (pp. 304–317). IGI Global.
28. Ghosh, A., Edwards, D. J., & Hosseini, M. R., (2021). Patterns and trends in internet of things (IoT) research: Future applications in the construction industry. *Engineering, Construction and Architectural Management, 28*(2), 457–481.
29. Giroux, G., (2008). What went wrong? Accounting fraud and lessons from the recent scandals. *Social Research*, 1205–1238.
30. Groot, T., & Budding, T., (2008). New public management's current issues and future prospects. *Financial Accountability & Management, 24*(1), 1–13.
31. Haller, A., (2002). Financial accounting developments in the European Union: Past events and future prospects. *European Accounting Review, 11*(1), 153–190.
32. Héritier, A., (1996). The accommodation of diversity in European policy-making and its outcomes: Regulatory policy as a patchwork. *Journal of European Public Policy, 3*(2), 149–167.
33. Hijink, S., & Veld, L., (2019). *Sustainability Reporting.* Available at SSRN 3436226.
34. Hodge, F. D., Kennedy, J. J., & Maines, L. A., (2004). Does search-facilitating technology improve the transparency of financial reporting? *The Accounting Review, 79*(3), 687–703.
35. Horngren, C. T., Bhimani, A., Datar, S. M., & Foster, G., (2002). *Management and Cost Accounting* (Vol. 1, pp. 1–17). Harlow: Financial Times/Prentice Hall.

36. Hull, J., (2012). *Risk Management and Financial Institutions, + Web Site* (Vol. 733). John Wiley & Sons.
37. Hunter, S. A., & Smith, M., (2009). Impact of internet financial reporting on emerging markets. *Journal of International Business Research, 8*(2), 21–41.
38. Ilg, P., (2019). How to foster green product innovation in an inert sector. *Journal of Innovation & Knowledge, 4*(2), 129–138.
39. Jaijairam, P., (2017). Ethics in accounting. *Journal of Finance and Accountancy, 23*, 1–13.
40. Kapellas, K., & Siougle, G., (2017). Financial reporting practices and investment decisions: A review of the literature. *Industrial Engineering & Management, 6*(04), 1–9.
41. Kern, A. P., & Formoso, C. T., (2006). A model for integrating cost management and production planning and control in construction. *Journal of Financial Management of Property and Construction, 1*, 1–13.
42. Kinney, Jr. W. R., (1999). Auditor independence: A burdensome constraint or core value? *Accounting Horizons, 13*(1), 69.
43. Kokina, J., & Blanchette, S., (2019). Early evidence of digital labor in accounting: Innovation with robotic process automation. *International Journal of Accounting Information Systems, 35*, 100431.
44. Lerrick, A., (2005). A leap of faith for sovereign default: From IMF judgment calls to automatic incentives. *Cato J., 25*, 25.
45. Li, J., (2021). Simulation of enterprise accounting information system based on improved neural network and cloud computing platform. *Journal of Ambient Intelligence and Humanized Computing*, 1–14.
46. Li, X., (2022). Optimization of accounting information system for enterprises in smart city by intelligent sensor under the internet of things. *Wireless Communications and Mobile Computing, 2022*.
47. Llewellyn, D. T., (2005). Trust and confidence in financial services: A strategic challenge. *Journal of Financial Regulation and Compliance, 13*(4), 333–346.
48. Lobo, G. J., & Zhou, J., (2006). Did conservatism in financial reporting increase after the sarbanes-oxley act? Initial evidence. *Accounting Horizons, 20*(1), 57–73.
49. Lytras, M. D., & Visvizi, A., (2021). Artificial intelligence and cognitive computing: Methods, technologies, systems, applications and policy making. *Sustainability, 13*(7), 3598.
50. Maas, K., & Liket, K., (2011). Social impact measurement: Classification of methods. *Environmental Management Accounting and Supply Chain Management*, 171–202.
51. Makarenko, I., (2017). Public companies non-financial reporting and audit in Ukraine: Challenges and prospects. *Accounting and Financial Control, 1*(1), 32–38.
52. Mbatha, N., & Ngibe, M., (2017). Factors affecting financial stability of small and medium enterprises: A case study of emerging markets. *Risk Governance & Control: Financial Markets & Institutions, 7*(1), 7–17.

53. Miller, H., (1972). Environmental complexity and financial reports. *The Accounting Review, 47*(1), 31–37.
54. Mills, L. F., (1996). Corporate tax compliance and financial reporting. *National Tax Journal, 49*(3), 421–435.
55. Mohamed, E. K., & Lashine, S. H., (2003). Accounting knowledge and skills and the challenges of a global business environment. *Managerial Finance, 29*(7), 3–16.
56. Mullins, J. W., (1996). Early growth decisions of entrepreneurs: The influence of competency and prior performance under changing market conditions. *Journal of Business Venturing, 11*(2), 89–105.
57. Mulvey, J. M., Rosenbaum, D. P., & Shetty, B., (1997). Strategic financial risk management and operations research. *European Journal of Operational Research, 97*(1), 1–16.
58. Murodovich, G. R., & Ziyadullaevna, B. S., (2022). Prospects for use of digital information technologies in accounting. *American Journal of Social and Humanitarian Research, 3*(12), 244–253.
59. Mutiso, A., & Kamau, C., (2013). Factors influencing complexity in financial report preparation-evidence from the banking sector in Kenya. *Journal of Economics and Business Research, 19*(1), 219–236.
60. Nagendran, M., Chen, Y., Lovejoy, C. A., Gordon, A. C., Komorowski, M., Harvey, H., & Maruthappu, M., (2020). Artificial intelligence versus clinicians: Systematic review of design, reporting standards, and claims of deep learning studies. *BMJ, 368*.
61. Ndofor, H. A., Wesley, C., & Priem, R. L., (2015). Providing CEOs with opportunities to cheat: The effects of complexity-based information asymmetries on financial reporting fraud. *Journal of Management, 41*(6), 1774–1797.
62. Park, A., & Ravenel, C., (2013). Integrating sustainability into capital markets: Bloomberg LP and ESG's quantitative legitimacy. *Journal of Applied Corporate Finance, 25*(3), 62–67.
63. Pothumsetty, R., (2020). Implementation of artificial intelligence and machine learning in financial services. *International Research Journal of Engineering and Technology, 7*(03).
64. Prevedello, L. M., Andriole, K. P., Hanson, R., Kelly, P., & Khorasani, R., (2010). Business intelligence tools for radiology: Creating a prototype model using open-source tools. *Journal of Digital Imaging, 23*, 133–141.
65. Rahman, A. R. A., & Rahim, A., (2003). Accounting regulatory issues on investments in Islamic bonds. *International Journal of Islamic Financial Services, 4*(4), 1–11.
66. Randall, R. F., (1999). New challenges in finance. *Strategic Finance, 80*(9), 30.
67. Reddy, Y. V., (1999). Financial sector reform: Review and prospects. *Reserve Bank of India Bulletin, 53*(1), 33–94.

68. Rezaee, Z., & Turner, J. L., (2002). XBRL-based financial reporting: Challenges and opportunities for government accountants. *The Journal of Government Financial Management, 51*(2), 16.
69. Rose, J. M., (2007). Attention to evidence of aggressive financial reporting and intentional misstatement judgments: Effects of experience and trust. *Behavioral Research in Accounting, 19*(1), 215–229.
70. Roychowdhury, S., Shroff, N., & Verdi, R. S., (2019). The effects of financial reporting and disclosure on corporate investment: A review. *Journal of Accounting and Economics, 68*(2, 3), 101246.
71. Salterio, S., & Legresley, P., (2010). *Developing a Culture of Reporting Transparency and Accountability: The Lessons Learned from the Voluntary Sector Reporting Awards for Excellence in Financial Reporting Transparency*. Available at SSRN 1722930.
72. Sarbanes, P., (2002). Sarbanes-Oxley act of 2002. In: *The Public Company Accounting Reform and Investor Protection Act* (Vol. 55). Washington DC: US Congress.
73. Satava, D., Caldwell, C., & Richards, L., (2006). Ethics and the auditing culture: Rethinking the foundation of accounting and auditing. *Journal of Business Ethics, 64*, 271–284.
74. Scholes, M. S., Wilson, G. P., & Wolfson, M. A., (1990). Tax planning, regulatory capital planning, and financial reporting strategy for commercial banks. *The Review of Financial Studies, 3*(4), 625–650.
75. Shao, C., Yang, Y., Juneja, S., & GSeetharam, T., (2022). IoT data visualization for business intelligence in corporate finance. *Information Processing & Management, 59*(1), 102736.
76. Sims, R. R., & Brinkmann, J., (2003). Enron ethics (or: Culture matters more than codes). *Journal of Business Ethics, 45*, 243–256.
77. Soederberg, S., (2004). Unravelling Washington's judgment calls: The cases of the Malaysian and Chilean capital controls. *Antipode, 36*(1), 43–65.
78. Taghipour, M., Soofi, M. E., Mahboobi, M., & Abdi, J., (2020). Application of cloud computing in system management in order to control the process. *Management, 3*(3), 34–55.
79. Taipaleenmäki, J., & Ikäheimo, S., (2013). On the convergence of management accounting and financial accounting–the role of information technology in accounting change. *International Journal of Accounting Information Systems, 14*(4), 321–348.
80. Tang, C. P., Huang, T. C. K., & Wang, S. T., (2018). The impact of internet of things implementation on firm performance. *Telematics and Informatics, 35*(7), 2038–2053.
81. Tang, D. Y., & Yan, H., (2010). Market conditions, default risk and credit spreads. *Journal of Banking & Finance, 34*(4), 743–753.
82. Tepalagul, N., & Lin, L., (2015). Auditor independence and audit quality: A literature review. *Journal of Accounting, Auditing & Finance, 30*(1), 101–121.

83. Verma, A., Lamsal, K., & Verma, P., (2022). An investigation of skill requirements in artificial intelligence and machine learning job advertisements. *Industry and Higher Education, 36*(1), 63–73.
84. Wagenhofer, A., (2016). Exploiting regulatory changes for research in management accounting. *Management Accounting Research, 31*, 112–117.
85. Xia, B. S., & Gong, P., (2014). Review of business intelligence through data analysis. *Benchmarking: An International Journal, 21*(2), 300–311.
86. Yatskiv, S., Voytyuk, I., Yatskiv, N., Kushnir, O., Trufanova, Y., & Panasyuk, V., (2019). Improved method of software automation testing based on the robotic process automation technology. In: *2019 9th International Conference on Advanced Computer Information Technologies (ACIT)* (pp. 293–296). IEEE.
87. Young, J. J., (1996). Institutional thinking: The case of financial instruments. *Accounting, Organizations and Society, 21*(5), 487–512.
88. Zaychenko, I., Smirnova, A., Shytova, Y., Mutalieva, B., & Pimenov, N., (2021). Digital logistics transformation: Implementing the internet of things (IoT). In: *Technological Transformation: A New Role for Human, Machines and Management: TT-2020* (pp. 189–200). Springer International Publishing.
89. Zilgalvis, P., (2019). The role of the state in the innovation triangle: Law and policy fostering the optimal regulatory, business and innovation policy environment. *New Models of Financing and Financial Reporting for European SMEs: A Practitioner's View*, 23–38.

INDEX

B

C

I

J

L

M

N

Printed in the United States
by Baker & Taylor Publisher Services